Great Expectations

Also by Noemie Emery

Washington: A Biography

Alexander Hamilton: An Intimate Portrait

Great Expectations

THE TROUBLED LIVES OF POLITICAL FAMILIES

Noemie Emery

BICENTENNIAL
1807
⊛WILEY
2007
BICENTENNIAL

John Wiley & Sons, Inc.

For Trude Lash

Published by John Wiley & Sons, Inc., Hoboken, New Jersey
Published simultaneously in Canada

Design and composition by Navta Associates, Inc.

For general information about our other products and services, please contact our Customer Care Department within the United States at (800) 762-2974, outside the United States at (317) 572-3993 or fax (317) 572-4002.

Wiley also publishes its books in a variety of electronic formats. Some content that appears in print may not be available in electronic books. For more information about Wiley products, visit our web site at www.wiley.com.

Library of Congress Cataloging-in-Publication Data:

Emery, Noemie, date.
 Great expectations : the troubled lives of political families / Noemie Emery.
 p. cm.
 Includes index.
 ISBN-13 978-0-471-23489-0 (cloth)
 ISBN-10 0-471-23489-3 (cloth)
1. Politicians—United States—Biography. 2. Politicians—United States—Family relationships. 3. Politicians—Mental health—United States. 4. Family—United States—Case studies. 5. Fathers and sons—United States—Case studies. 6. United States—Biography. 7. United States—Politics and government—Miscellanea. I. Title.
 E176.E54 2007
 973.09'9—dc22

2006010288

Printed in the United States of America

10 9 8 7 6 5 4 3 2 1

Contents

Preface

This is a book that defies definition, in a genre few words can explain. It is a social, political, and family history, but it is not the tale of a man, a movement, or a family. Rather, it is a story about a phenomenon—the pressures placed on young men in a specialized setting—as it works its way out over time. It is an eccentric, even tangential, approach that views many lives from one unique angle and tends to downplay, while understanding, the rest. Many things of great interest are therefore left out. The redemptive tale of Alice Roosevelt Longworth and her daughter and granddaughter is omitted completely, and the epic philandering of John Kennedy, itself the subject of endless conjecture, is mentioned only in terms of the additional pressure it put on his brother Bob's life. This is not the place to go for the definitive view of these men and their families, or of their views or their impact on history. Nor is it the place to go for political arguments. Most of the time, parties are not even mentioned, and policies are addressed only when weighted by family matters. Not every politician starts off his career with a ringing attack on the policy views of his ambassador father, as did John Kennedy, or has the words of his president father quoted against him while running for president, as did the younger George Bush.

This book has percolated through a lifetime of viewing politics as a great human drama, where complex, driven people vie for huge stakes. It was my luck as a child to have met Trude Lash, who died in 2004 at age ninety-five after an epic life that took her from pre-Hitler Germany to the FDR White House, to politics and education concerns in postwar Manhattan, where she became my mother's friend, and then mine. It was in the townhouse on West 11th Street in Greenwich Village that she shared with her husband, Joseph, (the author of *Eleanor and Franklin* and numerous histories) that I first saw another dimension to history: I learned what it was like to be close to a president's family, and to see large figures as human and unhappy people, with secrets and strains of their own. Trude and her husband read everything that I wrote, did not turn against me when I stopped being a Democrat, and were the best of friends and most helpful of tutors. I am deeply sorry I could not discuss this book with them, and miss them each day that I live.

I am grateful to Bill Kristol, Fred Barnes, and John Podhoretz, who conceived the idea of a center-right weekly and got Rupert Murdoch to fund it, and in September 1995 unleashed the *Weekly Standard* on a helpless and terrified universe. There I found a home, a hangout, the friendship of many remarkable writers, an ideal venue for my preferred form of writing, and the original outlet—in features and book reviews—for some of the words in this book. Among the *Standard*'s many exceptional features is its proximity in several ways to the American Enterprise Institute, a farm team and resource to some administrations, but to me a free university offering courses in government, only with much better food. On nearly any day, one can find people munching away on various foodstuffs as they absorb verbal sparrings among pundits, presidential advisers, and would-be prime ministers, enlivened by protests and/or armed security. It was there that I heard presidential biographers discussing their subjects, campaign managers discussing their candidates, and participants on a panel on terrorism on October 6, 2000, predict a calamitous attack on the American mainland within the next one or two years. The sustenance offered is not always ephemeral. At the AEI there is not only free lunch, there are also free coffee and cookies, and often free cheese and free wine.

I am grateful too to the numerous people whose efforts supported my own. I was inspired by books by Peter Collier and David Horowitz, who refined and defined the family saga; by Richard Brookhiser; and by Paul C. Nagel, whose book I was reading when it occurred to me that the death of Charles Adams in a Manhattan hovel in 1800 at age twenty-nine of acute alcoholism was not unlike that in 1984 of David Kennedy at age twenty-eight of a drug overdose in a motel in Palm Beach, and might be related to it in curious ways.

It was shortly after this that Karlyn Bowman led me to Deborah Grosvenor, who helped shape this thought into a proposal, who led me in turn to Hana Lane at John Wiley & Sons, who helped shape the proposal into a book. Advice, support, and encouragement came from other writers and friends, among them Fred Barnes, Jeffrey Bell, Karlyn Bowman, Jody Bottum, Danielle Crittenden, Stephanie Deutsch, David Frum, Bill Kristol, Michael and Barbara Ledeen, Michael Novak, Richard Starr, James Woolsey, and Claudia Winkler, who delighted us all by becoming Claudia Anderson and bringing her husband, Bill, into our midst.

In 2004, I wrote a piece that compared President Bush to the great racehorse Seabiscuit (both misunderestimated by uppity critics), which led to an e-mail friendship with Laura Hillenbrand, a spectacular writer, a generous friend to human and equine good causes, and the reason I now read *Bloodhorse* and *Thoroughbred Times* every morning, along with *Instapundit*, the *Corner*, and *Powerline*. "You can't write a book without a dog," Michael Ledeen once told me, and knowing this (and that one needed a dog for a true friend in Washington), I took two with me when I moved down from New York. They—and their heirs—have been loving companions. There are other friends in other places who have also been stalwarts. You know who you are.

Introduction

On the afternoon of November 20, 2001, on what would have been the seventy-sixth birthday of Robert F. Kennedy, the building that housed the Department of Justice was renamed in his honor, before a large crowd of his friends and relations and the current president of the United States. It was a festival of the well connected and the genealogically privileged, among them George W. Bush, the forty-third president, a son of George H. W. Bush, the forty-first president, and a brother of Governor Jeb Bush of Florida; Senator Edward M. Kennedy, a brother of the late Robert Kennedy and of John F. Kennedy, the thirty-fifth president, the father of Rhode Island congressman Patrick J. Kennedy; and some of Robert Kennedy's numerous children, including ex-Congressman Joseph P. Kennedy II, once thought a shoo-in for much higher office, and his older sister, Kathleen Kennedy Townsend, then considered an oncoming governor. All listened as

Joe Kennedy II read aloud the account that his father once gave of how he had managed to rise at age thirty-five to the position of attorney general from his humble start as a low-ranking lawyer in the Department of Justice. "I worked hard, I studied, I applied myself, and then my brother was elected president of the United States."

All laughed, for the underground joke that connected those present was the fact that none of them would have been in that room, or possibly even in politics, if they had not been related to two former presidents—George H. W. Bush and John Kennedy—who themselves had been children of rich and richly connected millionaire fathers who had also held high public office, and that Bush himself had become president when he narrowly defeated Albert Gore Jr., the son of a powerful Tennessee senator who had groomed his son for the White House since birth. All were in politics because of their fathers and families, and all belonged to that small group of people, beginning with John Quincy Adams at the birth of the country, who had been raised to believe they ought to be president, and if they weren't, they in some sense had failed. Success was in that room, but there also was darkness, the result of a mixture of pressure and privilege, of ambition passed on secondhand. George W. Bush and Ted Kennedy had fought drinking problems, as had Ted Kennedy's sons. Robert Kennedy's children had buried two brothers: one from a drug overdose, one in a freak accident in the midst of a scandal. A niece of George W. Bush was treated for drug problems while her brother was being promoted as a rising political star. None of this would have surprised the members of the John Adams family, who had seen similar troubles play out over two generations: the two Adams presidents each had three sons, one who contrived to fulfill his ambitions and two who broke under the pressure and drank. Of these six sons, four became alcoholics, three died around age thirty, and one, enmeshed in financial and sexual scandals, probably took his own life.

The families themselves have a resemblance that is not wholly a matter of chance. They tend to relate to the average family much as the army relates to civilian experience: they have a much more driven and disciplined manner of living, with assigned duties, much drill, much attention given to rank and to order, and quasi courts-martial, followed by shunning when somebody fails or flunks out. Disloyalty to the family, regarded as treason, is heavily punished. Much value is placed on esprit de corps. Physical tests, as in Marine boot camp, are common and are seen as good training for future engagements. Theodore Roosevelt led children and guests on obstacle courses that were exhausting and dangerous. The playing fields of Hyannis became an American version of Eton's—a trying locale for the building of character. ("We don't want losers around here," said Joseph P. Kennedy.) What went on in the Kennedy compound was not very different from what went on at Walker's Point in Maine, where the large, driven Bush clan went for its revels, and where George Herbert Walker and his daughter Dorothy (the mother of George H. W. and the grandmother of Jeb and George W.) instilled what emerged as the family credo: that life was essentially broken down into a series of competitions that had to be won at all costs. As Bill Minutaglio reports in *First Son*, the book he wrote about George Bush the younger, "For years in the Bush-Walker household there would be an endless series of measuring moments codified by what was sometimes called 'The Rankings,' an oft-debated statistical grid that placed various children and grandchildren at differing levels of skills." Because the young Al Gore was an only son who had only one, much older, sister, his father would set him to rigorous farmwork and, as he grew older, would challenge him to a series of contests at push-ups, which the older man now and then won. The Kennedys were often referred to as speaking their own private family shorthand or reading one another's thoughts through half phrases. As Elizabeth Mitchell writes in her book on the Bushes, "George Bush's former staffers would remark on how the family members talked to each other in code."

In average families, most parents study their children to find and encourage their interests and talents. In dynastic ones, children are often endowed with a destiny, while their extraneous interests are viewed as distractions and quickly and harshly suppressed. From John Adams's sons down to John Kennedy Jr., a long line of reluctant political sons have been pushed into going to law school. Kennedy wanted to go on the stage and might well have proved quite a good actor. Ted Roosevelt Jr. longed to be a great soldier and finally was one. Al Gore, as well as John Quincy Adams, yearned for the life of the mind. The more usual family works for the personal happiness of each of its members. In the dynastic family, this becomes less important, or rather each member is expected to find personal fulfillment in advancing the family goals. Roles are often assigned, based on sex or birth order, with girls and younger sons cast, sometimes unwillingly, as supporting players to the family stars. In some families, a first son can be passed over for a more promising junior; in others, primogeniture remains the unbreakable rule. The family is sometimes seen as a fighting force, almost at war with the universe. Unconditional surrender is the goal.

The dynastic drive tends to start with the father, who may have had dreams of his own. "To Joe, his children were extensions of himself," FDR aide Tom Corcoran said of Joseph P. Kennedy. "If you have the progenitor's sense, you play the game differently than if you only want for yourself." John Adams had it, but not every president did; Albert Gore Sr. had it, but not every senator did; Joseph Kennedy had it, but not every self-made tycoon did. Resentment seems a rich soil for dynastic fantasies. A vain man, John Adams felt himself unfairly passed over for less worthy people. Joseph Kennedy resented the WASPs, who had treated the Irish like refuse. The elder Al Gore had been WASP enough but the wrong kind completely: a poor white from the hollows of Appalachia who spent his whole life erasing his roots. Adams lost the presidency after one term to Thomas Jefferson and felt himself unfairly slighted. Theodore Roosevelt lost his last race, a third-party presidential run in 1912, embittering all of his children. Joe Kennedy's hopes were dashed by world war and by Franklin D. Roosevelt. But if a father's thwarted ambition can lead him to lean ever more on his children, his losses can set off a spark in a son. The senior Al Gore lost to Bill Brock in 1970, a slight his son Al still refers to in speeches. Senator Birch Bayh lost to Dan Quayle in 1980; his son Evan is seen as a possible president. Andrew Cuomo ran for governor of New York in 2002, hoping to pay back the man who unseated his father. In his first big election, George W. Bush defeated Ann Richards, who in the Democratic convention in 1988 had verbally savaged his father. His father won but then lost four years later to a ticket that featured Al Gore as the candidate for vice president. Gore then lost, in a battle of dynasts, to the elder Bush's avenger, young George.

Failure may spur on revenge in most of these cases, but it is not always the seminal cause. John Adams was training his sons to be president before the country or office existed. Joe Kennedy himself hoped to be president up to 1940, when the son he had trained for that office turned twenty-five. The elder Gore's hopes for national office did not end until the Democratic convention in 1956, when the vice presidential nomination went to Estes

Kefauver. Young Al was then eight. It may mean something that Gore, Adams, and Kennedy had all raised their families from obscurity to very great power in less than a lifetime, and they might have felt driven to lock in their accomplishments. Michael Beschloss notes that Kennedy "once quoted Bacon to the effect that every progenitor of a great family possesses qualities of both good and evil," and Henry Luce has said it would take "an exceptional dramatist" to describe the dimensions of Kennedy's character. As Doris Kearns Goodwin has written, Kennedy "called for Joe Junior to make restitution for all that he himself had been unable to accomplish. It was as if Joe Junior's life belonged to Joe Senior, as a second life for himself."

A "second life" for an ambitious father means a son has no life of his own. Or rather, no life that he shapes to his wishes but instead a life that is foisted on him, to which he adapts or against which he rebels. Significantly, dynastic children often divide into "good sons," who do their best to fulfill parental exactions, and spectacular flameouts, whose failures are marked and perverse. Among the good sons have been John Quincy Adams and his good son, Charles Francis; the ever-dutiful Ted Roosevelt Jr.; three of the four sons of Joseph P. Kennedy; and, of course, Albert Gore Jr., on whom his mother bestowed the ultimate accolade: "He always did everything we wanted," she said. Among the variations, one sees a John Quincy Adams, a Ted Roosevelt Jr., a Robert F. Kennedy, who devotes his whole life to the family image; a John Kennedy, who remakes his whole life to become the popular leader his father insists on; an Albert Gore Jr., who takes on a career he dislikes. The good son may survive, in a manner of speaking, but he may not survive without damage. He can live with a permanent sense of anxiety. He can live with the sense of being less than his father or siblings, like the Adams sons and the two younger Kennedy brothers. He can be steered into a life that is not of his choosing in a field that is not quite his own. Adams, Gore, and John Kennedy went through brief phases of semirebellion. In middle age, Al Gore went through a series of crises, in which he read, and wrote, books about put-upon children driven by demanding parents into uncongenial patterns of life.

The opposite of the good son is the bad seed, the dark side of the coin of parental exaction, who not only fails to fulfill the demands of his family but mocks and denies its pretensions. Among the bad seeds have been Charles and Thomas Adams, two of the three sons of John and Abigail Adams; John and George Washington Adams, two of the three sons of John Quincy Adams; Kermit, the alcoholic third son of Theodore Roosevelt; three of the four sons of Franklin and Eleanor Roosevelt; and several sons of Robert F. Kennedy, who himself had never been president but headed his family's dominant line. We see here the inverse of the family's claims to hold power: if the family wants to seem moral and disciplined, the bad seed may be dissolute; if it wants to seem active, the bad seed may be indolent; if it wants to seem driven by generous instincts, the bad seed may wallow in greed.

The Adamses wanted their sons to be moral and masterful; of their six sons in two generations, they had four who were neither and three who were dissolute. With a father elected four times and a mother widely regarded as saintlike, the Roosevelt boys cheerfully looted their family legacy. David Kennedy, whose 1962 photo showing him outside the White House was inscribed "a future president inspects his property" by his uncle the president, resembled instead the renegade Adamses, dying at twenty-nine of the drugs the Adamses would surely have taken had they been available. His stunning slide down resembles eerily that of George Washington Adams, including the latter's nihilism and excessive drinking.

Charles and George had been the un-Adamses; the Roosevelt boys the un–Franklin and Eleanor; and David in turn had been the un-Kennedy, trolling for drugs in the ghettos his father had tried to inspire. Expectations pitched too high can in their turn result in a counterreaction: a preemptive form of defense.

Some sons rebel as they honor their fathers, both promoting and slighting the name. One case in point may be Edmund Brown Jr., the namesake and son of a popular governor, who seemed to have copied his father's career path while at the same time he made war on his father's ideas. (The relationship of the odd, mod, and quirky Brown with his much more traditional father is one of the oddest in politics, along with the story of Brown and his sister, who tried to push him aside as the family spokesman when she ran for governor in 1994 and lost.) In a class all his own is Edward M. Kennedy, the bad seed and good son all in one package, at once the persistent and dutiful family workhorse and the flamboyant and raucous disgrace. For decades, he has maintained an exquisite balance between effort and excess, his hard work securing his place in his state and the Senate; his numerous scandals making him unelectable as a national candidate, the dynastic destiny he seems to flinch from and fear. Some of his nephews have followed this pattern, seeking a path of careerist ascension while indulging at times in the kind of behavior that tends to negate these ambitions. Small wonder that in 1998 the magazine *Capital Style* named Ted's niece Kathleen "the Last Viable Kennedy," the only one left with a plausible future. In a family studded with crown princes and namesakes, the one left standing was the last person one thought of, the one outside of the matrix of great expectations—a girl.

Dynastic women have tended to have their own patterns, although these are frequently hidden from view. Joe Kennedy's money and will won his children a seat at the table, but Rose

Kennedy's genes made them great politicians. A daughter of a notable mayor of Boston, she had political instincts that were better than Joe's. Pauline Gore, Al's mother, was one of the few women to earn a law degree in the 1930s, and was regarded as brighter than her senator husband. "Pauline was the brains, and Albert was the pretty blond," as David Maraniss quotes a Tennessee journalist. Had her husband achieved their ambitions, she would have been a co-president, years before Hillary Clinton. When he failed twice to be picked for a national ticket, she transferred her dreams to young Al. "Smile. Relax. Attack," Pauline Gore advised the young Albert. Tougher and feistier than her president-husband, Barbara Bush was more of a partner in the family enterprise than she ever let on. "We're pretty much alike," George W. Bush has said of his mother. "I don't mind a battle. She doesn't mind a battle. I've got my father's eyes and my mother's mouth." "Like George W. Bush, Al Gore did not marry his mother; he became her," ran an assessment in *Harper's Bazaar*.

Sisters have often been shadow inheritors, heirs to careers that never developed. "I always believed that if she had been a man, she rather than my father would have been president," said Alice Roosevelt Longworth of her Aunt Bamie, TR's older sister. Bamie was not, so she became a political hostess and backstairs adviser to statesmen, her brother included. Alice herself might have been the crown prince had her gender been different. It wasn't, so she opted for living through men: her husband, Speaker of the House Nicholas Longworth, and her half brother, Ted. Had her marriage been good, had her brother been president, she might have become a wise counselor. Neither occurred, and she lived out her long life in negative efforts, attacking her father's successors and foes.

"If that girl had balls, she would have been a hell of a politician," was Joe Kennedy's take on his third daughter, Eunice. Had she been a boy, some people think, she would have been tapped in 1946 for the safe seat in Boston, instead of her brother, the shy, sickly Jack. In 1986, when the same seat came open, it went to Bobby's oldest son, Joe Kennedy II, and not to his older, more disciplined sister. Joe got the safe seat and the family backing. Kathleen followed her husband to the Maryland suburbs, ran in a Republican district, and lost.

Kathleen soldiered on, took dull jobs in government, and was tapped in 1994 as lieutenant governor in her adopted home state. In the wake of the death of John Kennedy Jr., she was anointed the star of the family and talked up for a place on a national ticket, even before ever winning a race on her own. (When she did run for governor, in the 2002 midterms, she lost.) For dynastic girls, this can be a mixed blessing. On the one hand, their ambitions may no longer be thwarted. On the other hand, they may now be subjected to the same pressures that have done such great damage to boys.

The Adamses of Braintree may seem far removed from the Gores of Tennessee, the Bushes of Texas and Florida, and the Kennedys of just about anywhere, but it is the differences that may be misleading, and the similarities that may be the real thing. Read about the Adams family in the year 1800, and they could be the Kennedys of the mid-1980s, with all of the troubled and crumbling marriages, the drinkers and dopers, the burdened and over-taxed heirs. There is no "Kennedy curse," just a dynastic one, which for two-hundred-plus years has woven its way through the life of the country. It has produced presidents, statesmen, and slow-motion suicides. And it is not over yet.

CHAPTER 1

Adamses

Late in his life, Joseph P. Kennedy would compare himself to John Adams, another Massachusetts native and former ambassador, and, like himself, a fanatical parent who cherished great hopes for his sons. Had he known more about Adams, he might have said less about him. Like the Kennedys, the Adamses had commingled glory and ruin. Few things would happen to succeeding dynasties that this first family would not foreshadow or foresee. "The Adams children were told that to be less than excellent in matters great and small meant that they were ultimately betraying their family," writes Charles Nagel in *Descent from Glory*. Kennedys were told they must win and not cry. Successive lines of Adams sons and Kennedy brothers would think themselves less than the men they succeeded. The Kennedys called themselves a "clan" or a nation. The Adamses thought of themselves as a "race." Ties within these clusters were strong and long lasting. Children

---

were not happy far from their parents or siblings, who were also a burden. Dreams of escape were not rare. In 1801, John Adams's youngest son, Thomas, wanted to move west, to "honest, though homely, independence." In 1961, Ted Kennedy wanted to move west, where, in a new place, with new people, he could "succeed or fail on his own." John Adams ordered Thomas to practice law in the East, where he would supplement his small income. Joe Kennedy ordered Ted to stay in Massachusetts, where he paid for his son's Senate campaign.

Dynastic pressures would shatter the life of Joan Kennedy. As Nagel writes of the wife of one Adams grandson, "The intense Adams world left Abby uncertain about who or what she ought to be." The quiet weddings planned by Joan Bennett and Jacqueline Bouvier became grand celebrations of family power. So did the small celebration planned by John Quincy's son, George Washington Adams, when he graduated from Harvard in 1819. "He wanted a small party," writes Nagel. "John Quincy would not leave it at that, but summoned the governor, the college president, and other dignitaries who, it was felt, should be acknowledging an Adams event."

The Adamses tended to massage the truth when it became inconvenient, blurring or hiding unfortunate incidents. Charles, the reprobate son of John and Abigail Adams, was hurriedly buried and not referred to thereafter. The papers of the even more scandalous George Washington Adams were burned. His responsible younger brother, Charles Francis, "tried to make respectable what little could be allowed to survive of George's story," says Nagel. "He . . . consigned most of George's papers to the flames, and in the process turned the errant brother into a pathetic but safely vague memory."

The retarded Rosemary Kennedy was passed off as "shy" and

said to be teaching at the institution in which she really was being cared for. John Kennedy's unstable back became a war injury. His Addison's disease was turned into malaria. His sister Kathleen's death in a plane crash with the man she planned to run off with became the result of a chance ride with a friend. Fixated on image, these families were also concerned with performance, which became an obsession. Children were pushed to and beyond their apparent potential by the unyielding force of parental exactions. Sometimes they found new and deep-hidden talents. Sometimes they broke.

With an odd sense of prescience, John and Abigail Adams began raising their sons to be president years before their country declared independence, and twenty years before the office itself was conceived. Growing up, three generations would absorb a message both complex and destructive that focused on two central points. One was that the Adamses were or should be superior to all other people. The other was that all the Adamses were inferior to past generations, who happened to have come before. For Adams descendants, it put them in a double bind of guilt and resentment: guilt at not living up to their ancestral glories; resentment at others who made off with the tributes—fame, office, honor, and the devotion of followers—that they thought they deserved for themselves. For over a century and for four generations, Adamses were always important, always world famous, and always significant, but they were never the greatest of their generations, never the dominant or formative figures, never the ones who gave their name to an era, a movement, a great school of thought.

And they resented it: John Adams looked down on George Washington (and all other founders), John Quincy looked down on Andrew Jackson, Charles Francis looked down on Abraham Lincoln, and Henry looked down on Theodore Roosevelt, all of whom were considered by the Adamses as unlettered, ignorant, unworthy, flamboyant, or coarse. In his long career, John Adams would be a leading member of Congress, a notable diplomat, an ambassador to the Court of St. James's and other notable postings, and the first vice president, and the second president, of the United States. But he was always somehow in the shadow of others: the substitute, the also-ran, the second best. In France, he was mistaken for his cousin Sam ("le fameux Adams") and outshone by the wiles of Benjamin Franklin. Back in the States, he was once again in the shadow of Washington, who by that time had achieved demigod status, and overshadowed in the executive branch by Alexander Hamilton and Thomas Jefferson, the two rising stars of the cabinet. As president, his administration was secretly run by and loyal to Hamilton, and after one term he was defeated by Jefferson, who had been his vice president, and was, unlike him, a master of popular politics.

He left office in 1801, angry at everyone, including his voters and countrymen. As Richard Brookhiser writes, "Adams found himself in yet another new situation—the first loser in American presidential history. . . . His retirement . . . was almost as long as his national career. . . . He was the first loser, and his loss, coming at the end of a long, laborious, and in many ways great career, seemed to negate it. He brooded, he remembered, he justified himself." But if he was a loser compared to the others, he was in some ways ahead of them all: Washington had no children, Madison had no children, Jefferson had been left with only two living daughters, and Hamilton had many children, but his oldest and favorite, the one he was grooming for greatness and glory, threw his life away in a duel in 1801. Adams, however, had three sons, all of whom could be raised to succeed and surpass him. He was convinced they would.

John Quincy, born in 1767, two years after his big sister Abigail, was the ideal firstborn son for an ambitious couple: bright, conscientious, driven by duty, and terribly eager to please. As a child, he blamed himself when he wanted to play and not study Latin. At six, he had secretly cried in fear and frustration when he failed to understand or appreciate *Paradise Lost*. Said his biographer, Robert V. Remini, "Johnny . . . was perpetually lectured about how he was the oldest son and had to set an example. . . . He had been born with great gifts . . . and was expected to live up to them, and become a great man." At eleven, he had become so advanced that his father decided to take him to Paris, where he hobnobbed cheerfully with Franklin and Jefferson, becoming so proficient at the French language that he was sent to Russia with the American legate without his father when he was only fourteen. Returning, he went as his father's secretary to The Hague and then London, serving until both he and his father were called home seven years later when his father was tapped to become the vice president, when John Quincy himself was twenty-one.

Having spent his youth as a small adult mingling with great men in Europe, he was unprepared for the culture shock back home in Quincy, where his parents forced him into the law via Harvard, related to their plans for his future achievement. He did not resist, but he fell into depressions that carried him close to the edge of a breakdown. As Nagel writes, "His recurring self-image, a 'mere cypher,' unemployed and without character, made him so depressed that he became frightened. His troubled sleep was interrupted by the 'most extravagant dreams.'" In 1794, when John Quincy was twenty-seven, Washington put him out of his very real misery, naming him ambassador to the Netherlands, where he launched into his adult, and his proper, career. He was now more at home but still not free of pressure. As he wrote in his diary, "I have indeed long known that my father is far more anxious for my advancement . . . than I have ever been or shall be." In Europe in 1797 when his father at last became president, his son did not greet the prospect with unalloyed pleasure. As he wrote to the young woman he was planning to marry, it meant something more that he had to live up to. His father had gone to Harvard; he went to Harvard. His father practiced law; he too had done so, if only unhappily. His father had been an ambassador; he was an ambassador. Now, with his father as president, a new bar had risen. Would he have to be president too?

Johnny's success in the eyes of the world and his parents raised the stakes for his two younger brothers: Charles, born in 1769 and described as charming and delicate, and Thomas, born three years later and referred to as slower and shy. At age six, Thomas had started a sullen resistance, refusing to write to his parents in Europe and seeming relieved when they traveled out of the country, leaving him in the care of an aunt and an uncle, with whom he lived a quiet life on their farm. But if Thomas withdrew, Charles showed a tendency to break under pressure as his parents pushed him along in his big brother's footsteps. John Quincy had been taken abroad at the age of eleven and rapidly dazzled the great men of Europe. Charles, taken abroad at age nine, had cried, become homesick and sickly, and been forced to go home. Sent to Harvard (of course) in the wake of his brother, he had begun to drink heavily and had shown his reaction to his parents' strict lectures by joining in some kind of campus disturbance, in which he had run naked through the college square. This was not what his parents wanted to see in an offspring, and when they went to New York in 1789 to join the new government, they had Charles with them in tow. When they moved to Philadelphia the next year they left him behind, but insisted that a reluctant Thomas live with them when he graduated from Harvard that June. An unhappy Thomas joined them in September, writing to his aunt and uncle that he wished he were back on the farm with them, and telling John Quincy that he wished he were working at anything at all but the law. His parents ignored him and put him on retainer, and began criticizing his work habits and friends. Under this barrage, his meager store of self-confidence began to unravel. "I never was much in love with myself, and I feel less so than ever," he confessed to his mother, dreaming of his aunt's peaceful farm back in Haverhill or of a new home in the West.

Temporarily, Thomas's problem was solved by John Quincy, who took him along as his secretary when Washington sent him to Holland, hoping to separate him from their parents and thereby restore his morale. But by this time, Charles had become a distraction that no amount of good intentions could rectify. He had passed the bar, and in 1795 had annoyed his parents by marrying Sally Smith, sister of the ne'er-do-well colonel who was making his sister Nabby's life miserable. Shortly thereafter, he had begun to withdraw from his family, choosing to ignore their badgering letters or making only evasive replies. Working sporadically, he had managed to squander or lose over two thousand dollars of John Quincy's money, which had caused him to drink even more. In 1799, on a surprise visit to Nabby, Abigail found she had taken in Sally and her two children because Charles had vanished. On December 1, 1800, Charles died of cirrhosis alone in New York City, becoming the first of two Adams male children to die while their father was leaving the presidency. "Little was heard about Charles after his death, for the family wanted to forget him," writes Nagel, adding that "burial in the family vault . . . was denied him." Charles's fate was seen as such an embarrassment that it was left to Thomas to deliver his epitaph: "Let silence reign forever over his tomb."

Thomas himself had ended his European sojourn in much the same state as he had begun it, longing for a quiet life of peace, domestic tranquillity, and the "mediocre successes" his mother and father abhorred. At a loose end after being dropped from his post by President Jefferson, John Quincy invited his brother, now nearing thirty, to join him in a new life in the West. Just as Thomas warmed up to the prospect—"I am your man for a new country and manual labor," he had said to his brother—Abigail intervened and summoned him back home to Quincy. There he would stay, depressed and unhappy, for the next thirty years of his life. In 1805, his father and brother secured him a seat in the Massachusetts state legislature, hoping to give him a start in the family business. He dropped out in less than a year. His drinking increased, as did his depression. When his mother died in 1819, he and his family moved in with his father, who became their sole source of support. Six months after this, he vanished in Boston, sending John Quincy's wife and his sons on a desperate search of the city. Days later he surfaced, contrite and hungover, to crawl back to the family nest. He continued to talk periodically of the new life he still longed for, asking his brother to finance these ventures but in reality going no farther than Boston, to which he repaired in his cups. On one such occasion, his carriage turned over, but Thomas survived. His liver, however, had started to fail him, and it was a relief to him and to all around him when he died at last on March 12, 1832, the second of two Adams brothers raised to be leaders, who could not, in the end, lead themselves.

With Charles dead, and Thomas established as tactically useless, the family burdens devolved even more on John Quincy, who did more than his best to measure up. As a senator (1802), ambassador, secretary of state, and finally president, he would emerge as someone more than fanatically driven; rising at six, five, and even four in the morning, he would walk four miles, light his own fire, and read his Bible in Greek before breakfast. He also rode horseback, swam, wrote and translated poetry, and measured the length of his stride so that he could tell, to the inch or the minute, exactly how far he had walked. "Often he shifted from project to project in silent protest against the number of projects he loaded himself with," says Richard Brookhiser. "In the mid-afternoon, he might lapse into vacancy—other people would call it resting— which made him push himself all the more. A man who was not as intelligent, talented, and healthy as he was would have destroyed himself. He did his best." To the end of his life, he believed that he had failed to live up to his father's example. It was in this spirit of compulsion and urgency that he tried to bring up his three sons.

John Quincy had been born to a provincial lawyer of no great importance, and his father did not become president until his son was twenty-nine. By contrast, John Quincy's first son, born in Berlin on April 12, 1801, was already the grandson of an American president and the son of a rising member of the political classes, who bade fair to stand in his shoes. Expectations for his sons were thus exponentially greater than those he or his brother had faced. Naming his first son George Washington and his second son John, he soon had three sons, two named for presidents, on whom he exerted the unending pressures his parents had once placed on him. His wife, Louisa Catherine, a sensitive woman with no interest in power, had tried to cushion the impact on them, protesting vehemently when John Quincy, appointed ambassador to Russia in 1807 by President Madison, told her she must leave her two older children in Quincy when they went to St. Petersburg, taking with her only Charles Francis, age two. Enraged, she gave in, but never forgave her husband or his ambitions. "To the end of time, life, to me, will be a succession of miseries," she proclaimed as she set off for Russia. As it concerned the lives of her two older children, she would be proven all too correct.

Charles Francis, the third son, grew up self-possessed at the czar's court in Russia, learning to speak French, Russian, and German, attending schools for diplomats' children, going to fancy dress balls and parties, and thinking it normal (writes Francis Russell) that while out perhaps for a walk with his father, "they might stop to chat with the Czar." His brothers at home were less fortunate. John Quincy attempted to raise them long distance, with an unending series of hectoring letters that stressed self-control, duty, and the need to live up to their forebears' example; as he later insisted, "My sons have not only their own honor but that of two preceding generations to sustain." It was, as Doug Wead writes in *All the Presidents' Children*, "a tense atmosphere of high expectations, lonely abandonment, and sometimes well-intentioned personal rejection, meant to provide motivation" but that more frequently crippled morale.

When the family was reunited in 1815 in London and then returned two years later to Washington, the two older boys had their father again, but not as a comforting presence. When John and Charles Francis did poorly at Harvard, he refused to let them come home for their Christmas vacation, saying he would feel nothing but "sorrow and shame" at their presence, to say nothing of grief and "disgust." The "disgust" increased a year later when John was expelled and summoned to Washington, where he would atone for his sins. He would spend the rest of his life doing chores for his father, among them the running of a flour mill in Rock Creek Park in the city, which he proceeded to run into the ground. His work at the mill kept him tied to his father and to his repeated harsh judgments. Depressed by his failures, John began drinking. It was coming perilously close to the drama John Quincy had seen play itself out in regard to his parents and brothers, but he seemed unable to change his behavior, much less to check his sons' slide.

George graduated from Harvard in 1821, in a ceremony planned as his coming-out party before the state's leading political figures, to let them know that a new Adams star had arrived. The plan, duly mapped out by his father years earlier, was to have him clerk in the law office of Daniel Webster until the time came for him to seek office, but nothing would work out as planned. Poetic and dreamy (he once won a poetry contest, beating out Ralph Waldo Emerson), George had even less taste for the law than his father and was soon spending his time in his grandfather's library, soaking up fanciful tales. From Washington as secretary of state (and after 1825 as the president), John Quincy continued the deluge of letters, similar to the ones he himself had once suffered, telling a terrified George he was obliged to burnish the name of his family.

It was becoming apparent that George could barely stand up for his own. His father's demands drove him into a state of paralysis, in which, in a direct inversion of his father's example, he slept late, worked little, drank heavily, and lost himself in an imagined world. Nagel cites a manuscript fragment from 1825 in which George confessed to "a wild imagination and no mental discipline," a "penchant for fanciful literature," including "narrations of crime, tales of terrible depravity, mysterious horror, and supernatural power," as well as a craving for stories of suicide, which he traced to his parents' desertion of himself and his brother between 1809 and 1815.

In 1826, John Quincy got George a seat in the Massachusetts

state legislature, hoping to jump-start his career in electoral politics. It was the same thing he and his father had done years earlier for his brother Thomas, and once more the results were predictable: George would drop out after several months. The next crisis came with the death of John Adams, who left most of his land to John Quincy, who decided to survey it himself. He also insisted that George must assist him, a test the younger man failed. "When George faltered," writes Nagel, "his father taunted his son, embarrassing him before the strangers who made up the surveying party. . . . This was the final blow, and George collapsed, in the belief, as his mother put it, 'That he is unfit for the society or the duties for which other men are born.'"

Afraid now to move lest he anger his father, George stayed in his room, running up debts of over three thousand dollars, and became unable to pay his own rent. He refused to answer his father's letters, afraid his father had heard of his latest disaster: a maid in a friend's house had borne him a child and was threatening to let the news out. In the spring of 1829, John Quincy, having lost the presidency to Andrew Jackson some months earlier, summoned George to come down to Washington to help his mother and father move home. It was a well-meant attempt to repair their relations, but George by this time was "quivering" in fear of the reproaches he believed that his father would give. Charles Francis, who had been with him in Boston, thought George had seemed "disarranged" but not desperate. "I never suspected alienation of mind or he should never have gone," Charles Francis wrote later. "I went to his room and examined his papers. They display nothing but pain, mental agitation about his future prospects . . . but no despair."

Nonetheless, George was distraught when he boarded the

steamer *Benjamin Franklin* at Providence on April 29 for the trip down to Washington. By nightfall, he was pacing the decks, complaining of voices coming up from the engine room, and asking the captain to put him ashore. Minutes later, he jumped, or fell, into the water. Six weeks later, on June 10, his body washed up on City Island, ten miles off New York City. He was the second son of an Adams to die as his father left office, and his life had been a long series of self-induced failures. He was then twenty-eight years old.

The family member charged with winding up the tangled affairs of George Washington Adams was Charles Francis, who had taken on himself the generational role of guardian of the family image and name. He did this by burning most of George's papers, sanitizing his reputation, and settling the legal issues surrounding the illegitimate child, among them the people trying to blackmail the family. When his brother John finally drank himself to death at age thirty-one, five years later, it would put the cap on a two-generation story of ruin and privilege, in which the casualties outnumbered the survivors by a ratio of two to one. Charles, who had seen firsthand the decline not only of his brothers but also of his Uncle Thomas (whom he described as a brute and a bully), had no illusions about what ambition had done to his family. He and his mother had been appalled when his father, still smarting from the humiliation of losing his office and reeling from the terrible death of his firstborn, chose at this time to get back into politics, entering Congress as an antislavery soldier, where he stayed until his collapse on the floor of the House sixteen years later, dying in a small anteroom off the House chamber at age eighty-one. This did not appeal to the cool, private Charles, who intended to shield himself and his children from the deadly effects of dynastic compulsion. Reconciling this wish with his own sense of family duty would be the struggle and work of his life.

When George died, Charles was just twenty-two, but he seemed in some ways an old man already, exhausted by the dramas he had seen wrack his family. He had seen two brothers and an uncle drink themselves senseless; he had watched his parents fight over his father's ambition; he himself bore the name of the first Adams loser, who had drunk himself to death at thirty-one. On top of all this, he detested politics, both for its own sake and for what it had done to his family. As Shepherd writes, "He understood the impact on the family of the political life, and he wished to avoid it." As Nagel says, "Even as a young man, [he] was restrained and contained . . . [and] determined to move through life cautiously. . . . [He] had a remarkable understanding of his family's burdens. . . . For him, life meant anxiety and tension from the start." The tension came from the disconnect between his own interests and what he referred to as "my peculiar situation" as "the third of a distinguished line." What he meant was that he did not see himself as a free man regarding his own future but someone doomed to walk a fine line between his own wishes and his fears that he would let down his family. "All his inclinations ran counter to his responsibilities, except for one: his inclination to do his duty," as Brookhiser tells us. Ambition was gone, and all that remained was anxiety. As he wrote when he reluctantly ran for the first time in 1840, "If it is to be my portion to throw away my life in politics and squabbling, I am prepared to submit to it, but not to rejoice."

Dealing with the numerous people eager to make political capital out of the last living Adams of his generation, Charles Francis doled himself out in small, careful doses, allowing himself to be used now and then for some noble purpose, and then going back

to his books. In 1840, he ran for the first time for the Massachusetts state legislature but became so depressed he dropped out six
years later. In 1848, he ran for vice president on the Free Soil
ticket, doubtless pushed on by the death of his father into making
a statement of principle. In 1858, he ran for his father's old seat in
the House, landing himself in the Secession Congress, one of the
most crucial in history. His heart was in none of it. Faced in 1872
with the ultimate menace—being drafted to run on a reform ticket
for president—he fled not only the field but the country, taking his
wife on a trip to Geneva, from where he wrote home terse letters
expressing lack of interest, saying that if he had to fight for the
honor, he preferred to have his name withdrawn. "Not only did he
refuse to campaign," Otto Friedrich, biographer of his son's wife,
Clover, informs us, "but he refused to authorize anyone else, not
even his sons, to organize support on his behalf."

This quiet man's claim to the notice of history rests on the six
years that he spent in London as American ambassador to the
Court of St. James's, the third Adams in a row to have held that
position. Of course, Adams would hold it reluctantly. As his son
Charles Francis II would write later, news of his appointment "fell
on our breakfast table like a veritable bombshell. . . . My father
looked dismayed. . . . The great opportunity of his life when suddenly thrust upon him caused a sincere feeling of consternation.
He really felt that he was being called on to make a great personal
and political sacrifice." Yet it turned out to be the one public post
for which he was suited, combining great responsibility with great
independence, great prestige, and no partisan clamoring. For
once, his cold nature would work in his favor. Coolly, he worked
around the inclination of the British (and their large population of
mill workers) to support the cotton-rich states of the Confederacy,
telling the prime minister when the British were about to sell

ironclads built in a Liverpool shipyard to the South, "It would be superfluous for me to point out to your Lordship that this means war." In the end, Britain stayed neutral, which was a huge win for the Union and for its Adams ambassador. What mattered to him was that he had at last performed an act on a par with those performed by his forebears and on the very same theater of battle. As he wrote, in the only praise he would ever bestow on himself, "The ambition I had to make myself a position not unworthy of my name and race has been gratified. All the common conditions of man's life have been fulfilled."

One area where Charles Francis parted ways with his father was in the raising of his four sons. "The history of my family is not a pleasant one," he had written. "It is one of great triumphs in the world, but of deep groans within, one of extraordinary brilliance and deep, corroding mortification. . . . I would not have any of my children particularly distinguished at the price of such a penalty on the rest." And so he did not. In his correspondence, there are no letters resembling the ones John or John Quincy had sent to their children, warning that if they failed to be great, or be president, they would disgrace their name and themselves before God. Yet the weight of the past was never absent, even if it was only inferred: Charles Francis's firstborn son, the fourth John Adams and the second John Quincy, a young man of modest gifts and more modest ambitions, was stunned as a young man to be introduced to a crowd as a "descendant of three men who either had been president or ought to have been, and as a prospective president himself." There was nothing John Quincy II wanted less. Charles Francis could lighten his touch, but he could not undo the burden of history that was to hover above all his male children, this time less a goad than an unwanted responsibility and irritant that quietly distorted as it somehow diminished their lives.

Charles Francis had opened the door for his children to back their way out of the family enterprise, and in differing ways they all did. Only one—John Quincy Adams II—ever again held public office, and all of those that he held were minor because he preferred to run races he was likely to lose. His real wish, like that of Thomas, his great-uncle and John Quincy's brother, was to live a quiet life in a bucolic setting, and for the most part he did so, troubled by the feeling he was supposed to want more but not enough to disturb his tranquillity. "I want to be left alone," he said frequently. "I will not be a public man, or lose my life in a vain struggle for nothing. . . . I am determined to live my life to please myself."

It was a different story with the second son, Charles Francis II, who steered his ambitions out of the family channel, determined to do nothing done by his forebears and everything they did not do. "Out of his ambition, his hunger for attention, . . . his need to dominate, and his desire for material success, he would stand apart from his family," Nagel informs us. "[He] undertook to be an Adams on his own terms." He took pleasure in shocking his fastidious parents when he joined the Union Army in 1861, a life they considered too coarse for an Adams, and appalled them still more when he came out of the army and went, not into the law or writing or politics, but into commercial and business endeavors. Unfortunately, his acumen failed to match his ambitions, and his main creation in business was debt. Having become president in 1884 (not of the United States but of the Union Pacific Railroad), he was forced to resign six years later, handing over the reins to Jay Gould. He then turned his eyes to the family fortune, bequeathed to the boys by their very rich mother, borrowing more than two million dollars to purchase new lands in the West. Then came the crash of 1893, which cost the family hundreds of thousands of dollars, its unit cohesion, and even some cherished ancestral holdings, which Charles had used as collateral. "Rather than leading the Adamses to a glorious career, he had created a nightmare," says Nagel. "Every member of the fourth generation . . . carried financial and emotional scars."

It was after this that Charles was forced to retreat to the family business of writing, usually about his family members, although with a style more lively, more brusque, more skeptical, and therefore more readable than the turgid approach of much of his family. Of this retreat he said with his usual candor, "I go out of the present world, which I can't manage, into the past, where I am master." This became the byword of his whole generation as it continued its measured decline.

Escaping from the world to the assessment of it became the approach of the two younger sons, Brooks and Henry, who made their careers out of efforts to venerate the family legacy and then to explain, to themselves and to others, why they had failed to come up to the mark. The answer they reached was that the culture had failed them: the world had declined so much since the days of their forebears that great careers such as theirs were not possible. Brooks explained in a series of treatises that civilizations, like humans, have a determinate life span, and theirs was approaching debility. This approach had the benefit of allowing him to lift his failure to act from his own shoulders, or, as Nagel tells us, "His theory that civilization suffered from diminishing energy allowed him to blame the decline of his family line on forces beyond his control."

Henry had the harder job of reconciling his belief that he deserved to hold power with the fact that he lacked the will to fight for it, and with his resentment of people who did. Raised to believe, as he wrote, that "a president was a given in every respectable family," he gave rise to stories while he was at Harvard that he sat in his room waiting for someone to draft him for office. When nobody did so, he sulked. "Adams held no office," he wrote in his memoir, referring to himself in the third person, "and when his friends asked him the reason he . . . preferred to answer simply that no president had ever invited him to fill one. . . . Adams saw no office that he wanted and he gravely thought that . . . he was more likely to be a useful citizen without office. . . . He felt quite satisfied to look on." What he saw when he looked on caused him to shudder. Along with his father, he thought Lincoln a boor who was over his head in the social milieu of the White House, and Grant distressed him still more. "Grant fretted and irritated him," he wrote. "He should have been extinct for ages. . . . He had no right to exist." Returning from Harvard, where he had waited out the Grant administration teaching history courses, he settled into a house on Lafayette Square across from the White House and set himself up as a writer and critic, with his wife, Marion (Clover) Hooper, a difficult woman from an overbred family, who dabbled in photography. His great-grandmother Abigail had run a farm and looked after the family interests during a war, and his grandmother, Louisa Catherine, had traveled alone with her infant son through a fierce Russian winter. Clover, however, could not stand up to the death of her father, and she killed herself by drinking developing fluid, alone in her darkroom, while Henry was out for a walk.

After her death, Henry's mood darkened, as if the world, which rejected his claims to preeminence, had overwhelmed and then taken his wife. He burrowed still further into his cocoon of a house, surrounded by beautiful objects and rancorous thoughts. Oliver Wendell Holmes noted his tendency to turn everything to "dust and ashes." "He lacks generosity," writes Edmund Morris, finding him "contemptuous of politicians and practical achievers, paranoid about Jews, and above all, mistrustful of himself." "I regard the universe as a preposterous fraud, and human beings as fit for feeding swine," he once uttered. "Hating vindictively as I do our whole fabric and conception of society, I shall be glad to see the whole thing destroyed and swept away." The reverse of the passion that drove his forebears to create a great nation, this attitude perhaps was its residue. "As democracy in America progressed, the capacity of the Adamses for national leadership declined," Daniel Boorstin writes cruelly. "Men of large talents found themselves conspicuously unable to come to terms with their noble inheritance. . . . By the end of the nineteenth century, these most articulate Adamses had begun to luxuriate in their own decadence. They made a literary profession of saying nay to the world." Now and then, this bile would break out in what Brookhiser calls "pustules," which still contain an honest account of Henry's failings: "Not a Polish Jew from Warsaw or Cracow—not a furtive Yaccob or Ysaac still reeking of the ghetto, snarling a weird Yiddish to the officers of the customs—but had a keener instinct and intenser energy and a freer hand than he."

Henry lashed out not only at immigrants come to "corrupt" his own country, but also at the native born who had dared to rise. As his entire family had despised Andrew Jackson, they had also looked down on Abraham Lincoln, and of course on Grant, a failed president who nonetheless was also a great writer and general. Even among their own social equals, they were quick to condemn those with the ambition and energy they had so come to lack. Henry was appalled and repelled by the young Theodore Roosevelt, whom he described as "repulsively fascinating." Roosevelt's sin was his "chronic excitement," his drive, and his sheer will to power. But Henry might have said the same thing of the younger John Adams, a blunt middle-class man of no social standing and, of course, no inherited wealth.

Increasingly at odds with the world they lived in, the Adams brothers turned ever more inward, "fascinated," as Nagel had put it, with the prospect of their own dissolution. "Do you think I deserve to stand with the rest of my family?" Brooks would ask plaintively. At other times, he took note of his private futility. "I leave nothing behind . . . I go out like a candle," he said. Henry meanwhile had gone backward in time, into the past that had always consoled him since he had gone to England with his father during the Civil War. During the Grant administration, he had sought solace at Harvard, immersed in the medieval world that he found more compatible. Now he went back into it again, seeking "a world that sensitive and timid souls could regard without a shudder" because he could not now look at his own. As it was, the Middle Ages were themselves reeking with squalor and violence, but in looking at history one can choose one's own pieces, and the past he evoked was his mental cathedral, of Mont-Saint-Michel and Chartres. It was his final escape from the family industry. "By giving time, talent and money to venerating the world as it had been 800 years before, Henry went as far and as boldly as possible from the Adams legacy," Nagel informs us. "[He] had to run away from the family's policy of doing something, as well as from Boston . . . finally trading the tawdry present" for the imagined, less challenging past.

This had all been foreseen, years earlier, by none other than John Adams himself. "I must study politics and war, so that my sons may have the liberty to study mathematics and philosophy," he had written. "My sons ought to study mathematics and philosophy . . . commerce and agriculture, in order to give their children a right to study painting, poetry, music, architecture, statuary, tap-estry, and porcelain." The Adamses had suffered a surfeit of porce-lain, becoming refined at the cost of their vigor, moving from fundamental to marginal preoccupations, from the essential to the ornamental, and from the sublime to the ridiculous. In the process, they had been marginalized, by nobody but themselves. "Probably no child, born in the year, held better cards than he," Henry wrote of his birth as the grandson and great-grandson of presidents. But "he lost himself in the study of it, [and] never got to the point of playing the game." The game would go on now, absent his family. But others were in the wings.

CHAPTER 2

Roosevelts

One of those entertained by Henry Adams in his big house on
O H Street was Theodore Roosevelt, whose second wife,
Edith, had been one of Adams's favorites, admitted to the small
group of well-bred and literate women with whom he had
deigned to take tea. Adams had known TR's father, the first
Theodore Roosevelt, a loved and respected New York philanthro-
pist, who had died suddenly at age forty-six in 1877, in the
middle of a hot battle in New York state politics, in which he was
bearing the flag of reform. The papers mourned that a light
had gone out in the city, but he had left behind a tightly knit
and remarkable family, including two girls who would one day
become active in politics and one son who became a phenomenon. His other son, Elliott, would become an alcoholic and die in
his thirties, having first fathered a future first lady. But his elder
son, Theodore, would seize his baton and charge forward with it,

into the wilds of partisan politics, where no one of his class (or of Adams's) had chosen to venture for years.

Elected at age twenty-three to the New York state legislature, where he caused a sensation with his pince-nez and accent, he began a stunning ascent to the great heights of power, derailed only briefly in 1884 when his lovely young bride died in childbirth, in the same house and on the same day as Theodore's mother, still a great beauty at age forty-eight. Stunned by these blows, he had fled to the West to bury his grief in relentless activity. After two years he returned, to wed Edith Carow, his childhood sweetheart, have five more children, and resume his relentless ascent.

In the next fifteen years, he would rise like an arrow, serving as civil service commissioner (in which post he met Adams), police commissioner of New York City, assistant secretary of the navy, colonel in the Rough Riders (and hero of Cuba), and governor of New York. Even before this, he had loomed as a hero and outsize figure, a writer of books and a reader of many, a hunter and rancher, a man of exceptional talents and appetites—too many, it seemed, for some in his party, who thought they had forced him into semiretirement by running him as vice president with William McKinley, who was reelected easily in November 1900. But ten months later, McKinley was dead, and Roosevelt at forty-two had become the youngest president in American history and surely the liveliest. Adams, from his place on the sidelines, had watched this with dread. "Roosevelt . . . lived naturally in a restless agitation that would have worn out most tempers in a month, and his first year of the presidency showed chronic excitement that made a friend tremble," wrote Adams. "Roosevelt's friends knew that his restless and combative energy was more than abnormal. . . . More than any man living, [he] showed the singular primitive quality that belongs to ultimate matter. . . . He was pure act."

This chronic excitement that appalled Henry Adams enchanted the nation and the world. Never before had a leader been such a celebrity, not merely a simple political holder of office but a personality of huge and exacting dimensions, a cultural hero, a star. In many ways the first president of the modern era, he was also a genius at public relations; not until John Kennedy sixty years later would there be a president so adept at co-opting and using the press. As would Kennedy, Roosevelt made friends with reporters and mastered the art of giving them access in return for extensive and favorable coverage—he was the first president to hold "backgrounders" (leaking information under the cover of "highly placed sources"), the first to understand the ebbs and flows of the news cycle and to ride them for greater effect. Like Kennedy, he knew how to market himself and his family to build up political capital. His second wife, Edith, was too reserved and withdrawn to relish exposure, but Alice, the daughter of his star-crossed first marriage, was only too eager to make up the deficit, creating a sensation matched only later on in the century by Jacqueline Kennedy and Princess Diana, becoming known the world over for her style, her dress, and her quips. Songs would be written for and about her. On her trip in 1905 to the Far East, she was treated like royalty. Her White House wedding to Congressman Nicholas Longworth of Ohio was an extravaganza, played as a royal event. If some of her actions had a cutting edge to them, it just added interest. This interest kept up for almost a century. The most enduring of all of the children of presidents, she died in 1980 at age ninety-six, a persistent presence and a lifelong political star.

Equally endearing, although less controversial, were the five younger children, a sort of Our Gang in the White House, in some sense the whole country's children, an image their father encouraged. Pictures of the two youngest sons, Archie and

Quentin, lining up for morning drill with the White House police force were circulated just as assiduously as those sixty years later of Caroline and John Jr. dancing in John Kennedy's office or John Jr. peeking out from under his father's big desk. The whole country knew that the Roosevelt children kept pet snakes and ferrets and that Quentin had once tried to cheer up his sick brother Archie by bringing their pony up to his room. There is no record of Theodore ever telling his sons, as John and John Quincy Adams had told their children, that if they did not grow up to be great or be president, they would have failed and disgraced themselves and their families. But a cult was created around him that swept up his offspring, making them celebrities while they were still children and creating expectations on the part of the public that turned into a force of their own.

The burden fell most heavily on the eldest son, Ted, who seemed to know from the first what it was he was facing. "Don't you think it handicaps a boy to be the son of a man like Father, and especially to have the same name?" he is supposed to have said to a family blacksmith. "There can never be another Theodore Roosevelt. I will always be honest and upright, and I hope one day to be a great soldier, but I will always be known as Theodore Roosevelt's son." At age ten, he suffered from serious headaches, and doctors warned his father that the boy faced a breakdown if the pressures on him could not be lifted. Theodore tried, and to some extent did so, but when the boy wanted to go to West Point and become a professional soldier, he was talked out of it by his strong-minded father, who sent him to Harvard instead. The pressures were less direct on the second son, Kermit, who inherited the more intellectual side of his father's cluster of talents, and on the younger sons, Archie and Quentin. But all faced the challenge of becoming men under the shadow of the signature male of his generation: the model for many of courage and leadership, and one that the public demanded they live up to.

Of the millions of boys who looked up to TR as a model, none worshipped him more than his fifth cousin, Franklin, born in 1882, the year that Theodore went into politics, two years older than Alice, and an important six years older than Ted. He was the only child of the second marriage of his widowed father, who had once cast his eye on TR's big sister but been steered instead to a much younger beauty, who gave their young son his stunning good looks. Thirty years younger than her new husband, Sara Delano soon gave her heart to this child, all but smothering him in a tide of protective affection from which he frequently longed to escape. Overmothered, with a sickly and elderly father (who died in 1900 when his son was in college), Franklin early on had fastened on Theodore, as a role model, as an example on whom to pin his ambitions, and as his professional model for life.

"I think Franklin always intended to go into politics," his wife would say later. "I think Uncle Ted was responsible for that." Says Geoffrey Ward, his biographer, "As he grew, Franklin followed every stage of TR's career with eager admiration, even adopting TR's pince-nez and adjectives . . . cheerfully enduring the teasing of Harvard teammates . . . who liked to call him 'Kermit,' after the second and hardest drinking of the president's four sons."

Partly to get closer to the president's family, he became engaged at twenty-two to Eleanor, daughter of Theodore's dead brother Elliott, and married her on St. Patrick's Day in 1905, in a ceremony in which the president gave her away. The one step he would take away from his cousin the president was the decision he made to run as a Democrat, sensing that with four Roosevelt sons (and numerous nephews), he would be lost in the crush in the president's party or pushed to the back of the line. The back of the line was a place where he had no intention of staying. Three years later, Franklin would tell fellow clerks at the law firm he worked for that he intended to go into politics and to follow the TR career path— state legislator, assistant secretary of the navy, governor of New York, and then president—every step of the way.

When Franklin began his career, with Theodore's blessing, he never imagined he might have to battle his cousin himself. He entered politics in 1910 at twenty-eight, more than a year after TR had left office, having handed off the presidency to his handpicked successor, William Howard Taft, his best friend. But Theodore, who had become president at forty-two, was still only fifty, and the longing for "chronic excitement" that had made him a legend made him feel bored and underused in private life. In no time at all, he had begun to assail his successor, and by late 1911 he had decided, although privately, to run for president again.

This decision would fall like an ax through the Republican Party and cause immense strains in the Roosevelt family, where two young men the president took a paternal interest in had made commitments to other men. Alice's husband, Nicholas Longworth, was a Taft Republican, who sat in Taft's old Cincinnati House district, and Franklin had pledged himself to Woodrow Wilson, the reform governor who sat in the mansion in Trenton, New Jersey, and who had come to power as a progressive reformer, with a platform like Theodore's own. In a difficult meeting at Sagamore Hill, TR and his son-in-law agreed that Nick ought to sit out the election, campaigning neither for his patron nor for his father-in-law. Franklin, however, was forced to choose sides: at the Democrats' June convention in Baltimore, he actively worked to put Wilson over, ensuring his victory over Champ Clark, a traditional Democrat, for whose nomination Theodore "prayed." He understood that with Clark in the race, progressive Democrats would move to his standard and help elect him. With Wilson, they would stay with their party, and with TR and Taft splitting the votes of Republicans, TR and Taft would both lose.

In the end, this was exactly what happened: TR lost, although he managed to beat out Taft for second place in the contest. Several young Roosevelt in-laws and cousins, trying to start their careers in this cycle, also were crushed by the split in their party. TR would come back, but Nick Longworth lost (for the moment) his own seat in Congress and was forced to return to his home in Ohio, where a furious Alice fought with his mother and sisters. The one Roosevelt to emerge well from what was in effect a familial catastrophe was, of course, Franklin, who was not only reelected to his seat in the legislature but soon after the election was given TR's old post in the Navy Department by a Democratic Party that realized, not for the first or last time, the benefits that could fall to it by showcasing a Roosevelt of its own.

Franklin took office in what was step two of his grand plan to repeat the career of his cousin in March 1913, to a chorus of speculation from the press and his colleagues that presumed just that. "His distinguished cousin TR went from that place to the presidency. May history repeat itself," his new boss, Josephus Daniels, wrote in his diary. "He's Following in Teddy's Footsteps" went one newspaper headline. And from Teddy himself came this note of approval: "It is interesting that you yourself are in another place which I myself once held. I am sure you will enjoy yourself . . . and that you will do capital work." A professional politician himself since the start of his twenties, he understood the ambitions and pressures of other political people and did not blame them when his interests were crossed. In 1912, he had understood the problems both of Nick Longworth and Franklin and did not expect them to sacrifice themselves to his ambitions.

In 1914, campaigning in New York for Republican candidates, he refused an invitation from Franklin's mother to stay overnight as her houseguest because it might hurt Franklin if word should get out.

Democrat as he was, Franklin, who had moved his family into Bamie's big house on N Street, was much more in tune on foreign affairs with his cousin than with either his boss or his president, and after 1914 when war broke out in Europe, he acted as Theodore's spokesman and agent, pressing his pleas for an interventionist policy in what was then largely a pacifist government. He lobbied the administration for a major arms buildup. He created a rescue squad and asked for permission, which was denied him, to bring the fleet north from Guantanamo Bay. He intervened to get Theodore an interview with the president, in which TR, ailing and overweight, begged to be permitted to lead a squadron to Europe. (This was denied him.) In March 1917, Franklin and Theodore both attended a meeting in New York of interventionists, mainly TR's old Republican allies, in which both of the Roosevelts made the strongest pitches for war.

When war began shortly thereafter, Franklin asked to be sent to Europe, a request denied by the president. But all five of TR's children by his second wife would be in the thick of the battle, including Ethel, TR's younger daughter, who had married a doctor and gone to France as a war nurse in 1914. All four of his sons would show daredevil courage. Kermit joined the British Army in the Middle East and won a British Military Cross when he captured the remnants of a Turkish platoon outside Baghdad. Archie won the Croix de Guerre when he was wounded by shrapnel in his left arm and left leg. Ted Jr. was gassed on the Marne, received a Silver Star for a raid into enemy country, and received the Croix de Guerre when shot and wounded behind his left knee. Three days before young Ted had been wounded, the Roosevelts learned that Quentin, the baby, then age nineteen, had been shot down and killed while in flight behind enemy lines. It was a blow from which Theodore never recovered. Obese and ailing, the victim of his many exertions and appetites, he had been hospitalized in the summer for various ailments. Now he spent much of his time in the nursery at Sagamore Hill, saying, "Poor Quinnikins" over and over as he rocked back and forth in his chair. At ten in the evening on January 5, 1919, he told his wife that he felt his heart and his lungs were not working. In the early hours of January 6, Theodore Roosevelt died.

The king was dead, and the crown prince was being set up to succeed him, the issue in question being just who the prince was. There was Franklin, already well launched in politics, who had been Theodore's policy aide and his agent, even across party lines. But it was Ted Jr. who had lived from his boyhood with great expectations, having been written up and described as the heir to his father, who had been not only a spectacular president but the most outsize man in American life. Like everyone else in the Oyster Bay family, Ted had grown up in the shadow of Theodore, awed by him, desperately anxious to win his approval, and convinced he was never quite doing enough. As the war ended, Ted's lifelong anxiety—that he would never live up to the idea of his father—was matched by a novel and different fear: that Franklin was stealing his name and his future and might emerge as the Roosevelt heir. There was Franklin's habit of copying Theodore's gestures, his use of the name to help win him attention and office, the careful copying, through several offices, of the pattern of TR's career. (Young Ted, of course, later would do the same.) Franklin doubtless believed he had rights in the matter, having advanced Theodore's cause in the Navy Department at some risk to himself and his party. It did not seem so to Ted, who had launched himself on the same career pattern, winning election to the New York state assembly in 1919. At the Republican convention the next year, Ted and Alice gained a symbolic advance when they threw their support to Warren G. Harding in return for his promise that he would support thirty-three-year-old Ted when he ran for governor of New York four years later. But this paled in comparison to the boost the Democrats had given thirty-eight-year-old Franklin when he was nominated to run as vice president, partly because of his skill and his promise but largely because of his name.

James M. Cox, the nondescript nominee of the Democrats, sent his appealing young running mate out to the West, where his charm, ebullience, and family connections rapidly made him a national favorite, especially to voters who seemed to see in him the second coming of the great and lamented TR. But with Ted's future at stake, his aunts and cousins ardently backed the Republican ticket. As Linda Donn writes in her book on the Roosevelt cousins, "The Oyster Bay Roosevelts despised Harding, but they campaigned for him in order to block Franklin's progress and ensure that Harding would help Ted." And the Republicans, eager to keep the Roosevelt name for their party, sent Ted himself out to trail after Franklin, disputing his claims to the Theodore mantle and reminding people just who was the genuine heir.

Many things about Franklin seemed to irritate Ted, but it was the common idea that he was one of Theodore's children—"I voted for your father!" people would shout at the Democrat—that seemed to disturb him the most. Contrasting the wartime service and sacrifice of himself and his brothers with the comfortable life Franklin had been living in Washington, he implicitly declared him unworthy of the Rough Rider legacy, and one day in Wyoming, he became more explicit: "He is a maverick. He does not bear the brand of our family," Ted stated, giving voice to the latent strains that had roiled the family since at least 1912.

In retrospect, Alice thought Franklin should have said, "I wear no man's brand" and brushed it off lightly, but no such response had been possible. "Franklin . . . took it in the spirit it was meant (i.e., meanly), and got very annoyed, and that was the beginning of very bad feeling," she said. The year 1920, which ended in a Republican win, was nothing less than round one in the family drama, in which both the future and claims to the past were at stake. Franklin was not blamed for the Democrats' loss and was seen as a rising star in his party. A grateful Harding put Ted in the Navy Department, in the same job once held by his father (and Franklin), from which he proceeded to plot his own future, on the lines he and his half sister Alice had planned. He would run for governor in 1924, run for reelection two years later, and be ready in 1928 to make his own run for president. And sure enough, there would soon be another Roosevelt governor, and a Roosevelt president, and a grandchild of the first Theodore Roosevelt would once again live in the White House. But it wouldn't be Ted.

Alice and Eleanor, the daughters of the strong and "weak" Roosevelts, respectively, had gone from troubled childhoods into difficult marriages, and the problems stemming from these sad situations would linger through both of their lives. Neither grew up in a normal home with both of her natural parents: each had a dead mother, an absentee father she could not see too often, and a sense of not wholly belonging at home. Eleanor had a girlhood that was famous and frightening: with a distant mother, who died when her daughter was eight, and a disgraced, drunken father who died two years later, she was then handed off to eccentric relations in conditions TR's youngest, Corinne, would call "grim."

Alice's girlhood was not quite so dramatic, but it too contained numerous strains. After her mother died at her birth, a distraught TR handed her off to his big sister Bamie while he went West to repair his crushed spirits, returning to claim her some three years later when he was married to his second wife. Alice in time became close to her stepmother, Edith, and she was greatly loved by all her half siblings, but there were strange things around her that were never explained: she was always called "Sister" because her father found her real name too painful to mention, and her birthday was never celebrated in her family, since it had been the worst day of her father's young life. Her father's absence—and refusal to talk of her mother—left deep scars on Alice, to whom the reasons were never explained.

"Psychologists are unanimous in saying TR's first born is the virtual poster child of an abandoned baby," writes Douglas Wead in *All the Presidents' Children.* "Popular as she may have been, Alice Roosevelt Longworth is viewed by many historians as a woman who lived in great pain." Alice's cousin Nicholas Roosevelt called her a "brilliant but basically unhappy person," and her diary entries, quoted by Linda Donn in *The Roosevelt Cousins,* show that under the brave show she put on in public, she thought herself "nondescript" and inadequate. Making an impression on Theodore became the goal of her life, first through stunts done to gain his attention, then by making herself a valued political aide. Wead quotes a friend saying that Alice was capable of loving one person at a time, and for much of her life, that person was Theodore. Donn quotes psychiatrist Lawrence S. Kubie as saying that as an adult Alice carried around with her an enormous collection of Theodore's speeches and writings, and she was "enslaved to her father's memory" to a truly astounding degree. His death would do nothing to change this devotion. Instead, it would only grow worse.

Each girl had made an important political marriage: Eleanor to her fifth cousin Franklin, Alice to Nicholas Longworth, a congressman from Cincinnati and a rising Republican star. But within twelve years each had begun to unravel: by 1912, Alice had mentioned divorce to her scandalized family, and, some years later, Franklin had strayed. "I shall never be able to hold him, he is so attractive!" Eleanor had once cried to Alice's half sister, Ethel. And in 1918 she found out she had not: he had fallen in love with Lucy Paige Mercer, a beautiful girl from a good but poor family who had come to work for the Roosevelts in 1913. Still fragile from the strains of her perilous childhood, Eleanor was all but destroyed. "In the months after she had learned of the affair, her face had taken on a ravaged look," Collier and Horowitz write in their family history. "The betrayal was something she had so often imagined in the early years of their marriage that when it finally happened, it had all the force of a prophesy fulfilled."

On the campaign trail in 1920, Franklin's adviser Louis Howe had been so stunned by Eleanor's misery that he began to nudge her into a new life in politics, where she could build a future independent of Franklin while still in some sense remaining his partner in the one interest they could still share. As a young woman, she had begun finding her way into settlement houses. There was a strong strain of activism in the Roosevelt women: Bamie had been an adviser to numerous statesmen (her brother included), her cousins and aunts would speak at conventions, and her cousin Corinne (daughter of TR's baby sister) was starting a lifelong career in Connecticut politics, where she lived with her husband, Joseph Wright Alsop IV. When Franklin moved back to New York to make money, Eleanor began making her way into New York state politics, through a series of women's and liberal lobbies that worked with the governor, Alfred E. Smith. Homeless in some sense for much of her life, displaced in her own home by her husband's mother, Eleanor found her real home in cause-driven politics, among peers who could share her new interests.

Within a few years, she had risen to new heights of power, chairing committees, helping draft platforms, and speaking all over the state. Power intrigued her, but the real payoff appeared to be in the friends she was making, who gave her a kind of acceptance she had never experienced and became her alternative family. "At first tentative in her overtures, she became emboldened as she struck up successful relationships with women her own age," Collier and Horowitz tell us, "acknowledging the deep hunger for friendship she had previously suppressed." In time, she all but surrendered the big house at Hyde Park to Franklin and his mother and moved to the small cottage built on the estate where she lived and held court with her retinue. Franklin would joke of the "she-males" she befriended, but they and their causes had been her salvation. "Before this, Eleanor had merely hoped for an absence of pain," Collier wrote of her life since Franklin's affair was uncovered. "Now the possibility of a different kind of life had been revealed." At home in the world for the first time in years, she had no intention of yielding her frail grip on power or on the new peace that came with it. When a challenge arose, she would fight it intensely, even from her own father's brother's first son.

Eleanor had responded to the collapse of her marriage by establishing a new home in politics, with the friends she found in it. Alice responded to the collapse of hers by transferring her romantic affections to William E. Borah (the Idaho senator who some people thought resembled her father) and her dynastic ambitions to her half brother Ted, who returned a war hero at age thirty-one to the family future he had faced all his life. No matter that he had never before shown a talent for politics; Republican leaders were panting to run him, and TR enthusiasts all over the country were looking for an outlet for the fierce emotions they had been holding in check with some difficulty since the third-party loss in 1912.

"Ted's life was governed by a cruel combination of filial loyalty and the unspoken demands of others . . . and the strain was evident," Donn tells us, complicated by the threat of Franklin, who had stolen a march on him while Ted had been in the army, and before that, making money to sustain his projected career. Ted had the name and the descent from the hero, but Franklin was not without things that had evened the score and perhaps reversed it: he was six crucial years older; he had a history of working with TR in politics; he had run on a national ticket and had also held two public offices; he had a soothing, mellifluous baritone, whereas Ted had the high-pitched squeak of his father; and he was tall, slender, graceful, and almost too handsome. Ted was smaller and always looked agitated, with overlarge features in too small a face. Lucy Mercer aside, Franklin had a life that was almost too easy: the doted-on son of an elderly father, just the right age to ride Theodore's coattails, he had missed both the emotional trials of Alice and Eleanor and the trial by fire of Theodore's sons in the war. There was resentment of this in the Oyster Bay family, which called him "Feather Duster" in reference to his facile charm and perceived lack of consequence. And then, in August 1921, the charm on the life of Franklin D. Roosevelt would come to a sudden and terrible end.

On the evening of August 21, Franklin, then thirty-nine, went to bed at his vacation home on Campobello Island in Canada, after a long day of swimming and sailing, with a sore throat and what he thought were sore muscles. In the morning, he could not leave his bed. For the rest of his life, he would be confined to a wheelchair, and he would not again stand, much less walk, on his own. Ahead would be more than six years of grim efforts first to defeat, and then build a new life around, his profound disabilities; but not for a moment did he even seem to dream of dropping his plan to follow TR to the White House, through very much the same route. With his doctors, at least, he was unceasingly cheerful, so much so that it seemed almost as if this charming, facile, and coddled young man had been looking all the time for a test to at last prove himself Theodore's equal and the right man to bid for his legacy. For the next seven years, he would often be absent from politics as he tried to build up his legs and his body, often at the spa resort of Warm Springs in Georgia, which he made a national center for the treatment of polio. But he never lost track of the political universe and remained connected to it by Louis Howe, his political manager, as well as by Eleanor, who through her own blooming career kept the family name current in politics (and also picked up a great many tidbits, which she passed on to him via Howe).

Franklin never developed a sick man's psychology, and, building his arms and shoulders up to a wrestler's proportions, he projected an image of robust vitality. He never surrendered his cheerful benevolence. When he made his first visit on crutches back to his old office, he slipped and fell in the lobby. People around him were frightened and horrified; Roosevelt laughed. Another time, his cousin Nicholas Roosevelt saw him fall getting out of an auto; again he laughed merrily. Perhaps this was a ploy to short-circuit the pity of others; perhaps it was a firebreak against any despair that he might have felt privately; but in public at least he conveyed the belief that all would be well if it were not well already, a sense that became the core of his public persona and one that would serve him brilliantly as he tried to steer the country through two of its most long-term and nerve-wracking crises: the Great Depression and the Second World War.

"Clearly, the illness strengthened his tendency to dissimulate, to charm people while revealing as little about himself as possible," Roy Jenkins wrote in his short biography. "He increasingly kept his views secret behind a surface of optimistic geniality. It was not entirely a coincidence that he signaled his return . . . by what became famous as his 'Happy Warrior' speech, and that eight years later, the campaign song was 'Happy Days Are Here Again.'"

Through it all, what braced and propelled him was his unchanged desire to follow TR to the White House, further sparked by the bad blood that had sprung up between himself and Ted Jr. Frances Perkins, who had known him from his first days in the state legislature, and would serve as his secretary of labor in Albany and then Washington, noted that during this period one of his prime motivations was to "outshine his cousin Ted."

Any illusions that Franklin was now out of politics ended on the afternoon of June 26, 1924, when Franklin, leaning on crutches with his legs locked in braces, took fifteen steps from his chair to the lectern at Madison Square Garden to put the name of Alfred E. Smith before the convention as a candidate for president of the United States. As he spoke, the sun broke though a cloud bank over the roof of the garden and bathed his face and his figure in light. Theoretically, he was endorsing Smith, then New York's governor, but in reality he was making his own reintroduction, and the "Happy Warrior" that he spoke of was nobody but himself. Shortly after, he went back to Warm Springs, leaving his future to shine in the mind of his party and the field for the moment to Eleanor and to Ted. Franklin's speech had done more for him than it had for its subject, who lost the nomination on the 105th ballot and was thus forced to defend his old seat as governor. Ted, now thirty-six, after five years in politics, was making his bid to become the next Governor Roosevelt. And Eleanor, eager to save the new life she was building, was ready to stand in his way.

Still wounded from the Lucy Mercer debacle, Eleanor had seemed indifferent to Franklin's great triumph, to the extent that she left it out of her memoir, citing instead as the highlight of the convention her reunion with a childhood friend. Al Smith, however, was a different story: he was her patron, the friend and patron of the new friends she was making, and a central figure in the new life in politics she had struggled to build for herself. She had been devastated by his loss in the convention to John H. Davis, the Democrat picked to oppose Calvin Coolidge in the November election. But now that he was forced to run for reelection as governor, she had no intention of seeing him lose to the opposite party, much less to her cousin Ted.

On September 26, the day after the Republicans chose Ted as their candidate, she had taken the floor at the state convention of the Democrats to second Smith's nomination in a caustic speech that poured scorn on Ted as an inadequate pushover candidate and a "nice young man" in the grip of unsavory friends. Some observers were stunned at this outbreak of family warfare, but Ted had some problems that were rather more serious: he had chosen to run in a statewide race after only five years in politics (and having run only once in his assembly district), and, unlike Franklin, who had found his own style in his trial by polio, he could not find a voice of his own. People attending the convention to see the second coming of Theodore Roosevelt found instead a slight, earnest, anxious young man, straining to project an image of vigor and instead sounding strident and shrill. Cartoonists drew him as a tiny figure, all but submerged in the voluminous folds of his dead father's uniform; opponents railed at him as a small child playing at being a grown-up; editorialists mocked him for trying to imitate his dead father's gestures and voice.

As if trying to show where his heart really was, Ted tried to campaign on his impressive war record and held flag-waving rallies surrounded by veterans. But he was fighting not only one, but two major enemies: Smith, a veteran campaigner and genuine success story from the Lower East Side of Manhattan, and his own father, whose galvanic memory made all around him seem dim by comparison, including, alas, his own sons. He was also damaged by an implied connection to one of the many scandals of the Harding administration, the transfer of oil leases at Teapot Dome in Wyoming that briefly had been under his control in the Navy Department but in which he had played no real part. It was at this point that Eleanor moved in for the kill, dressing a car in a papier-mâché "teapot" in which she trailed Ted as he made campaign speeches, interrupting him with blasts of steam from its improvised "spout." On Election Day, Ted lost the state by a hundred thousand votes out of a three-million-vote total, and his dream of succeeding his father was shattered. Eleanor for her part had emerged as a vengeful, and powerful, player. And Franklin's own rise had begun.

Theodore Roosevelt Jr. would lead a life rich in accomplishment, in business, the arts, and government, serving on the board of the American Express Corporation and as vice president of the publishing firm of Doubleday Doran, and doing good works, as his grandfather before him, in a range of wholly commendable causes, helping found the American Legion and working hard on behalf of civil rights interests. Yet for the next sixteen years, his life would be shaped by his loss to Al Smith in the 1924 election, first in a dogged effort to claw his way back into politics and then in an effort to deal with his loss. At first he seemed stunned, and a little off balance, deprived of the cause that had been his life's mission and the goal he had held all his life. As his wife would write later, this was the most difficult part of their life together, adding that his business career "was nothing but the means to an end," which of course had been politics, driven by a "strong feeling that he must prove worthy of the father whom he adored."

Party leaders were happy enough to send him out on the road to rip into Democrats, and his attacks on Al Smith in the 1926 and 1928 elections were strident enough to make people gasp as they listened. But his poor performance in 1924 had discouraged the powers that be in his party, and his appeals for a chance to run once more for office—to run for governor again in the 1926 election and to run with Herbert Hoover in 1928 as his running mate—were politely and firmly turned down. That was the year Henry F. Pringle, who would write books about Al Smith and about young Ted's father, published a book that correctly diagnosed the source of young Theodore's problems: he was the victim of outsize expectations, and he had been brought along much too fast. "The most casual analysis of the record reveals that he was rushed along too swiftly. He should have remained in Albany for several years, and there learned the ABC's of the political game. He was far from mature politically when he went to Washington, and additionally handicapped by comparisons to his father. Roosevelt is still immature," Pringle added. "Just turned forty, he has little concept of what it is all about."

In 1928, Hoover was elected president, the same year that Franklin became New York's second Roosevelt governor, and, under heavy pressure from Ted's wife and Alice, named Ted governor-general of Puerto Rico, a post upgraded a year later when he was appointed governor of the Philippines. Because the posts did not demand the use of political talents, Ted was successful, but he could not have been encouraged by this conversation between two Puerto Ricans, as reported in the *New York Times*:

> "Roosevelt is coming to be governor."
> "What Roosevelt?"
> "The son of the President."
> "The son of the President is the governor of New York."

What Ted and his family had secretly feared since the first race run by Franklin—and especially since the 1920 election when frenzied crowds hailed him as a child of Theodore—had finally started to happen in earnest: Franklin had stolen both his name and his future and emerged as the family heir. Franklin had, like Ted, begun his career by idolizing and imitating the older man and hitching a ride on the tail of his rocket, but what Ted didn't realize was that Franklin the candidate had deepened and altered and emerged as a star on his own.

Some similarities would always remain: Franklin and Theodore both believed in proactive policies; both projected vigor and optimism. But over the years, Franklin had gradually dropped the Theodore tics he picked up as a schoolboy, much as he dropped the pince-nez. Franklin had less genius than Theodore but better emotional balance; less intensity but more ingenuity, more subtlety, less bombast, more guile. "Franklin admired his cousin extravagantly . . . but his basic personality was quite different," says Geoffrey Ward, his biographer, noting that "intrinsic differences between them finally made Franklin's almost worshipful imitation of his cousin impossible to sustain. . . . The mature FDR was neither shrill nor bellicose nor hyperkinetic. . . .

His own distinctive personality emerged slowly but steadily. . . . He was simply not credible trying to seem like someone he was not." If the fading glamor of Theodore's name had had some part in 1928 in Franklin's election as governor, it was Franklin himself who won the landslide he earned two years later, and later on, in his presidency, he built for himself his own large devout following. It was only close to the end of the twentieth century, when both men were long dead, that interest revived in their vital connection, although both still stood tall on their own.

Ted was in Manila on November 4, 1932, when he learned by radio that Franklin had been elected president of the United States. This time, he knew that his hopes were now ended. "I believe the chances of me 'coming back' politically are now non-existent," he wrote to his mother. "That chapter of our lives is definitely closed." To Franklin, of course, it was a brand-new beginning. Collier quotes Bamie's son as saying, "Power released something essential in him . . . a confidence, a joy, a reminiscence of the tireless ardor that had characterized TR in his day."

For the Oyster Bay branch, it meant something quite different: a sideways retreat into resentment and memory that seemed now to freeze them in time. More and more, they clung fast to TR and his greatness as a buffer against more recent history. Increasingly, the idea grew among them that Franklin had "stolen" Ted Jr.'s career. Edith remained deeply embittered. Enraged at the hundreds of letters that arrived at Sagamore Hill congratulating her on the presidential campaign being waged by her "child," she appeared late in October at a packed Hoover rally, where, "dressed all in black . . . her pale face burning," she ripped into the man who had, in her opinion, rudely displaced her first son. A few weeks later, she and Ted were both scandalized when Kermit and his wife, Belle (who would later become part of the FDR circle), accepted an invitation to cruise on Vincent Astor's yacht *Nourmahal* in a party that included the president-elect. Ted's wife later recorded what happened when a reporter asked her husband why his brother had gone on a cruise with his rival. "Before he could answer, [Edith's] gentle voice came across the table. . . . 'Because his mother was not there!'"

Ted himself remained locked in reflexive hostility, so constricted by it that when Franklin narrowly escaped assassination (by a bullet that killed Chicago mayor Anton Cermak, who had been sitting beside him), he could not give a simple statement about it without carefully weighing all the possible nuances again and again in his mind. "I was shocked," he later wrote to his mother, but "I could not let the matter go for fear of being called surly, but at the same time I must not slop over" and let people think he was "curry[ing] favor" with the man who had beaten him out. His real feelings would burst out in a note he would write after hearing that Alice had gone to the White House: "I could not help feeling it was like behaving in like fashion to an enemy in time of war."

Alice was the one most conflicted in the interfamily battle: she was drawn to Franklin, whom she saw as a kindred spirit and a co-conspirator in her war against stuffiness: the two had enjoyed themselves greatly in World War I Washington when they had "spied" on an acquaintance thought to be passing on to the Germans Allied secrets she had unearthed in the course of a love affair with Bernard Baruch. At the same time, she remained locked in her father obsession and could not resist tossing hand grenades over the barricades, such as the assertion, made in a 1936 newspaper column, that while Theodore had successfully battled asthma to become a vigorous athlete, Franklin had merely adjusted to the limitations forced on him by polio and was now trying to get the depression-wracked country to adjust to the same crippled fate. This was grossly unfair, because the disease that he had could not be conquered, and, as Alice said later, "This quite rightly made him hopping mad." "I could have had a lot of fun with Franklin if only the damned old presidency hadn't come between us," Alice wrote later. But come between them it had, and with it had come her old fear that his success might diminish her father, and so she kept sniping. The end came when in 1940 she said she would "vote for Hitler" before casting a vote for her cousin. With that, her invitations to the FDR White House dried up.

What contact there was between the two branches was kept up by the families of Theodore's sisters: Bamie, and the youngest, Corinne. In 1924, on her Teapot tour of the state, Eleanor had crossed the state line to Bamie's big house in Connecticut and asked for a bed for the night. Appalled as she was by the spectacle of her favorite niece attacking the son and namesake of her beloved dead brother, the dutiful aunt took her in. "Mother liked Eleanor, so she just swallowed it," Bamie's son said. Another point of contact was made by Corinne, who in 1932 turned down a chance to speak at the Republican convention because she did not want to campaign against Eleanor's husband. (In return, the president-elect and Mrs. Roosevelt were honored guests at her funeral when she died the next year.) Corinne's daughter, Corinne Robinson Alsop, a first cousin to Alice and Eleanor, remained close to both when they no longer were close to each other, and she balanced her role as a power in Republican politics with her status as Eleanor's friend. After seconding the nomination in 1936 of Alf Landon to run against Franklin, she went home to her Connecticut district to instruct her voters in splitting their tickets, to keep down-ticket Republican candidates from being wiped out in the oncoming

FDR landslide. After that, unwilling to miss a good family party, she invited herself to Franklin's inaugural ball.

Two of her sons, Stewart Alsop and Joseph Wright Alsop V, arguably the best political journalists of the twentieth century, also bridged the family chasm, being equally welcome in the FDR White House and the big house on Massachusetts Avenue near Dupont Circle where Alice Roosevelt Longworth held court. Corinne sent Eleanor an effusive letter when the First Lady, enraged when the Daughters of the American Revolution refused to allow Marian Anderson to sing in their concert hall, arranged for her to perform at the Lincoln Memorial. Theodore had been the president who lowered the color bar at the White House, inviting Booker T. Washington to several lunches, and Ted Jr. was active in civil rights causes, sitting on the boards of Howard University and the NAACP. At one on so much, the clans were divided by grievance and memory. And so it went on.

As the 1930s ground to an end, Alice and Ted slipped into a mode of reflexive hostility, much as they had earlier with other successors and rivals, such as Woodrow Wilson and Taft. Himself the father of a large loving family, Ted took perverse pleasure in the scandals that sprang up around FDR's children, whose lives in their parents' unhappy household were now bearing turbulent fruit. Periodically, he emerged to deliver harsh critiques of Franklin, whose New Deal, so he claimed, betrayed Theodore's legacy. He was suspicious of FDR on domestic policy, and when fascism bloomed as a menace in Europe, he was suspicious of him on that, too. "I am bitterly fearful of Franklin," he had written to Alice. "He is itching to get into this situation, partly as a means of bolstering himself." With Ted in this mood, it was easy for Alice to pull him with her into America First, the anti-interventionist group she had helped establish, in much the same spirit that, twenty years earlier, she had rallied opposition against Wilson's League of Nations. Alice was happy enough tossing spitballs at Franklin, but the dutiful Ted was a different matter completely, and he soon began having doubts. Was this really what his father would have wanted? Would his bellicose father have backed isolation? Before World War I, TR and Franklin had stood together for a common front with the Allies. Would TR once more have been standing with Franklin? Was it possible Franklin was right?

This seemingly closed circle of ongoing grievance was ruptured at last by the war. Distressed by conversations he had overheard suggesting that members should refuse to enlist if war did in fact come to the country, Ted severed his ties to America First. He asked George Marshall, chief of staff of the army, to put him back on active duty, and he was given command of his old unit, the 26th infantry, in April 1941. Four days after Pearl Harbor, Franklin raised him to the rank of brigadier general, and he was sent to Fort Blanding, where his son Quentin joined him. Archie, now forty-six, and still suffering the effects of the wounds that had won him a 100 percent disability, wanted so badly to get back into action that he took the extraordinary step of writing to Franklin, an ice breaker that, as Collier and Horowitz noted, "would grow into a wary collaboration as the war progressed."

But no one was more eager to see war than Kermit, who looked to it to give him a path back to his father and redeem the squandered promise of his youth. Once thought the most brilliant of all TR's sons, a gifted writer, explorer, and linguist, a man who spoke Urdu and Romany and read Cervantes in Spanish as he rode on the subway, Kermit was breaking under the strain of being a Roosevelt, or at least being the kind of Roosevelt his father had been. Like his brothers, Kermit had been raised to be a great man, a scholar, and a hero. But since the Great Crash, the one he resembled most had been Elliott, TR's black sheep brother (and Eleanor's father), who had gone in for heavy drinking, what were referred to at the time as "lower-class women," and absences of weeks, if not months, from his home. Enlisting in the British Army (as he had in his first war), he had performed bravely at the battle of Narvik in Norway in June 1940 as the Nazis had overrun western Europe. But this brave start was also the end of his comeback: sent next to Egypt, Kermit fell ill with malarial fever and was sent back to America the following year.

Back at home, with no prospect of action, he started once more to drink with a vengeance. He spent the next year and a half disappearing from sight, going on benders, or taking "cures" in the hospitals into which Archie would check him, which seemed to do him no good. For a time in 1941, Franklin sent the FBI out to find him, after he disappeared for some months with a mistress. When found, he begged to go back into battle, as if it were his one hope in life. Searching for a place to put him where he could do the least damage, Franklin and General George C. Marshall had him sent to a base in Alaska, in the armed forces, yet out of harm's way. But there was little to do there, and he had ample time to dwell on his demons. On the night of July 3, 1943, the second son of Theodore Roosevelt took his service revolver and shot himself in the head.

When this occurred, Archie was already in action, having forced his way into a combat unit then in New Guinea, showing such remarkable courage that a key mountain peak on one of the islands was named "Roosevelt Ridge" in his honor. But it was Ted in the end who emerged as a legend, performing a spectacular role in the D-day invasion, winning every decoration that the U.S. ground forces could give. Under arms, he was back in his element, in the world he had loved as a child, free of resentment for the first time since the 1924 election, and of anxiety for the first time in years. "Ted is very well, and far happier than he has been for some years," his wife would write gratefully. "He has got his teeth into something he knows he can do supremely well." If Ted, as his cousin Nicholas noted, "had not inherited his father's flair for politics," he had more than inherited his feeling for war. "Fearless, brave, tireless, with a strong sense of responsibility and a truly great gift for inspiring his men, he was at his best in war," Nicholas added. "It was as a personal leader of troops under fire or in difficulties that he was at his best. . . . He knew by their first names more than 1000 men in his division. . . . The wiser among the general officers regarded him as worth a division himself because of his great gift of leadership and his rare capacity for heartening a whole front line."

At the front, he was known for two affectations: his jeep, painted with the words "Rough Rider," and his cane, which he leaned on through two great invasions, to ease the pain of his arthritic hip. On D-day, he and his son Quentin were the sole father-and-son team to hit the beaches together (although at different locations), and each man would emerge unscathed. As he landed on Utah Beach, Ted saw his troops had disembarked by mistake about a mile south of their true destination, in a spot massively raked by enemy fire. "Immediately organizing a counterattack . . . he began personally shuttling groups of soldiers to the protection of a sea wall," writes Peter Collier. "He was under constant enemy fire for several hours, propping himself up on his cane." General Omar Bradley would call this the bravest feat he had ever seen done by an American soldier, and Ted would be played by Henry Fonda in the epic film *The Longest Day*. Eisenhower was about to raise him to the rank of major general on the evening of July 14 when Quentin arrived to visit his father.

Ted appeared drawn but exceedingly happy, telling his son he felt "whole." Back at his unit, Quentin was awakened at three the next morning and told that his father was dead.

About the time that Ted died while on duty in Normandy, Franklin had started to fail. Just sixty-one, all at once he appeared twenty years older, suddenly haggard, his neck thin, his face gray. Drained by twelve years of unending crisis, he had served three terms, one more than any other man in American history; he had held the country together in the face of a hard and protracted depression and then faced a malignant and barbarous international menace to which he had been unable to alert his own country until it was almost too late. His troubles began when he returned from the Tehran Conference in December 1943, feeling drained and lethargic, and an examination on March 28 the year after found him in cardiac failure, with blood pressure levels that skyrocketed to 240/130 at the Quebec Conference in September 1944. Nonetheless, he insisted on running for a fourth term that autumn, although leading Democrats were so concerned that they had forced Henry Wallace off the ticket at the July convention, replacing him there with Harry S. Truman, considered a much sounder choice. Truman saw FDR at the White House on August 18, and he later wrote, "Physically, he's just going to pieces." In February, Winston Churchill's physician saw him at Yalta and wrote in his diary, "He has all the symptoms of hardening of the arteries. . . . I give him only a few months to live."

In his last months, one of those Franklin saw most was Archie, who had been sent home from the Pacific wounded in action, the only man in the history of the U.S. armed forces to receive a 100 percent disability twice. Once back, he began agitating to be sent back to the front, even when felled by a bout of malaria that side-lined him in the fall. Once over that, he went to the White House to make his case to his cousin in person. They had, FDR told Archie's wife, a "nice chat." At the end, Archie pressed into the president's hand the battered cigarette case he had carried with him through seventy-six days in action: a sign that the worst of the family battles was over, burned out in the fires of war. Archie would write Franklin later that they could both take pride in what they and their kin had done to ensure the oncoming victory: "It seems to me that regardless of the bitterness that many people feel toward the 'Hyde Park' Roosevelts or the 'Oyster Bay' Roosevelts, they have to admit that the whole clan has turned out to a man." FDR sympathized with Archie's desire to get back in action. But the president, who had taken Kermit's widow, Belle, under his wing and was engaged in a correspondence with Archie's wife, Grace, did not want to send Theodore's last living son back into battle, and he wrote to Marshall that Archie was "too old and too sick" to go back. Franklin was still brooding about the best way to break this to Archie when he went off for a short vacation at Warm Springs in Georgia on April 10. His old love, Lucy Mercer, was with him on the morning of April 12 when he raised his hand to his head and complained of a headache. Minutes later, the president died.

"It was like the magnificent climax of a great play," Quentin Roosevelt wrote to his mother when Ted died in Normandy. Franklin's death in Warm Springs about eight months later—of much the same cause and for much the same reason—rang down Act II in the Roosevelt drama, a long-running, intense, and popular saga that had mesmerized the world for fifty years. Alice and Eleanor would live on, very much their old selves, world famous until the days they expired: Eleanor in 1962, ever the activist; Alice in 1980, having been the scourge and the delight of a series of presidents, at the ripe old age of ninety-six.

But with the deaths of the "boys," the main story had ended— the war for possession of Theodore's mantle that the president himself had had some part in starting, when, along with his own brood of four lively boys, he took his young cousin Franklin under his wing. Who won the battle? Both did. TR at heart was a warrior manqué, who longed all his life for distinction in battle, who wanted to charge into every war going, and never got over the shame of the fact that his father, because he had married a woman from Georgia, had sent a substitute to fight for him in the Civil War. So frantic was he for his own "crowded hour" that in 1898 he was prepared to leave his gravely ill wife to charge into Cuba. "I made up my mind," he would tell a friend later, "that I would not allow even a death to stand in my way." But what he confronted, in both the White House and Cuba, was child's play to what would be faced by his heirs. No one was more aware of this than the old lion himself. "I walk with my head higher because of him," he would say to Ted's wife. "My war was a bow-and-arrow affair compared to Ted's, and no one knows it better than I." It was Franklin who followed his path, almost step by step, into the White House and then into history. But it was Ted who fulfilled his old longing for battlefield glory, dying a hero and a different kind of great man.

In 1946, Ted's oldest son Teddy returned from the navy a hero and was seized on at once, as his father before him, as a glowing political property. He dutifully served one term as Pennsylvania's secretary of commerce and then came under "incredible pressure" to run for higher state office. "Articles began to appear . . . calling Teddy the 'hidden weapon' of the Republican Party," his mother wrote later. Only one thing appeared to cloud his bright future:

politics made him physically ill. At last, his distraught wife appealed to his mother. "I answered that no one should ever go into politics without an overwhelming urge to do so," she wrote back, doubtless recalling her husband, and adding that "Teddy could fulfill his duty to his country in other ways." With this, the Oyster Bay branch would bow out of history, into worthy careers in more private venues, untroubled by genius or tragedy.

Things were different on the FDR side of the family, where the splendid records his sons had racked up in the armed services were the sole bright spots in lives marked by scandal before them, and scandal and failure ahead. Raised in a highly dysfunctional household, caught in the cross fires between their mother and father (and in the war of long standing between Sara and Eleanor), they had emerged as adults both ruthless and rattled, raised by parents distracted by their own problems and unwilling to rein in their children out of guilt. When FDR was elected president in 1932, his sons were old enough to want to fully exploit his high office and immature enough to be exploited by others, who flattered and used them. They were also filled with resentments against both of their parents, which they worked out in varying ways—writing tell-all books that told ugly secrets or sometimes invented them, going to work for political enemies, and getting enmeshed in scandals that tarnished their name. "They were either seeking acceptance or intimacy . . . or they were as far away as they could get," writes Doug Wead in *All the Presidents' Children*. "Some of them traded shamelessly on their father's name, even while they sought their own identity. Two sons worked for their father's bitterest enemies, and another married into a family that openly despised him. One lobbied against parts of his legislative program in Congress. Another endorsed his father's opponent when he ran for a third term."

The youngest son, John, ran as far as he could from the family business, becoming a Republican, marrying a socialite whose father hated his parents, and taking a job as a salesclerk in Filene's department store in Boston, where he worked his way up to a business career. His other three brothers had different ambitions. By the end of FDR's second term, Franklin Jr. had made headlines for mischief in the schools he attended; Elliott had been married twice, was deeply in debt, and had been involved in a scheme to sell military planes to the Soviet Union; and Jimmy, the eldest, was so entangled in charges of conflict of interest that he was forced wto reveal his tax returns to reporters from *Collier's*. He once approached William O. Douglas, then head of the Securities and Exchange Commission, to do a favor for a friend who had a case coming up before that regulatory body. When Douglas refused, Jimmy told him that "now that the Democrats were in office . . . it was their turn to make money." Douglas repeated all this to the president, who, when he heard it, put his head down and cried.

Nonetheless, neither Franklin nor Eleanor ever attempted to control their children, who returned from the armed forces more determined than ever to cash in on their parents' estate. Although hostile to each other (and Elliott), Jimmy and Franklin divided the coasts in their first tries at politics: Jimmy making his move in California, where he had gone before the war to make money in movies; Franklin staking his claim in the family fief of New York. With the magic name and the robust good looks of his father, Franklin Jr. won a House seat in 1949, and his future seemed boundless. But the only impression he made was a bad one, and when he ran for attorney general in 1954, he lost. In California, Jimmy tried to run for governor in 1950 from a standing start as state party chairman and was trounced by Earl Warren, as his mother had predicted. Four years later, in the midst of a new bout of personal scandal, he decided to run for a seat in the House, in spite of a warning from his sister's new husband that his race would embarrass the family. "You may subconsciously believe that your rehabilitation is only through the ballot-box," Dr. James Halstead had warned him. "But don't forget . . . people will give their approval . . . only because you are your father's son." This was doubtless true, but it was enough to win him election, and he served six terms, none with distinction. But all hope of high office was gone.

Still hoping for a political comeback, FDR Jr. attached himself to the 1960 campaign of John Kennedy, son of his father's old backer-turned-rival, who had all the focus, direction, and discipline the Roosevelt children were lacking, selling him the one asset he still had to offer—his name. When the Catholic Kennedy ran into trouble in West Virginia, a state that had once worshipped President Roosevelt, Franklin sent out a mass mailing under his name with the Hyde Park postmark, making it seem like a voice from the grave. JFK paid him off with a subcabinet post but tended to use him as a gofer and lackey, sending him to chaperone Jacqueline Kennedy when she took a cruise on the yacht of Aristotle Onassis shortly after the death of her premature baby. Soon after Franklin's return from this aquatic idyll, President Kennedy was murdered in Dallas, and his last ties to power were snapped.

Even when out of the business of politics, the Roosevelts continued to embarrass their family in novel and startling ways. It soon took a scorecard to keep up with their marriages, which amounted to nineteen among the five siblings, with two brothers racking up five apiece. Several wrote so-called insider accounts of their parents' unhappy marriage, which differed widely in the blame they assigned to each party but had the aggregate effect of making them seem unattractive, profiting from their parents while dragging them down. A cheerfully amoral hustler who managed to become a black sheep in even this family, Elliott forged a career living off his mother, first selling off properties from the Hyde Park estate, then becoming her "agent" for embarrassing television and advertising endeavors, and finally, long after her death, lending his name to a series of novels that featured her as an amateur detective, a sort of Miss Marple on the Potomac, solving a number of capital crimes. "Puncturing the myths that others created about their parents became for them an obscure way of asserting a principle," writes Peter Collier. It was the flip side of what had occurred in the Oyster Bay family, in which obsessive worship of the great man in their background had paralyzed some of the family members, casting them in the role of perpetual acolytes, frozen in place and irrelevance. For the Hyde Park branch, desecration became a perverse form of calling, on the theory that if they could not rise up to the heights of their parents, they could at least drag them down to their level.

In the twentieth century, two spectacular Roosevelt presidents had had four sons apiece, who gave rise to a fever of great expectations that somehow had failed to come true. TR's son, Ted Jr., was a good man who suffered because he was not a great politician. For the FDR sons, greatness was out of the question, and goodness not even attempted, as they set out to pillage the house of their parents and buried themselves in its crash. As a result, the presidential estate that might have gone to Theodore's children went to Franklin, a fifth cousin and a Democrat. And the Democratic future that might have belonged to his children went to his enemy's sons.

CHAPTER 3

Kennedys: Rise

When Eleanor Roosevelt arrived at the Democratic convention in Los Angeles in July 1960, she was appalled to realize that three of her sons were actively working against her own candidate and for the son of a man she detested and her husband had come to despise. A millionaire born in the Irish wards of East Boston, Joseph P. Kennedy had been one of the few financiers to back Franklin in 1932 when he had first run for president, and he had served with distinction as the first head of the Securities and Exchange Commission, an agency created in 1934. But his stint as ambassador to the Court of St. James's had been a catastrophe, and he emerged as a hindrance, and then a pariah, forced by ill will to retire from politics and to pin all his hopes on his sons.

It is this that makes him different from dynasts before him, who were subtly different in attitude. Other dynasts had wanted their sons to succeed, to further the work of their lifetimes. For

Kennedy, his sons *were* the work of his lifetime, and all that he did was subsumed in their cause. His sole interest in the fortune he made was in having it serve as a base for his children. He supported Roosevelt in the depths of the Depression because he thought he was the one man in the country who could save the free enterprise system and, with it, his children's inheritance. He was drawn to isolationism, and then to appeasement, because he believed, all too correctly, that war would endanger the lives of his sons. "The only occupation to which he ever committed himself was fatherhood," writes his biographer, Richard J. Whelan. "He felt an extraordinary responsibility for, and participation in, the success of his children. . . . What the Roosevelts lacked, the Kennedys possessed in abundance. Because of these qualities, the Kennedys ironically could even press into service the underexploited Roosevelt fame."

Kennedy was born in 1888, the grandson of refugees from the great Irish famine, and the immense divide in his hometown of Boston between the Protestant natives and the Catholic Irish—a chasm just inches away from a legal apartheid—was the formative fact of his life. Life for the Irish and the Yankees was separate and wholly unequal: the Irish could live in a parallel universe, with their own separate rankings and rituals, but social acceptance and genuine power would always be out of their reach. Some biographers trace his roaring ambition to the day when he and his Catholic friends were denied admission to the best clubs in Harvard, a lesson to him of the force he was facing, and a warning that accepting conventions would do him no good. "It was a devastating experience," writes Doris Kearns Goodwin. "He looked at himself in a different way, and from then on he realized that he was going to have to fight that world. . . . He would have to mount an attack, and in some ways . . . his whole career from then on, the money, the kids, the presidency, was his attack on that whole Brahmin world."

Like FDR, Kennedy made the best political marriage he could within his own orbit, marrying Rose Fitzgerald, the favorite daughter of the mayor of Boston, the king of the small Irish universe. He also set out to make large sums of money, in a financial career that was as lucrative and dazzling as it was uncentered and hard to describe. He produced little, founded no companies, and left little behind as tangible proof of his efforts. "He gave his occupation as 'capitalist' in 1932," Whelan tells us, but calls this a "bare description of a man perpetually in motion, an entrepreneur who plunged into situations promising wealth and prestige and pulled out quickly when the possibilities were exhausted." "He got into the movie business early and made money; he got out of the stock market in May, 1929, when everyone else seemed to be getting in," Michael Barone tells us. "Throughout his career, [he] had an instinct for numbers and an eye for the opportunities that others failed to see."

By the age of thirty, Kennedy had made his first million; by his midthirties, he controlled one of the great American fortunes. Doubtless he had always intended to turn his eye toward politics, but the crash of 1929 and the depression that followed accelerated this change, and for two different reasons: he was afraid that financial and social collapse would erode his children's security, and he was correctly convinced that power in the next several decades would accrue to the people in government. In the year he helped Roosevelt make his first run for power, he welcomed into his family the last of the nine children for whom he would try to do everything: Joe Jr., born in 1915; John Fitzgerald, born two years later; and then the others, the girls and small children: Rosemary, Kathleen, Eunice, Patricia, Robert, Jean, and the youngest, Edward Moore Kennedy, born on Washington's Birthday in 1932.

Kennedy joined the FDR team at its inception, starting a complex, often tortured relationship that lasted for nearly ten years. At first, all was sunshine, at least on the surface. Between 1930 and 1932, Kennedy raised hundreds of thousands of dollars, contributed thousands more of his own money, and at the Chicago convention helped break up a menacing deadlock when he convinced William Randolph Hearst, who controlled the California delegation, to come over to Roosevelt's side.

Pretending an affinity that neither man really felt, he hosted the president's party for long liquid nights in the mansion he leased in the Maryland countryside. He showered care and advice on the president's children, making a special pet out of the gullible Jimmy, whom he used to get business deals. Apparently on the grounds that he would know which abuses to look for because he had presumably done them, Roosevelt made him head of the Securities and Exchange Commission, where he performed brilliantly, boosting his stock as a possible candidate. But it was the Court of St. James's that was to be his undoing, proving that whatever his skills might have been in the market, his political eye was not keen. He was never the Nazi some detractors have made him, but he proved so obtuse to the great dangers posed by the Axis, so naive in his hopes that it could be bargained with, and so defeatist at the prospect of raising resistance that he was seen, quite correctly, as one of its tools.

His motives, as always, were familial and personal. "I should like to ask you," he wrote in a line that Roosevelt made him take out of a speech about Munich, "if you know of any dispute or controversy existing in the world which is worth the life of your son, or of anyone else's son." But Roosevelt, who was now going around him to deal directly with Churchill and others, saw Kennedy as a bomb to be defused with great caution as he gingerly went about the delicate business of preparing the country for war. Isolated in the administration, Kennedy was now detested in Britain, especially after bombing raids started in June 1940 and the country was facing the Axis alone. Back home, Kennedy was forced into endorsing Roosevelt when he ran for a third term, and he soon cut his own throat in an unguarded interview, in which he said that democracy was finished in Britain and war would also finish it in the United States. The damage was such that he would never recover. The job of climbing the redoubts of power would fall to his more politic sons.

One son in particular would be groomed to wield power, and in some ways he seemed the ideal. "He is going to be president of the United States," Honey Fitz told the press when his first grandson was born on July 16, 1915. "His mother and father have already decided he is going to Harvard. . . . Then he's going to be a captain of industry until it's time for him to be president for two or three terms." The captain of industry was not in the cards, because Joe kept his children remote from his interests in business, but as Joe Jr. grew—bright, handsome, sturdy, and successful in everything— the president part seemed increasingly plausible. As Jack would write later with some tinge of envy, "He had great physical courage and stamina, a complete confidence in himself which never faltered, and he did everything with a great verve." His parents adored him, as did his young siblings, to whom he behaved as a sort of third parent, showering them with parental affection. "Very early in life he acquired a sense of responsibility," Jack later noted. "He would spend long hours throwing a football with Bobby, swimming with Teddy, and teaching the younger girls how to sail."

There was friction only with the second son, Jack, two years younger, and smaller and sickly, the only one big enough to be competition while never quite able to win. First in Boston; then in New York, where Kennedy in 1926 moved his family; in the Palm Beach mansion he bought in 1932 as a winter retreat for the family; and especially at Hyannis, the Cape Cod "cottage" that Kennedy bought in 1928 to give his young children the Brahmin experience, life was a series of fierce competitions, in which young Joe won and Jack lost. Joe Jr. was tall, strong, and robust, with a disciplined intellect; Jack was scrawnier, frequently bedridden, with a more quirky and less tidy mind. Joe obeyed his parents and teachers in everything; Jack would stage quiet and subtle rebellions. Joe did everything at the height of his powers; Jack chronically underperformed in his studies, except for the rare moments his interest was piqued. At Choate, where Joe won the Harvard trophy for all-around excellence, Jack (with two other boys who also had star older brothers) formed a club called the Muckers, which specialized in subversion, and nearly got them expelled. Joe Sr., who could see his namesake moving in a measured pace to the White House via the governor's mansion, despaired frequently of his second son's progress. "The happy-go-lucky manner with a degree of indifference . . . does not portend well for his future development," Joe Sr. wrote to Jack's headmaster. To his oldest son, who functioned as both Jack's goad and his protector, he added, "Mr. Ayres told me that he has one of the few great minds he has ever had in history, yet they all recognize the fact that he lacks any sense of responsibility, and it will be too bad if with the brains he has he really doesn't go as far up the ladder as he should."

Joe Jr. grew up shaped by his father's ambition, which he adopted and took as his own; Jack, in the shadow of the brother he envied, resented, and idolized, stressing his qualities that were those least like Joe's. If Joe was obedient, he was subversive; if Joe was orderly, he was untidy; if Joe applied himself, he adopted a facade of unconcern. He was clever enough to know he was undermining himself with this attitude, as he explained to a psychiatrist called in by Choate. "My brother is the efficient one in the family. I am the boy that doesn't get things done. If my brother were not so efficient, it would be easier," he said to the doctor. "He does it so much easier than I." As the doctor noted, he was "in a trap . . . he has established a reputation . . . for thoughtlessness, sloppiness, and inefficiency, and he feels entirely at home in the role. . . . Jack is apparently avoiding comparison and withdraws from the race . . . in order to convince himself that he is not trying," convinced that if he tried, he would lose. In view of his later career, it is likely he was suppressing some of his own more aggressive and leaderly qualities as falling into the sphere that belonged to young Joe. "A good deal of his trouble is due to comparison with an older brother," the doctor reported, correctly. Despite his strenuous efforts to appear carefree and careless, Jack was diagnosed at seventeen with a spastic colon and incipient ulcers, conditions related to stress.

At the same time, as Jack would come to see later, being perfect was not always that simple for Joe. "Though a glance at Joe's record shows that he had great success, things did not come particularly easy for him," Jack would write later, adding that "I do not think I can ever remember him to sit back in a chair and relax." Many would find him overly serious; a friend in London described him as "struggling to 'do the world one better, to have the last word, to be one-up on every person he encountered, be that person a brother or stranger,'" in competition with "life itself." Classmates and roommates at Harvard Law School (the one school to which Jack would not follow him) recalled him as under fierce and perpetual pressure, working "like a slave" to keep up with his studies, buying class notes on Harvard's "black market," and taking special lessons from a Boston judge who was a friend of his father's.

When Jack pulled himself up and started to shine intermittently, Joe became edgy. A roommate recalled Joe as "overwhelmed academically" and "increasingly jealous" of what he perceived to be Jack's easy successes," Edward Renahan writes in *The Kennedys at War*, his biography of the younger family members. "Joe once told me he thought Jack had some kind of lucky charm," a classmate remembered. "But he said the luck wouldn't last forever and Jack would be sunk in the long run. . . . He was clearly disapproving of Jack's relaxed attitude, and at the same time envious of how Jack's successes tended to pile up." When Jack was praised for a speech he had made, Joe enrolled at a school of public speaking; when Jack's senior thesis was made into a book, Joe told friends that "Jack's book wasn't much, and had been accomplished with a lot of help from professionals," the last part of which was true.

It was comments such as this that left Jack incredulous when Harold Laski, who had taught Joe Jr. in 1933 in his classes at the London School of Economics, told the family after Joe's death how fondly he remembered him for the kindness he had shown the class stars. "He was with me during a year when the three outstanding students . . . happened to be at once Socialists and poor Jews from the East End of London. Nothing was more admirable than Joe's attitude toward them, a deep respect for their ability, an ardent promise that one day he would know enough to argue with them on equal terms."

It is impossible to know how a mature Joe Kennedy Jr. would have stood up in politics, but, unlike the Adams sons or Ted Roosevelt Jr., he was not being pushed by external pressures into a line of work he found uncongenial or for which he had few natural skills. But his family's assumption that he would always succeed and excel exerted such pressure that he was unprepared to accept the possibility that he might not always have the last word, that someone somewhere might do something better or that he might be thwarted, if not by a rival, by circumstance. He was ill prepared to deal with frustration or failure, or to handle them well when they came.

Because Theodore Roosevelt's father had sent a substitute to the Civil War (he had married a woman from Georgia, whose brothers were in the Confederate Army), Theodore Roosevelt longed all his life to get into combat. Perhaps because Joseph P. Kennedy had avoided service in the First World War, and as an ambassador had been called an appeaser and coward, his two oldest sons were determined to get into battle; and once there, they were determined to shine. Relentlessly, they pushed their way into the service, pressed constantly for the most dangerous missions, and exposed themselves to the maximum risks. World War II has come down as a "good war," one that children of privilege flocked to get into (George H. W. Bush joined the navy the moment he became eighteen), but even in this context the drive of the Kennedy brothers was considered extreme. In two different wars, the sons of Theodore Roosevelt had shown similar tendencies: trying to live up to a mythical father. The job of the Kennedy brothers was still more complex: they had to refute the idea that their father (and they) were lacking in courage, they had to lay a foundation for future endeavors, and each had a mission that was wholly his own. Joe had to excel, to live up to the faith that his father had in him, and to establish himself as a possible president; Jack had to equal his brother, or perhaps outperform him. And their father, who had said no cause on earth was worth the loss of a child, had to watch for five years as his sons courted danger, with mixed feelings and terrible fears.

"I think Jack is not doing anything, and with your stand on

the war people will wonder what the devil I'm doing," Joe Jr. wrote to his father, explaining why he was dropping out of Harvard Law School to enlist in the navy days after Roosevelt declared a national state of emergency on May 26, 1941. He was sent to Squantum Naval Base in Massachusetts and then down to Jacksonville, Florida, to train as a pilot, knowing that Jack had failed his physical in an attempt to get into the army and that health problems were likely to keep him at home. But Jack, who had built up his back through strenuous exercise, badgered his father into pulling the strings that got him into naval intelligence in September, with the high rank of ensign, in the week Joe was getting his wings. As Joe's biographer put it, Jack had "wrecked his accomplishment. . . . As an older brother, Joe was proud, but as a previously undefeated contender for family honors, he was shattered. Lorelle Hearst found him worried about his brother's bad back and bitter at his father for not doing something to keep Jack out of uniform. He was annoyed too at having been so quickly and easily outranked."

In the next year while Joe was confined to hunting German submarines off Puerto Rico and the coast of Virginia, Jack was lobbying to see active service, despite back problems so bad he was considering surgery, and in the summer of 1942 was accepted to train to captain PT boats, the small swift vessels used to harass destroyers in the eastern Pacific theater of war. The attractions for Jack were the glamour and danger: "So far in the war the fatalities are ten men killed for every survivor," he cheerfully wrote his best friend. When his commander tried to keep him on to train other people, he protested bitterly, and in the early spring while a steaming Joe tried to press to see action in Europe, Jack was on his way to the Solomon Islands, in one of the war's most dangerous theaters. And there, some months later, the glory that Joe was so avidly seeking came instead to his young brother Jack.

At two thirty in the morning on August 2, in the Blackett Strait of the Solomon Islands, Jack's boat was sliced in half by a Japanese destroyer that killed two of the thirteen-man crew upon contact and severely wounded three others. Clinging to the wreck of the boat until it began sinking about ten hours later, the survivors swam for an island three miles distant, Jack pulling a severely burned shipmate by a strap that he held in his teeth. Half an hour after they landed (after six in the evening), Jack swam off again, hoping to hail another PT boat, and he did not return until noon the day after, when all the others believed he was dead. When their food supply—coconuts—ran out a day later, Jack organized a swim to an island half a mile distant, once again towing the injured. He made more fruitless swims into the open sea until August 6, when two islanders in a canoe carried a message Jack had scratched on a coconut to an American naval base. It was not until August 8 that they were finally rescued and brought back to a hospital base.

Joe Kennedy was famous for the lengths he would go to get publicity for himself and his family, but this time the media needed no prodding. "Kennedy's Son Is Hero in the Pacific" blared a front-page headline in the *Boston Globe*. His father, who had been told three days earlier that Jack was missing but had kept it a secret from everyone, heard the news of his rescue on a radio newscast, as did his mother, who had had no idea what was wrong. Joe Jr., in Florida, "got quite a fright" but did not contact his family for more than a week. "Considerably upset that during those few days after the news of Jack's rescue, we had no word from you," his father would scold him, apparently unaware of what he had done to provoke this reaction or what the dynastic dynamic could do.

In 1917, Ted Roosevelt Jr. had been a "very sad and envious

bunny," as his sister Ethel had put it, when his young brother Archie won a medal before him. As Renahan tells us in his study of the Roosevelt children, "He could stand Archie having either the wound or the medal, but that he should have both seemed to Ted unfair." Thus Joe was now the Kennedy son who was not a hero, a point brought home with some emphasis when he went home on September 6 for his father's fifty-fifth birthday. "To Ambassador Joe Kennedy, father of the hero, our own hero, Lieutenant John F. Kennedy of the United States navy," went one of the toasts. Joe smiled and drank with the others. Then he went upstairs and cried.

The war was now over for Jack, who would spend the next year in a series of hospitals, suffering from malaria and assorted back problems as his weight sank to 120 pounds. Joe's war, however, had only begun. By late September, he was stationed in England, flying twelve-hour sorties from bases in Cornwall, hunting submarines and U-boats in the waters near Brest. By May, he had racked up more than his quota of missions but elected to stay on over D-day, where he helped provide cover for the Allied invasion, flying continuous loops between Dover and Cherbourg as transports carrying the greatest invasion in history crossed the Channel below. One reason he stayed was to get in on a moment of history that would stand him in good stead if he did run for president. Another was the fact that he had not yet won a medal; all of his months of steady and dutiful effort had failed to yield the one single moment of maximum daring that would let him draw even with Jack. Jack had now won the Navy and Marine Corps medal, and his story, described in detail by his classmate John Hersey, had already appeared in the *New Yorker* and would find national exposure in *Reader's Digest* quite soon. "Joe's nerves were straining," his biographer tells us. "He became wilder, and even less cautious. . . .

He found a German U-boat grounded on the Brest peninsula, and was only driven off by anti-aircraft fire. . . . On his next hop, he flew against orders so close to the German-held island of Guernsey . . . that he drew flak from the enemy, to bring back a partly perforated plane." He always continued to seek and court danger: as a fellow pilot would recall many years later, "There was never an occasion that meant extra hazard [for which] Joe did not volunteer." But nothing happened, and near the end of July he seemed reconciled to going home without the medal for which he had lusted. And then, at the last moment, he chanced on the mission he sought.

For more than a year, V-1 rockets had rained down on London, launched from bases on German-occupied territory, in the Low Countries, and France. Incessant raids on these bases had failed to curtail this activity, and at last Allied forces came up with a plan: they would pack a plane with explosives, launch it in the air, and then transfer control to a mother ship flying beside it, which would guide it to crash into the base and explode. The pilot would switch to remote control and parachute out while the plane was still over England. This was the project that held such appeal for young Joe. In letters home, he hinted at something exciting, without giving too many details; to Jack, he said he had been made a promise of the Navy Cross. Shortly before six in the evening on August 12, the plane became airborne. One of those who saw it explode was Elliott Roosevelt, son of the president, in a plane flying escort that was so badly damaged by the blast's repercussions that it nearly went down. Joe Jr. was awarded the Navy Cross posthumously, as was his copilot. Joe Sr. would be shattered but not shattered enough to forgo his obsession. The Kennedy drama had lost its main linchpin. But the Kennedy dream would go on.

In the book of remembrance he had privately printed, Jack paid his brother the ultimate tribute, comparing him to his ideal, Raymond Asquith, the son of one of England's World War I prime ministers who died young, as did Joe, in a war. To Joe, Jack applied quotes from Winston Churchill (his father's enemy but one of his heroes): "He went to his fate cool, poised, resolute,"—and from his favorite writer, John Buchan, "He loved his youth, and his youth has become eternal. Debonair, brilliant, and brave, he is now part of that immortal England which knows not age or weariness nor defeat."

For his own part, he described his brother's life as "perfection." "His life as he lived and finally as he died could not have been improved on. . . . His worldly success was so assured and inevitable that his death seems to have cut into the natural order of things." For himself, Jack, the second son and the standby, who had defined himself in reaction to Joe, had suddenly become the first son in the family, heir to the family project of power and glory and his parents' now grief-deepened dreams. How much this was assumed, not only inside his family but by those in its orbit, was summed up in a letter that the headmaster at Choate sent to his parents: "I am certain he [Jack] never forgets that he must live Joe's life as well as his own." If there was any chance that he might perhaps forget, there was always his father: "I told him he had to," Joe told a reporter for *McCall's* magazine in 1957 when Jack was running for president. "I was the one. I told him Joe was dead, and it was . . . his responsibility to run for Congress. He didn't want to. He felt he didn't have the ability, and he still feels that way."

Comments made at the time seem to bear out this story. "I was drafted," Jack later said to Bob Consodine. "My father wanted his oldest son in politics. 'Wanted' isn't the right word, he demanded it. You know my father." "There goes the old man," he said to his friend Paul Fay at Hyannis that autumn. "There he goes, figuring out the next step. I'm it now . . . I've got to perform." He was not averse to the substance of politics—he was a history buff and news junkie—but he shrank from the role of the public performer, glad-hander, and maker of deals. "He was so shy he could hardly tell you his name," said George Smathers, who later would meet him in Congress, adding he talked about being a writer. Said the son of Jack's wartime flame, Inga Arvad, "she remembered him as pretty much of a quiet person who'd never been healthy . . . and wanted a quiet life of writing, some research, and teaching American history. That was his dream at that point." "If he [Joe] had lived, I'd have kept on being a writer," he told a reporter. His parents had thought he might work in an embassy. Another time, he said that if Joe had survived, he would have entered law school in the fall of 1946. Clearly, he was not eager to go to law school, but he did not seem inclined to lead other lives either, and he seemed to realize that having another son to live for and through was key to his father's stability. At the end of 1945, he moved into his grandfather's hotel room in Boston and prepared to run for an open House seat in the 11th congressional district in Boston and to take up his dead brother's life.

Skeletal, jaundiced, and leaning on crutches, Jack began his campaign, backed by his family, for an office he didn't seem to want very much in a city in which he hadn't lived for some years. "He was probably uncomfortable," said his father's friend Joe Timilty. "He was a stranger in Boston . . . he was extremely shy." His own father would watch in astonishment as his son approached a group of tough-looking men and began a conversation. "I would have given odds of 5000 to one that this . . . could never have happened," he said. Later, Jack would tell Smathers how hard he had found it. "He told me the agony he suffered in going around sticking out his hand to people he'd never met, never seen," Smathers said later. "Politics wasn't his bag at all." Often, he apologized for not being his brother. "I wish Joe was around. He would have been governor," he would say to people. "If he were alive, I'd never be in this. . . . I'm just filling his shoes."

When he won, he seemed more stranded than ever, as if washed up on an island he never expected to reach. "He was sort of drifting," said his father's friend, William O. Douglas. "He didn't know the first thing about what he was doing," said his first secretary, who found herself running his office. "He was sort of lost for a while. I don't think he knew if he really wanted politics—if he was going to remain with it—or what politics was going to do with him." What no one at the time could begin to imagine is that within ten years the center of gravity in the Kennedy enterprise would have shifted from Joe to an alliance of Jack and the then-unknown third brother, Bobby, and that Jack would have become an obsessed—and a great—politician with the highest of dreams of his own.

The transformation of Jack, the reluctant candidate and shy second son of the family, into JFK, a presence so immense that he still haunts the Democrats, is one of the strangest stories in the annals of politics and on the surface, at least, one of the hardest to quantify. Other good sons—the Adams boys and Ted Roosevelt Jr.—had been pushed into politics and there been unhappy; and FDR, a great politician, had elbowed his own way into a family drama; but not before this (and so far, not after) has a good son been pushed into politics as something so close to a featherless duckling and come out in the end as a swan. "Fascination began to grip me," he wrote later, when he was running for president, "and I realized how fully politics filled the Greek definition of happiness: 'A full use of your powers along lines of excellence in a life affording scope.'"

But fascination did not grip him at once or quickly, and there were some aspects he never got used to. He disliked adulation, was embarrassed by flattery, and hated the back slapping, the small talk, the clichés and "hokum" of too much political utterance. "I really hate this," he said in 1958, when facing a long day of stroking interest and ethnic groups. "I hate it," he said in 1960, when asked if he liked to campaign. At the time, people talked of his lack of ambition. "He was intelligent, but not very serious," David Ormsby-Gore had said of him. In retrospect, Joseph Alsop saw "only a small glimmer . . . of what would come later. . . . I found him surprisingly unambitous and uninterested in politics. He was plainly not entirely well." Still on crutches from a failed back operation, haunted by the deaths of his brother, his crewmen, his friends (and his sister, in a 1948 plane crash), turning yellow or green from his illness and treatment, he showed little interest in his political future and seemed more likely to talk about death. "Tell me, Teddy boy, what's the best way to die?" he asked one friend suddenly. On a fishing trip, he brought the matter up with George Smathers: "He wanted to know which I thought was better—freezing to death, drowning, or getting shot." At some length, he went into the pros and cons of each option. "He was against freezing because it took so long," Smathers said.

Slowly, however, he began to emerge from his ennui, following the pattern set in his school days when he would drift for months, suddenly pull off an impressive performance, and then lapse once again into indifference and negligence. But he had begun to sense that politics, far from being the false self he might be made to force himself into, could be instead the means by which he defined his identity, marked himself off from his father and brother, and asserted his own independence at last. It was no mistake that his first major speech, given in March 1947, only months after he had been sworn into office, was a ringing defense of the Marshall Plan and the Truman Doctrine, both of which were strongly opposed by his father; in the speech he also went out of his way to criticize the failed diplomacy of the pre–World War II era, in which his father played such a large part.

This was the start of a series of battles that he would wage to fend off his father, who was trying to re-create the sort of rapport he had had with Joe Jr., to little effect. There would be more speeches like this and many more arguments. "There was a real strain there," said Jack's friend Chuck Spalding. "They went for about a year without talking about these matters at all." By the time Jack ran for the Senate in 1952, they had nearly stopped talking of anything, and the rift put the campaign in danger. Trying to assert the control he had had in the previous races, the patriarch had virtually moved into headquarters and tried to dictate on matters of tactics and strategy, "insist[ing] that he okay ad expenditures, pass on advertising layouts, and ratify decisions involving campaign policy," say Collier and Horowitz. "He also caused such turmoil that the early stages of the campaign were marked by chaos that threatened to paralyze the whole effort, something Jack understood but was powerless to change." Realizing that only a family member could break up what looked like a family impasse, one of the aides called the third brother, Bobby, and urged him to come up to Boston. Reluctantly at first, Bobby, then twenty-six, moved up to Boston and into the heart of the Kennedy drama, a place he was never to cede.

Until then, Bobby, the third son and seventh child of Joe and Rose Kennedy, had been largely cut out of the family drama, too young for the adventures and losses that had defined his elders, too young to have known or traveled in the doomed prewar Europe; too young to absorb the London experience; too young, most of all, for the war. Ten years younger than his idol, Joe Jr., and a critical eight years younger than Jack, he had been too small or too awkward to prove himself alongside his adored older brothers: while they had won medals and headlines in the war's biggest theaters, he had been a young seaman on the destroyer *Joseph P. Kennedy Jr.* and had never seen action, a role that defined his place in the family's life. "Kennedy, for much of his young life, was an acolyte," writes Evan Thomas. "Left behind, unable to catch up to his war-hero brothers, he reconciled himself to a supporting role. He extolled their exploits, advanced the family cause, and carefully polished the Kennedy myth." In this cause, he would quickly discover a genius for management and establish himself as the indispensable Kennedy, the one at the heart and core of the family, the one who could balance the contending factions and make them more than the sum of the parts. He was the one person to whom his father would agree to yield power, the one Jack trusted and to whom he would sometimes defer. Soon Joe would see him as his heir and his soulmate, the one who would take his place after he had stepped down. "Charlie Bartlett . . . heard Bobby talking on the phone to his father," writes Thomas. "Yes, Dad," Bobby kept saying. "Yes, Dad." Bobby was not so much acquiescing to his father as humoring him. . . . At several important moments . . . RFK rejected his father's advice."

But Bobby's new role as his father's surrogate was less important than the bond he was forming with Jack. Almost at once, they fell into a pattern of interdependence that would last them the rest of Jack's life. Jack had idolized his older brother but resented and envied him; Bobby looked up to Jack with unalloyed adoration. Jack could remember when he had been the second-best son and a source of anxiety; Bobby remembered a successful and glamorous figure, a war hero, a writer of books. Jack and Joe Jr. had jostled for honors and standing; Bobby cheerfully ceded first place to his brother and always seemed happy to serve.

From the start, an unspoken bargain was struck, in which each in some sense would look out for the other: Bobby running interference for his brother and relieving him of the details he found unappealing; Jack relieving Bobby of the burdens of consequence, protecting him, with his charm, his power, and the power of office, from the many enemies that he made. In time, they would merge into one perfect political animal: emotive and rational, detached and empathetic, electric and cool. "With none of the competition and conflict that defined Jack's relationship with Joe Jr. . . . Bobby and Jack explored the opposite pole of synchrony and merging," writes Adam Bellow in *Nepotism*, adding that Bobby happily and without reservation "took a back seat to Jack." "Bobby . . . saw his brother as the family intellectual, and deeply admired him," said their friend and aide David Powers. "He saw Jack's enormous natural charm, which he could only envy, but never imitate. And he saw his brother on a clear path to the presidency, a path he could not even dream of for himself."

After this, their paths would never wholly diverge. When Jack went to the Senate, Bobby took a job in the same building as counsel to the Senate select committee on investigations, where for the next seven years, in a series of high-profile showdowns, he would indulge his penchant for appearing in his favorite guise as a moralist and crusader assailing the fortress of sin. In 1957, when Jack won a seat on the labor committee, they formed a brother act that transfixed the country as the two appeared side by side on the television screens of the nation, heads close together as they conferred on some issue, their chestnut locks almost entwined. "The . . . committee hearings made first rate theatre," writes Richard Mahoney. "National radio and television coverage was constant. . . . Beginning in March 1957, there was the first of a succession of stories in the major news magazines. . . . *Look*, which took 8,000 pictures of Jack and Bobby, gushed, 'Two boyish men from Boston, with healthy shocks of hair, a father rich and benevolent, and minds honed at Harvard and by foreign travel, have become hot tourist attractions in Washington.'"

In retrospect, it now appears clear that 1952 was the critical year in the rise of the Kennedys, the one that set the pattern for their future successes and enabled all that would come later on. Jack's upset Senate win put him on the path to becoming a national figure and placed him in the special assemblage of possible presidents. It was also the year of the great power shift in the family, the year Jack's ambition supplanted that of his father as the main driving force in the family project, and the year that Joe's role as the family mastermind gave way to the duo of Bobby and Jack. Joe would remain in the background as a powerful figure, immensely useful via his cash and connections, available for such gestures as the so-called loan of $500,000 to a Boston newspaper, which soon after would come out for Jack. But decisions from then on would be made by the brothers, who would defy their father at the 1956 convention with their decision to enter the race for vice president, which Jack lost, but from which he gained because it put his face on the national map.

But the main thing was the evolution of Jack into a great politician, something Joe might have hoped for but could not have foreseen. "He started to do his homework," said Tip O'Neill, who had taken his old seat in Congress. "Suddenly, he became an active person. Suddenly he became a person with a future. . . . 'Will you go out to Missouri . . . to Florida, to speak for the party?' You can't go to those places unless you have a knowledge of what is taking place." Reconnecting with Jack in the late 1950s, Joe Alsop found him serious, "far more engaged," and deeply intent on becoming the president. "When Kennedy was in the House, I thought he was a third-rater," said Congressman Richard Bolling. "A big change has come over Kennedy. . . . He's hardworking now, which certainly he wasn't in the House." Newly serious, he had also begun to emerge as a star. At the start of his career, he had thought he lacked the requisite "big personality," the back-slapping nature, the big voice and outgoing presence to command a large crowd in a hall. What no one expected was that television, which rose in lockstep with his career, and to some extent caused it, would nullify all of these so-called personal defects and convert them all into a charm. He had always been seductive in a one-on-one setting, and the camera, which could be brutal to the old-fashioned, barn-burning speaker, would pick up his quieter charm and project it, allowing him to approach voters in his favorite manner, one to one, as it were, in their homes. The charismatic presidents of the late twentieth century would be Jack, and Ronald Reagan, the latter trained in the underplayed art of film acting, who knew how to tone himself down for the camera and who, like Jack, would speak softly, shun bombast, and fillet his rivals with wit. Tracking Jack's rise with uncanny precision, television was unknown in 1946 when he made his first race in a district small enough for him to meet many voters; was more widespread in 1952 when he made his first run for state office; and was ubiquitous in 1960 when he took his campaign to the entire nation, and, in the opinion of many, won the election with his composed performance in the first debate. Television was almost as ubiquitous in 1956 when he made his breakthrough appearance at the Democratic convention, narrating a film at the start of the session that made him a star overnight.

"The Kennedy brothers learned something," writes Richard Mahoney. "Jack, good in person, was better on screen." As a writer, war hero, amateur historian, and now as a heartthrob, he had begun to emerge as a public celebrity, something he observed with his chronic detachment. "He . . . watched with fascination as he became an object of consumer culture," write Collier and Horowitz. "The whole Jack was coming to represent more than the sum of his parts." Not since Theodore Roosevelt had a political figure so enchanted the public, shown such a genius for public relations, or had so large and lively a family he was willing to use in his interests. The circus atmosphere that had surrounded TR now began to envelop the Kennedys and would do so for too many years.

By this time, "fascination" had come to consume him, about nearly all parts of political life. "It's a very interesting life," he said later. "It allows the full use of your powers. . . . There's the great chess game . . . the battle, the competition. There's the strategy, and which piece you move. . . . And then in government you can do something about what you think." Politics had become his obsession, his way of engaging with history on an intimate level; and the enemy too of his greatest foe, boredom, with its incessant challenge and battles. "The price of politics is high," he would say when he was running for president, "but think of all those people living average lives who never touch the excitement of it." By the end of the decade, he was talking of politics as if no other life work had ever been possible, and his lassitude was replaced by a desperate urgency. "I can't wait. I don't have time. I've got to do it now!" he told George Smathers, who had been afraid he was too sick to run for the Senate. Seven years later, he was still more compulsive, telling reporters "I must get it NOW! NOW!" The urgency may have stemmed from his terrible health and the large number of people he knew who had died young and suddenly, but he campaigned as if there would be no tomorrow, as had proven true for so many.

When Ben Bradlee met him in 1958, he found him obsessed about politics. "The thing about Jack now is that politics takes precedence over family, over religion, over everything," Bradlee noted. "It's his overwhelming drive." To some, it appeared all too sudden and startling. "His rise had indeed been swift, and his transformation dramatic," write Collier and Horowitz, "from a young, cynical, death-obsessed congressman to a presidential contender almost overnight." But it was not overnight, and it had not been an accident but a long course of discovery that may have surprised Jack himself. He had gone into politics, a friend said, without enthusiasm, but with curiosity, open to the idea that he might find himself in it. In it, he found a self he and some others had not known existed: a driver, a leader, a serious person, a charismatic figure, a star.

Jack never emerged as a man of the Senate, and for this reason he was often dismissed as a lightweight, especially by other senators who ran against him for president and whose records as legislators much outweighed his. But he had given his entire adult life to the study of international politics, and it was on this he intended to run. More than any president since John Quincy Adams, he had been steeped from his school days in great power politics, touring extensively in different countries, usually with entrée to very high circles and important and powerful men. In 1937, at the age of twenty, he and a friend had spent two months in Europe, including Hitler's Germany and Franco's Spain. In London, as the ambassador's son, he had a front seat at the failure of prewar diplomacy and gotten to know and see some of the actors, aside from his father. Before the war started, he went to Europe again, where he was received by his father's fellow ambassadors, including in Prague a reluctant George Kennan, who had no idea he was hosting a future president and boss. When he wrote his senior thesis (and first book, *Why England Slept*), it was based on what he had seen and not merely studied. And for further research, he went back to England and talked to friends of his father.

In 1945, Jack had gone as a reporter to the conference in San Francisco that set up the United Nations, and he later traveled in France, England, and Germany, where he interviewed Eisenhower twice. Although he was only twenty-nine when he first ran for Congress, he brought with him a storehouse of foreign experience, which he began to use as a member of Congress and made the basis of future campaigns. What set him apart from his potential rivals aside from his looks, hair, and money was the coherence and intensity of his views on foreign relations and the passion with which he began to propound them. They had been the background to his family life as he saw his father slip, fall, and be pilloried for his many misjudgments; they had been the proximate cause of his near death in the South Pacific and the deaths of his brother, his crewmen, his sister Kathleen's titled young husband, and of a great many friends. To Jack, the personal had become political, long before it emerged as a left-wing activist slogan, and it became the hook that would pull him out of his ennui and into the heart of his father's ambition, which he proceeded to claim as his own.

In March 1947, two months after having been sworn into office, John F. Kennedy made his first major speech as a member of Congress, backing the Marshall Plan and the Truman Doctrine, insisting that a strong defense was needed to deter aggression and citing Munich and pre–World War II appeasement policies as mistakes we must never repeat. Early in 1951, he made a six-week tour of western Europe, returning to make a radio address, and that fall spent seven weeks in the Near and Far East, traveling from Israel through Pakistan and Indochina to Japan. Through his career, he would establish himself as an aggressive and ardent cold warrior, running to the right of his opponents in all his elections, and criticizing Presidents Truman and Eisenhower (when he chose to do so) as insufficiently prepared and assertive. He attacked Truman for the "loss" of China to communists and Eisenhower for proposed cuts in the defense allotment, and in 1960 would run on the "missile gap," a charge that the administration had been negligent in maintaining defense capabilities. He insisted that the country must maintain unquestioned military supremacy over all comers, endorsed the domino theory, which claimed that weakness in even one world area would start a cascade of disaster, and attacked the "ideas of neutralism, resignation, isolation, and indifference" that marked his father's approaches to foreign affairs.

At the same time, he insisted that the country must break its pattern of reflexive support for the old colonial powers that were resisting communist-led insurgencies in third-world areas and ally itself with indigenous nationalist movements. "The most powerful single force in the world today . . . is neither communism nor capitalism," he insisted. "It is man's eternal desire to be free." His father believed in appeasing aggressors; he would resist them. His father believed the country ought to retreat within its own borders; he would guarantee the survival of numerous allies. His father saw democracy as weak and imperiled; he would exert every effort to see it prevail. This was no accident. "He began to see the erosion of Western influence . . . in terms analogous to the great international drama of his youth, when Europe faced the moral and political tensions that led to World War II, and when he had charged in his senior thesis that appeasement was the 'inevitable result' of 'slowness in rearming,'" as Collier and Horowitz explain.

In a speech in the Senate in 1958, he quoted Churchill so often that he was asked by a colleague, "if he meant that the situation . . . could be compared with the situation faced by the British in the late 1930's?" Jack replied, "The Senator is entirely correct." He was reliving history but casting himself in the role of his father's great enemy and with those who thought like his father as dangerous people, whose counsel must be overcome. He was selling himself as a Churchill for the new cold war era or what Churchill might have been like if he had looked like a film star, had a family as large and as lively as Theodore Roosevelt's, and had the good looks of TR's cousin Franklin. This mixture of a message of struggle and sacrifice coming from a figure unique in his glamour and dazzle was something entirely new for the country, and, if it unsettled some people and made them suspicious, it lured enough (110,000 more) into taking a chance on this exciting, unnerving, and sometimes inspiring figure. If he was more than the sum of his parts, it was those parts themselves, interesting, unlikely, and unique to his character, that made most of the difference: he had taken on his brother's life and taken it perhaps beyond his brother's capacities, in a way no one had ever foreseen. It was hardly the way that his parents had planned it, and he was not the one for whom his parents had planned it, but, as predicted forty-five years before by the mayor of Boston, the oldest living son of Joe and Rose Kennedy was elected president of the United States.

Joe's dream of power had come to fruition, but now he desired still more. It was Joe who insisted that Bobby be made attorney general and that Jack's Senate seat should be kept warm for Teddy, who could not run himself for two years. "The person who was primarily interested in having Ted run was my father," Bobby said later. "Just as I never would have been attorney general if it hadn't been for him, I don't think my younger brother would have been senator, nor would my older brother have been president." On policy matters, Jack did as he wanted, but on family matters his father still ruled. "I was against it, and we had some rather strong arguments," Bobby said of his own appointment. "He wouldn't hear of anything else." "Bobby is going to be attorney general," Joe said to Clark Clifford, who was sent down to argue with him by his son the president. And so it was. At a stretch, Bobby's appointment was plausible; he was just thirty-five, but he was the president-elect's campaign manager and political intimate and had spent years working with Senate committees on major investigations and campaigns.

Teddy was different. At twenty-eight, he had to wait more than a year before he could even run for the Senate, and his political experience consisted in coordinating the western states for his brother, all of which Jack had lost. Jack was appalled. "Your brother wants to announce that he's running for . . . what?" was his reaction when Bobby had called with the news. "I don't know why the House isn't good enough for Teddy, it was good enough for me," he told Charles Bartlett, afraid that a backlash could damage his standing. "Don't force him into politics, . . . let him be the playboy," he said to his father, echoing the sentiment he had once voiced to Bartlett: "If the old man would let Teddy alone, he would do what he likes to do, which is to chase broads in the South of France." Ted and his family had plans of their own, which were to move west to live independently. "Ted felt he was being pushed into public life. He could not do what he wanted," Ted's first wife would say later. "We wanted to move to Arizona. We thought we'd have fun and live our own lives." He had no more luck than the two sons of John Adams, who, seeking escape from their dominant parents, were forced in their turn to stay home. "I was there the night it was decided to move Teddy's residence out west," a housekeeper would tell Laurence Leamer. "Then, all of a sudden, . . . the decision was changed." Ted moved to Boston, where he worked in the office of the district attorney for Suffolk County, where it was apparent to everyone that he was biding his time there until a suitable seat opened up. Unable to get a straight answer from Ted about what his plans were, Ted's boss called his father. "He's running for the U.S. Senate," Joe told him. "Now, put him on the phone."

As a candidate, and then as a senator, Jack often held Ted at a distance, unwilling to be thought of as doing him favors excessively. ("Tough shit," he barked at his brother when Ted complained to him that one of his policies was causing him trouble at home.) Bobby and Jack, however, especially after the Bay of Pigs, when their trust in experts was compromised fatally, were welded together, functioning in effect as a single presence, running the country in tandem. Some distance remained. They did not often socialize, and whereas Bobby was an open book to his brother, the more elusive Jack Kennedy had facets Bobby seldom saw. The president and his wife disliked the raucous atmosphere at Hickory Hill and seldom went there, avoiding the pool parties that became notorious during the Camelot era. Nor were Bobby and Ethel often upstairs at the White House when the workday was done. The president "rigidly divided his relationships, separating 'staff' . . . from his social friends," Evan Thomas writes coolly. "RFK was, in a certain sense, staff."

Yet on the working level the two brothers blended into one unit, able to communicate in the family shorthand or even with no words at all. At any rate, Bobby functioned during Jack's term as his acting co-president, overseeing, along with his own war on crime and the civil rights crises, back-channel contacts with the Soviet Union, clandestine attempts to remove Fidel Castro from power, guerrilla wars in Southeast Asia and elsewhere, and the discussions leading to the resolution of the Cuban missile crisis in October 1962. In the unwritten bargain worked out between them, John Kennedy gave his brother entrée into all arms of the government, often letting him go around or overrule the decisions of others assumed to be in control. In return, Bobby picked up after and looked out for his brother, in all his complex areas of life. Before this, he had mediated the rocky passages in Jack's marriage to Jacqueline, being present at the stillbirth of their daughter in 1956 when Jack was off partying. Now the older brother's promiscuity emerged as a serious problem, giving a powerful weapon to Bobby's bête noire, J. Edgar Hoover, and paralyzing the attorney general in his turf battles with the FBI. Jack's rumored affair with an East German woman also caused problems, and Bobby's war on organized crime was compromised twice, once by his knowledge of the secret pact between the CIA and Mafia head Sam Giancana, and also by his brother's affair with Judith Campbell, who was also sleeping with the Mafia boss.

There was also the matter of Jack's tricky health and the dubious nostrums he took to curb pain and keep up his levels of energy. Being the keeper of this particular brother was no easy matter, and the strain was now evident. On November 20, 1963, Bobby turned thirty-eight, and his mood at a party was grim and sardonic as he spoke ironically and almost resentfully of the shocks he absorbed for his brother. Some people listening to him thought he was thinking of leaving the government or at least stepping back from some of his duties. Serving his brother or moving out on his own was the decision that faced him. Two days later, it was no longer his choice.

Late in John Adams's life, having seen two sons and two grandsons break under pressure, Adams would tell Charles Francis, the one strong son of his one strong son, that these trials had been sent to temper the pride of his family and spare it the more dire lashings of providence. "Had all his sons flourished," Paul Nagel informs us, "the world would have been obliged to crush such a family. "But while the world respects us, it at the same time pities our misfortune, and the pity destroys the envy which might otherwise arise." Now, in the 1960s, with three Kennedys flourishing, the world would begin to crush them. The first blow would strike at the end of Jack's first year in office, when Joe was felled by a massive stroke at his compound in Florida and rendered a permanent invalid. The tireless architect of the Kennedy project would be mute and helpless, unable to respond to, much less order, events. He was thus in a wheelchair in his home at Hyannis on the evening of November 22, 1963, when Ted and Eunice arrived to tell him that Jack had been murdered in Texas, killed by bullets from a sniper's rifle as his motorcade rode through the streets.

With this, Jack would change from a man to a legend, sanctified by the horrendous manner of his passing into a figure much larger than life. If the murdered Abraham Lincoln had become the lost father, Jack was now the lost son in perpetuity, a major difference being that Lincoln had no brothers in the Senate or Cabinet, seen by the world as the line of succession. Joe was no longer able to tell Bobby, as he had once said to Jack, that it was his duty to step in for his dead older brother, but Joe in this sense was no longer needed. The "Kennedy Party," and much of the world, assumed he would do so. It was now expected, as Lord Beaverbrook wrote to Rose Kennedy, that "Bobby will repeat Jack's career."

For the time being, Bobby was desolate, almost "devoured by grief." He seemed to contract until he appeared wasted, smaller than ever in his brother's clothes that he insisted on wearing, once risking his life by jumping off a boat into turbulent water to retrieve one of his brother's old jackets that had been blown overboard by the wind. He was "saved" from his grief by his hatred of Lyndon Johnson, his brother's vice president, whom he had frequently battled, viewing him as a usurper and a villain, much as Hamlet saw Claudius and Malcolm and Donalbain saw Macbeth. "Our president was a gentleman and a human being," he said, in a remarkable paraphrase of the Prince of Denmark. "This man is not. He's mean, bitter, vicious—and animal in many ways." As Johnson hit his stride in 1964 and began racking up triumphs in Congress, Bobby begrudged him the plaudits of others, as if every word buried his dead brother deeper. "Respect for Johnson did not come easily," says Jeff Shesol, the title of whose book *Mutual Contempt* explains everything. "He was having trouble simply calling Johnson "the President," a term Bobby reserved for his late brother. Usually, Johnson remained nameless, referred to by a simple "he" or "him," as in, "Can you believe what he just did?" "I can't stand the bastard," Bobby once said to a friend.

"All Adamses, when expelled from the corridors of power, were inclined to look on their successors as imposters," writes Otto Friedrich in *Clover*, his study of the suicidal wife of Henry Adams. They were not alone. Theodore Roosevelt resented his friend William Howard Taft from the day Taft took office. For Woodrow Wilson, who would beat them both four years later, he and his children cherished an enduring hatred. Like the "Roosevelt

Party" that was loyal to TR and his heirs even when none were in office, there was now a "Kennedy Party," in and around the national Democrats, which looked not to Johnson, John Kennedy's choice as his legal successor, but to Robert Kennedy, now a powerless Cabinet member about to leave office, as its only legitimate head. The fact that the Kennedys had been ousted by a criminal act, not by an election, only added to their sense of grievance and vengeance. Like the Taft-Roosevelt feud that in 1912 had split the Republican Party, as TR struggled to regain the office he had thoughtlessly vacated, the Democrats would be shaken and shattered by the dynastic drive of the Kennedy Party, as it struggled to get back its own.

Bobby's first move was to try to force his way onto the ticket with Johnson, where he thought he could get a head start on the next nomination or succeed directly if Johnson should die. (Johnson took Hubert Humphrey, a liberal senator.) His second was to move to New York, where he had spent part of his childhood, and run for the Senate, and he took his place alongside his one living brother in January 1965. There were now two Senators Kennedy, but their aims and ambitions were utterly different: Ted wished to stay in and work in the Senate; Bobby wanted to work toward the great restoration, not so much as officeholder as "head of the Kennedy wing of the party," a great prince in exile, head of a shadow administration representing what could and, by rights, should have been. He launched a series of overseas trips, in which he was greeted as a head of state, and presented himself as the ambassador of the shadow Kennedy government, addressing the crowds in the name of his brother, invoking both the late president's genuine virtues and others he never dreamed of possessing.

In domestic affairs, he started to dwell on poverty issues, adopting the causes of ghetto dwellers in the Bedford-Stuyvesant section of Brooklyn, migrant farm workers in California, American Indians, and starvation-stricken Mississippi Delta blacks. It was a way of challenging Johnson, author himself of his own War on Poverty, but there was a calculus here that was not wholly political. "Whatever the level of calculation in his adventures into this American netherworld," said Collier and Horowitz, "there was also a personal dimension for which there was no sufficient political explanation. . . . He went from one powerless and oppressed group to another like a detective obsessively following clues to a mystery which he knew was inside himself." In fact, he was drawn to the suffering because he had been suffering; drawn to the unlucky because he was unlucky; drawn to those without financial or political power because his fall from absolute power had been so sudden and shattering. Rich and powerful, a millionaire and a senator, he still felt bereft apart from his brother, alone in a strange land.

At the beginning, the implied promise of the Kennedy project was that Bobby would restore as much as possible what had been Jack's government, a prospect that seemed increasingly appealing as the 1960s wore on, riots broke out in American cities, and the attempt to prop up the Vietnamese government turned into America's war. But as he emerged from his dead brother's shadow, he became a whole other person, raw and engaged, where his brother had been detached and ironic—a man of stark contradictions in impulse and politics. John Kennedy had been the last iconic figure of the World War II–cold war establishment, a group that was elite, self-assured, and bipartisan. Robert Kennedy was the first iconic figure of the disruption that followed, and what made him so hot as a political figure was the fact that the era's sense of anger and perceived injustice mirrored what he felt in himself. It was unfair that some people were poor, unfair that race was a burden, unfair that young men, most of them poor, died in a war past explaining. It was unfair too that his brother was dead, unfair that he and his friends had lost power, unfair that, largely through his own efforts, a man he detested now sat in his dead brother's chair.

The new Bobby emerged as a creature of paradox. He was a martinet who could with some cause be considered ruthless, and a man who could cradle a child with a distended stomach whose body was covered with sores. He was enraged at a system that denied opportunity to some kinds of people and enraged at people who refused to seize opportunity, who languished on welfare and didn't try hard to achieve. Sometimes he sounded like a radical street organizer in his tirades against injustice, and sometimes he sounded like Ronald Reagan, the former film star and liberal activist turned conservative governor, in his critique of big government, moral indiscipline, and social decay. He was an opponent at once of welfare and privilege, a man who believed that the country had to do more for more people and who at the same time believed less and less in big government's power to do much of anything. He was both a uniter and a divider, a man who polarized people strongly in emotional terms, and at the same time he could reach across chasms: he appealed both to the blacks empowered by the civil rights laws and to the blue-collar whites who sometimes resented them; a man who believed in law and order and sometimes sympathized with those who protested; a man who could connect at once to the Green Berets he not so secretly idolized and to the students protesting them. Some people saw him as his brother's heir and the heir to the hope they believed he embodied; some saw him as the enemy of the order that reigned when his brother was president and that seemed to disappear soon after his murder.

Whatever he seemed, Bobby roused violent feelings, and he seemed to like doing it. Nostalgia for the Lost Prince, his brother, had become in the American memory merged with the frenzy of Bobby's agenda, which stemmed in turn from his ongoing sense of bereavement. Interviewing him in 1967 for *Life* magazine, the novelist Saul Bellow "was taken aback by the ferocity of his emotions" as he cursed out President Johnson, whom he seemed to feel was somehow to blame for the death of his brother. "He never stopped thinking about his brother," Bellow recalled. "He seemed to be continually grieving. He was literally, muscularly tense about it. His face was convulsed with some great emotional charge. He was nourishing his grief. It gave him energy." Bellow thought that he wanted it never to die.

It was perhaps because he longed so much for the direct battle against his brother's successor that Bobby was stunned into something close to paralysis when the chance to achieve it arrived. "He wanted the presidency so much he could taste it," an aide would say later. But when leaders of the burgeoning antiwar movement came to him and asked him to run against Johnson, he turned all of them down all the time. It was the start of a time when this man who loved starkly defined all-out combat would find himself more and more trapped in ambivalence: held back by many concerns from fighting the man he detested, then forced to fight proxies he couldn't quite hate. He was afraid people would say he was ruled by ambition and vengeance, afraid of splitting his ancestral party. Most of all, he was frightened of losing: no incumbent president had ever before been denied his party's nomination, and if he ran and was beaten, his chances of regaining the White House in the name of his brother were dead. But he regarded the right to challenge the president as his franchise and was stunned and unsettled when Eugene McCarthy, whom he looked down on, jumped in. Immediately, young supporters who had been his followers took off for New Hampshire to challenge the president; and part of his backing was slipping away.

"I think I blew it," he said on March 13, 1968, when returns from New Hampshire showed the unknown McCarthy a mere nine points away from the president and advisers told him he could have blown Johnson away. On March 16, he appeared in the Senate Office Building on the spot on which his brother had stood less than eight years ago, and, in the same opening sentence, declared he was running for president. In his second sentence, he stated he was not running to oppose any man. This was not the way Johnson saw it, as he later told his biographer. "The thing I feared from the first day of my presidency was actually coming true," he later explained to Doris Kearns Goodwin. "Robert Kennedy had openly announced his intention to reclaim the throne in the memory of his brother. And the American people, swayed by the magic of the name, were dancing in the streets." Fifteen days later, on March 31, in a surprise ending to a televised address to the nation, Johnson announced he was no longer a candidate. Bobby, having split his own base and lost millions of backers, now was deprived of his grand confrontation. He had to fight the wrong race, against the wrong people, on terms he had compromised. And he knew it was all his own fault.

Bobby, as Shesol writes, was "a little stupefied" by Johnson's demurral. "Attacking Johnson—or Johnson's war—was natural and almost effortless. . . . Now, overnight, his stump style was obsolete and his campaign virtually devoid of issues. . . . Kennedy was subdued, obviously deflated. There had been a cause in running against Johnson . . . a real challenge, a real adversary, emotion, and even 'fun.'" Now while Hubert Humphrey, Johnson's heir and vice president, waited to battle the primary winner, Kennedy had the job of attacking McCarthy, backed by many of his older supporters, and trying to explain why he deserved the nomination more than the man who had jumped in to fight Johnson while he himself had hung back. The closest he came to making the case that he was especially equipped to lead, and possibly to heal, the country was on the night of April 4, 1968, when he broke the news to a largely black audience in Indianapolis that Martin Luther King Jr. was dead.

"I had a member of my family killed, but he was killed by a white man," he said to his audience. "What we need in the United States is not division, what we need . . . is not hatred, what we need is not violence . . . but love and wisdom and compassion toward one another, and feeling of justice toward those who still suffer. . . . Let us dedicate ourselves to what the Greeks wrote so many years ago: to tame the savageness of man and to make gentle the life of the world." He also quoted from Aeschylus, the poet he had discovered after the death of his brother: "In our sleep, pain, which cannot forget, falls drop by drop upon the heart until, in our own despair, against our will, comes wisdom through the awful grace of God."

By this time, he was being steadily ground down by the strains he was under, as his biographer Evan Thomas, reveals. "When John Barlow Martin had joined the Kennedy campaign in April, he was startled by Kennedy's worn visage. The brown-blond hair was turning gray, and the once-boyish face was deeply lined. 'He really did not look young,' Martin wrote. 'He has aged more than he should since his brother's death.'" Columnist Joe Kraft had "never seen him look so bad, so tired; his blue eyes were standing out really like a death's head from his skull." He was, Thomas says, "an old man." He was exhausted, drained by the emotions he felt and those that he stirred in people around him, which boiled and seethed without stopping. Adulation, and violence, seemed to be hovering, in the frenetic way people clawed at him, pulling him out of his car in their excitement, grabbing his cufflinks and ripping his clothes. There were, of course, other reactions. "He's going to be shot," Martin quotes *Newsweek* correspondent John Lindsay. "Do you know what I think is going to happen to Bobby?" Jackie had asked when he started campaigning. "The same thing that happened to Jack." And then it did happen. It was late at night, not at midday; it was in California, not Texas; it was not outdoors in a motorcade during a precampaign fence-mending mission, but in the kitchen of the Ambassador Hotel in Los Angeles after a win in a primary; and it was not by a sniper's bullet from a very long distance, but from a fairly small handgun held at fairly short range. He did not die immediately, but two days later, having never again regained consciousness. Three brothers had died pursuing their father's ambition. And now there was one brother left.

CHAPTER 4

Kennedys: Decline and Fall

When Ted Kennedy was born, at the tail end of a long line of children that included three other brothers, it had never occurred to anyone that the last born and afterthought would ever emerge as the family head. Always good looking, big and good natured, he had somehow avoided the strains that had roiled the others: he had no health problems, like Jack; no personal problems with sibling complexities; no stress as the family fought its way upward; no pressures and risks in the war. He had not been pushed by his father, as were Jack and Joe Jr.; he did not push himself, unlike Bobby; and, as the last born, the pet, and the baby, he was surely not pressured by anyone else. Stranded midway between the big boys and the babies, Bobby fought constantly against his designation as a second-tier brother and fought all his life to keep up with the others.

But Ted accepted his role as the baby, with all of the gifts that came with it: the indulgence, the exemptions from the strictures that bound all the others, the unconditional favor and love. Always, he had trailed along in the wake of the others and coasted along on the tide of their efforts. Indulged as they were, Jack and Bobby had still had to work hard for their wins and had few easy victories: the Senate race in 1952 and the presidential race eight years later were long shots and hard won. Ted, in contrast, sailed into the Senate two years later in a display of sheer gall so completely appalling that even his brothers were mortified. His elections thereafter would be mere formalities, and his future seemed limitless. He of all men appeared to be endlessly fortunate. No one could imagine how soon or completely his luck would begin to run out.

Under the surface were some signs of trouble, signs that he had been coddled a little too much. When Joe Jr. had problems keeping up with his class work at law school, he hired more tutors for himself and worked even harder. Ted, however, cheated at Harvard and served a two-year term in the peacetime army before being allowed to return. He had permitted his father to order his life, allowing him to send him to Harvard, to send him to law school, to insist on his marriage to a beautiful girl with a suitable pedigree (against the misgivings of both of the parties), to order him then to run for the Senate, and to veto his plans to move west. Once in the Senate, he was shrewd enough to realize he was being resented and laughed at, and he went to great pains to defy expectations by working quite hard at his job.

Unlike his brothers, he was at home in the Senate and had hoped to stay in it for life. "At thirty-three, he was already an old Senate hand, finding the ritualized pace and articulated structure of Congress congenial," write Collier and Horowitz. "He had seen the Senate as his new frontier—a place spacious enough to allow him to grow into his future—which he warned would take decades to develop, not years." He seemed uneasy with talk that projected him as a possible president (after, of course, Jack and Bobby) and tried to shun comparisons with them, afraid he might not measure up. Described by Jack once as "not terribly quick," aware he had done nothing to earn his high station, he often had little faith in his talents or judgment. As Burton Hersh, a sympathetic biographer, tells us, "The others had worked for theirs, but celebrity broke over Edward Kennedy; he found it thrust on him early. It made him nervous underneath." This was the man who, still in his thirties, found himself heir to the Kennedy mantle, with all it had come to entail.

"At the age of thirty-six, with less than eight years' direct involvement in political life, the senator heard from every side that he had no choice, that there was no way he could stay in politics, and avoid being the Democratic standard bearer in 1972," Jack's friend Charles Bartlett wrote later. "Even if you say you have decided not to run," he was told, "they won't believe you or accept it. This was incredible pressure on a young man who inherited the Kennedy zest for competition but nursed no deep lust for power. . . . His brothers . . . left him a magic and heady legacy . . . a two-edged legacy for a young man geared to a less intense way of life."

As the pressure built, he began to crack visibly: Hersh writes that reporter John Lindsay of *Newsweek*, among many others, began to "pick up constant signals of deep-seated emotional disruption: a tendency to stop in mid-sentence, shift moods . . . break into unexpected tears." In the winter of 1968–1969, he crashed his car in Palm Beach, inexplicably missing a sharp turn on a road that he drove on frequently. On a trip to Alaska in April, he got roaring drunk on a flight back from Fairbanks, weaving down the aisles shouting "Eskimo power!" and holding a full cup of steaming hot coffee inches away from an infant's face. After this, a group of journalists, Lindsay among them, wrote internal memos to their organizations about his disintegrating emotional state. At last, Bartlett approached him directly: "All those young guys are pushing you, but take this thing and it will be a disaster," the newsman had told him. "You're just not as bright as Jack. You don't have the experience. You should lay off." Sometimes it seemed that he wanted to do so, but it also was clear that he could avoid the nomination only by doing something disastrous. And then, a little more than a year after the death of his brother Bobby, he did.

On Friday, July 18, 1969, Ted Kennedy was on Chappaquiddick Island, eight miles away from the Kennedy compound, hosting a reunion barbecue party for a cluster of people who had once worked on Bobby's campaign. Around eleven thirty that night, he left in his car with twenty-nine-year-old Mary Jo Kopechne, one of the six women present. Shortly after, his car went off Dike Bridge and plunged into the pond underneath it, turning over and filling with water. He got out of the car, went back to his hotel in Edgartown, and did not call police until nine the next morning, when other people had already reported the accident and Kopechne's body was being removed from the car.

Neither then nor in all the years after has he ever given an explanation of what he did in those hours that has made sense to anyone. The kindest interpretation was that he was in shock and denial, and the most prevalent one was that he was trying to concoct a story that would distance him from the scene of the accident or at least allow him to shirk some of the blame. "I went to pieces," a housekeeper heard him say to his speechless and paralyzed father. "I must have gone a little crazy. . . . I left the scene of an accident, and things aren't good." As details filtered out, conflicting with the news of the successful moon landing, a program launched by his brother Jack some years earlier, things became worse.

"A lot of people think that the one thing Ted should have done is to run to anybody and say, 'For Christ's sake, help me out, this girl's drowning!'" his brother-in-law Sargent Shriver said later. "And he didn't. . . . Why didn't he go to the first place where there was a light on? . . . Then it begins to look like instead of worrying about the girl he was worrying about himself, and that's what bugs people, that he connived, manipulated, to help himself."

This impression grew stronger when a swarm of courtiers who had worked for his brothers descended on the compound in Hyannis, isolated him from police and reporters, and began to spin and to "manage" the tragedy, as if it were a distraction that had come up quite suddenly in the course of an election campaign. Ted remained remote from these discussions, wandering in and out of the endless and ongoing meetings and taking long walks on the beach. "God damn it," he said to a friend on one of those outings. "All my life I've done everything they told me to do. Everything. I'm finished. I'm going to marry Helga [one of his girlfriends] and leave the Senate and go off with her." But he did not; he went back to the house and did as they told him, reciting a speech written by Jack's former wordsmith that made it appear as if he were the victim, and spoke for the first time of a family curse. Effective enough in his home state (where voters rejected his "offer" to step down from the Senate), the speech was a bomb in the rest of the country and became the second thing for which a great many people would never forgive him.

"Many in the press corps thought it reminded us of Nixon's 'Checkers' speech," said *Time* reporter Hays Gorey. "It did not ring true. It was highly political, and intended, obviously, to save his political neck." It did save his neck, but at the cost of his future, and of the mystique that had haloed his family since Jack and Joe Jr. volunteered for the navy, Joe Jr. took off on his suicide mission, and Jack made a late-night swim of a different variety. A meeting of Democrats to plan strategy based on the idea that Ted would be their next candidate adjourned and went home at the news of the accident. Ted Sorenson, planning a run for the Senate, excised all mention of Ted Kennedy from the book he was writing. And Joe Kennedy, with three sons dead and one facing the kind of disgrace the others could not have begun to imagine, had stopped eating. He died at age eighty-one four months later, seeming to realize that this last blow was fatal. Money and glamour aside, the Kennedy myth had been solidly grounded in courage and sacrifice. Now that was gone.

A tentative Ted returned to the Senate that fall as a newly ambiguous figure, at once the noble survivor of multiple tragedies and the instigator of tragedy on other people, by neglect and omission, if not by design. Almost at once, he began to carve out the pattern that would define him for the next several decades and firmly establish his public persona: on the one hand, an immensely skilled and hard-working senator, the very example of the worthy successor; on the other, a not infrequent tabloid embarrassment, the profligate heir at his worst. He hired a large crew of experts, creating what was perhaps the best staff in the Senate, worked them prodigiously, and then wore them out with his own dedication. And then there was the other side to his character.

"In Washington, it sometimes seems as if everyone knows someone who had slept with Kennedy, been invited to sleep with Kennedy, seen Kennedy drunk," wrote Michael Kelly. "A former midlevel Kennedy staffer . . . recalls one now ex-high ranking aide as a 'pimp . . . whose real position was to procure women. . . .' Howie Carr (a Boston columnist) . . . says it isn't considered summer in Cape Cod until the Senator drives on the sidewalk for the first time." Whether this was the cause of the slide in his family life or the reaction to it is unclear and perhaps unknowable, but the combined pressures of the expectations, assassinations, and accidents had taken a toll on the senator and on his family beyond that exacted from many in politics.

Stoically, Joan Kennedy had gone to the Kopechne funeral, but soon after, she miscarried, and she began drinking heavily. In reaction to this—and to fears that their father would be shot, like his brothers—all three of their children sought refuge in drinking or drugs. A nadir of sorts was reached in the life of Ted Kennedy in November 1973 when, as part of his efforts to support Bobby's children, he gave away Bobby's daughter Kathleen at her morning wedding and then returned to Georgetown University Hospital, where his oldest son, Teddy, stricken with cancer, was about to lose his right leg. This cavalcade of disasters in his private life, among other things, allowed him to sidestep the presidential contention in 1976, the second such race after Chappaquiddick, but it did not quell the hunger in Democrats to revive their past glories or avoid the disaster the Carter administration was quickly becoming.

By 1978, the pressure once more had become unrelenting. Polls among Democrats showed him leading the president by a 53 to 16 margin. "Kennedy right now can decide on his own volition whether he wants to be president," said Mervyn Field, the veteran pollster. "A moment of electric drama seems to be in store for this generation," enthused one reporter, "the moment when Ted Kennedy appears on the television screen saying, . . . 'Help me finish what my brothers began.'" Ted announced his candidacy at Faneuil Hall in Boston on November 7, 1979, surrounded by his brothers' widows and children, the third in a series of such announcements, whose tone was increasingly grim.

"At first, the assumption was that merely being available would be enough," wrote Collier and Horowitz. "It was almost as if the decision to finally do it . . . would in and of itself take care of all the loose ends." But the biggest loose end turned out to be Teddy, who from the start was an unnerving and unfocused presence and who appeared to mislay all his skills. Three days before he announced, he gave an interview to Roger Mudd and the CBS network in which he seemed unable to utter a sentence in English. "The reasons I would run is because I have a great belief in this country," he said when asked to explain why he was running for president. "The energies and resources of this nation, I think, should be focused on those problems in a way that brings a sense of restoration—in this country, by its people, to . . . in dealing with the problems that we face . . . and I basically feel that it's imperative for this country to move forward; that it just can't stand still or otherwise it moves backward. . . . Well, it's a—on—on what—on—you know, you have to come to grips with the—different issues that we're facing. I mean we can—we have to deal with the various questions that we're—we're talking about."

About Chappaquiddick, he had this to utter: "Oh that—there's—the problem is—from that night—I . . . found the conduct, the behavior, almost sort of beyond belief myself, I mean, that's why it's been—but I think that's, that's the way it is." In the campaign itself, he was no more coherent: "Roll up your sleeves and your mother and father," he exhorted one audience. "I'm an uphill struggle," he said at one time.

"His manner seemed desultory and uncertain," wrote Burton Hersh. "Whenever crowds responded listlessly, he attempted to harangue them to life." Voters who turned out to see him found none of the eloquence, fire, or urgency they had come to expect of the Kennedys and went away baffled. "Kennedy doesn't generate the excitement that John Kennedy did, nor the electricity that Robert Kennedy did," wrote Elizabeth Drew in the *New Yorker*. "He seems battened down and unnatural . . . the feeling one gets is of a man on the defensive . . . this is not, as yet, a joyous quest."

It was only when he had been decisively trounced in his earlier forays that he started to rally, finding his voice in a set of speeches and eking out several primary wins. "Reporters following him in 1980 noticed a sense of freedom growing in him as his chances faded," Garry Wills would write later. Hersh quoted an associate who had worked on the campaign, who had told him, "I have a personal hypothesis that he lacked confidence in his ability to be president, and one of the reasons his performance improved so drastically was in inverse relationship to how much he thought he had a chance to win." "I believe Ted has an unconscious drive to self-destruct," Jackie Kennedy once wrote to Roswell Gilpatric, deputy secretary of defense in the JFK era. "I think he knows he'll never live up to what people expect."

"Never, never, did Teddy want the job," said Jack's friend George Smathers. "The Kennedy crowd, the extended clan and their friends and allies were yearning for a new Camelot. They pushed him, tugged at him, and finally convinced him he could make it. . . . Jack and Bobby went into their campaigns with all guns blazing, Teddy walked in . . . half-heartedly, and it showed." It was considered shocking in 1968 when Bobby lost the Oregon primary, the first time a Kennedy had ever lost anything (discounting Jack's 1956 run for vice president). Ted, by contrast, lost twenty of twenty-five caucuses and twenty-four of thirty-four primaries, a stunning personal rejection by a party that in theory at least still claimed to worship the Kennedys. For the second time in ten years, he had derailed his own chance to be president, and this time, it would be the last.

Ted returned to the Senate in 1981 as a changed man in an altered political landscape, no longer a threat or a possible president, an outsider, and in a strange land. Republicans controlled the Senate for the first time since 1954 and were beginning a stretch of executive dominance: with the exception of 1993 and 1994, when Democrats briefly held the White House along with both houses of Congress, he would spend his career in opposition, usually in the Senate's minority party, no longer leading or trying to set an agenda but guarding old gains from attack. In this, he would prove a skillful and resolute fighter, "the Shadow President," as Hersh would describe him, increasingly a beleaguered lion in winter, bucking a stiff and cold wind. But hard times would bring out the best in the child of privilege, who had thrust away power when it was pushed on him but would prove his grit under adversity.

In the next two decades, he would become a great senator. As Norman Ornstein put it, "Kennedy is going to go down as one of the most significant senators in history, in terms of concrete things accomplished and put on the agenda that will get accomplished in the years to come." Mike Kelly produced grudging compliments: "Even a partial listing of the major bills in whose passage Kennedy has played a part is impressive. . . . He has become not only the most consistent counterforce to the long-running Republican administrations in pushing for government activism . . . but has also become adept at building Republican-Democratic, right-left coalitions that can endure passage of compromise domestic policy legislation. . . . He is increasingly successful and increasingly prolific. The 100th Congress (1987–1988) was the best period he or almost any senator has ever had."

But this was his reputation in Congress. To the public, he was seen increasingly as a figure of disrepute or even of ridicule, a regular feature on tabloid front pages, a constant target of late-night talk-show comedians and/or of parody skits. Stories circulated about the time he and a colleague roughed up a young waitress, the time he was found on a restaurant floor with a young female lobbyist, and the time he was photographed in flagrante delicto in a small boat. ("I see you've changed your position on offshore drilling," one colleague had said.) Still worse was the episode in 1991 in Palm Beach over Easter vacation when he woke his son Patrick and nephew William Kennedy Smith and took them both out on a round of late-night bar hopping, which resulted in Smith's well-publicized trial for rape. "Ted Kennedy has presided over his large dysfunctional clan as best he could, but he has apparently been more inclined to participate as an equal in their revels than to act as a stern authority figure," Adam Bellow has noted. "The real model for Ted Kennedy is not his own father but the corpulent palace eunuchs of the Ming dynasty or the sybaritic cardinals of sixteenth-century Rome, with their retinues of concubines, nephews, and bastards." As Ted's cousin Mary Lou McCarthy remarked, "No wonder the younger boys have all gotten in trouble. . . . With that as an example, my God."

Once by far the most handsome of four handsome brothers, he had by that time been coarsened beyond recognition: "Up close, the face is a shock," wrote Michael Kelly. "The skin has gone from red roses to gin blossoms. The tracery of burst capillaries shines faintly through the scaly scarlet patches that cover the bloated, mottled cheeks. The nose that was once straight and narrow is now swollen and bulbous . . . deep corrugations crease the forehead and angle from the nostrils and downturned corners of the mouth. The . . . teeth are the color of old piano keys. The eyes have yellowed, too, and they are so bloodshot it looks as if he's been weeping." As perhaps he had.

From the mid-1980s on, as it became clear that Ted would never be president, dynastic hopes were transferred to the third generation, whose older members had now arrived at their twenties and seemed poised to move up and move on. In 1988, Frank Mankewitz, who in 1968 had announced Bobby's death to the nation, foresaw "an avalanche of young Kennedys descending on Washington," an irresistible army of relatives. At the time, it appeared not unlikely: there were twenty-six Kennedy cousins, eighteen of them male, with a machine behind them built up through fifty years of arduous tilling in national politics, and a monstrous fan base of millions of people, ready to back them with huge sums of money and invest in them years of lost hopes. Kennedy runs would be both lavishly financed and mounted and heavily publicized. Kennedy boys would be scouted while still in their teens by political fixers and pressed into running for office, given the services of the most famous consultants and wordsmiths, surrounded when they campaigned by actors and athletes. And twenty years later, three would be dead, two involved in trials or scandals involving rape charges, and only one current in national politics—and no one, it seemed, in the wings.

At first, it had appeared fairly uncertain just who the main heirs might be. John Kennedy Jr. had the magic name and the descent from the president, not to mention the national memory of the heart-stopping moment when as a small boy he had saluted his dead father's coffin. But in 1964, his mother moved him to New York, taking him out of the Kennedy orbit and its highly energized ethos of politics. The focus then moved to the RFK children, brought up in the "alpha" Kennedy family by the most family minded of all of the brothers, who had the most completely recapitulated in his own household the conditions in which he was raised. He had tried to instill the esprit—and the purpose and discipline—that was his own father's legacy. But his sudden death in 1968 while just forty-two, when his oldest child was sixteen and his youngest not yet born, devastated his children, catching his sons at a critical moment and abandoning them in an era of vast social meltdown with no guide and no mentor in sight.

In his absence, it soon became evident how much he had been the heart and the soul of the family and how ill equipped his wife now was to replace him or to deal with her angry and traumatized children. By 1984, David, the third son, was dead of a drug overdose; most of the boys were in serious trouble, and the second son, Bobby Jr., was in the grip of a heroin problem that would become public years later when he was arrested, after having collapsed on a plane. None of this was unpredictable in the case of young boys deprived of their father and indulged as celebrities in a culture about to go off on a sex and drugs bender, but it did not compute with the habits of discipline that tend to produce a great leader. "We were all of us brought up to be president," said Christopher Lawford, son of the president's sister Patricia, who himself had drug problems. But they were not; they were only brought up to think that they should be—which isn't the same thing at all.

First out of the gate was Joe Kennedy II, Bobby's second born and the first Kennedy grandson, namesake of both the patriarch and the son he had groomed to be president, his very birth a political moment and key to the rise of his family: he had been born on September 24, 1952, right in the middle of Jack's run for the Senate, in which his birth and well-publicized christening had worked, in the words of a Lodge campaign worker, to "knock the stuffing out of our campaign." He was, like the second Joe Kennedy, the "lead-off hitter" for his generation, the one picked out for succession and carefully groomed: the one to whom his father wrote a letter after Jack had been murdered, the one who had been flown west to see his dying father with the rest of the grown-ups, the one who walked with his mother greeting the mourners on the funeral train bearing his father's body to Arlington, the one whose political future was a subject of interest among party leaders before he was out of his teens.

He was also the one perhaps set most adrift by the death of his father, who had been trying to ease him into the family business, who had groomed him to follow the family pattern and then died just as he was beginning to instruct him in how. He was also not a natural fit for the role of political star of the family: dyslexic and slow, he had problems in school and was lacking in confidence, which he attempted to make up for with bluster. "I'm like a bb rattling around in a boxcar," he told a friend during a tongue-tied discussion of the perils of being crown prince. He was also filled with an unfocused anger and an understandable set of conflicting emotions that no one had helped him resolve.

"He didn't have anybody he could lean on," his headmaster said later. "He seemed to think that he was supposed to have his father's death under control, but he didn't. He had a violent temper and would get this swollen look, as if he were about to burst at the seams." There was an accident in 1973, when a jeep he was driving flipped over, injuring his brother and paralyzing a young female passenger.

But after this, he calmed down, took a series of entry-level jobs in the government, and moved back to Boston to found Citizens Energy, a nonprofit concern that sold heating oil to the poor at prices below market value, which gave him a public name and a platform to run on when Jack's old seat, in the Massachusetts 8th district, opened up in 1986. "The Kennedy name set him apart from the field, and made him the front-runner," wrote Lawrence Leamer. "Richard Goodwin wrote speeches that sounded as if Joe were running for president, and Joe read them as if reading the words for the first time." He was not, of course, mature enough to be running for anything, but that bothered neither the voters nor the advisers pushing him. He was elected and sent into Congress, with the assumption that he was not stopping there.

Stressed as it was, Joe's life had been easy compared to that of his young cousin Patrick, the overlooked second son of Ted Kennedy, who until then had appeared as the consummate victim, on whom all the family pressures converged. Born four years after Jack's murder, he was just a year old when Bobby was murdered, and only age two when his father's misdeeds at Chappaquiddick ended forever his national future and set the family fortunes on their long downward arc. As a result, his mother had become a severe alcoholic and his father a sporadic one; their marriage broke down when Patrick was seven and formally ended when he was thirteen. Through his childhood, he had suffered severe bouts of asthma, a condition brought on by nervous anxiety, and he entered a program to cure his addiction to drugs and alcohol while in his late teens.

"My problem was low self-esteem and loneliness, and a sense of anxiety, and a feeling the world was overwhelming," he said. After dropping out of Georgetown University because of "the overwhelming presence of my family in Washington," he enrolled in Providence College, a small school in Rhode Island, and startled everyone by running for office when he was just twenty-one. He was the last one on earth his family thought of as suited for politics, but he had his own reasons for seizing the family legacy. It was, he explained, the only way he could think of to get the family's attention focused on him and his prospects. And, as one observer noted, "It provided structure, and gave him people who organized his life."

It was clear from the start that Patrick was running less as himself than as a generic Kennedy, a repository for the complex of emotions surrounding his family. At his first race, for a seat in the Rhode Island state assembly, he was surrounded by photogenic family members (including a reluctant John Kennedy Jr.), who on Election Day collared people outside polling places and posed for pictures with them before sending them in to vote. His father helped him with numerous appearances in this neighboring state in which he was popular, but even he was astounded to find later on that his son had spent the staggering sum of $92,000 to win a seat that paid the extravagant salary of $300 a year.

Four years after that, Patrick ran for the House from Rhode Island's 1st district in a campaign that seemed almost an afterthought, awash as he was in the rivers of money and the flood of celebrities that showed up to help him campaign. "The entire Kennedy dynasty mobilized," wrote Robert Dreyfus in *The Nation.* "Star-studded fund-raisers in Washington and Los Angeles included numerous Kennedys and friends like Peter Lawford, Sargent Shriver, Pierre Salinger, Jack Valenti, and Tip O'Neill helped Patrick amass $12 million. . . . Since then Kennedy has swamped his opponents, spending $1.2 million in 1998 against an opponent who raised just $29,000." Patrick was swept into Congress by money and family, and the Democrats put him to work using his family name to raise money for them, making him head of the Democratic Congressional Campaign Committee in 1998. In that capacity, he traveled the country, creating a club for $100,000-plus donors, whom he invited for picnics at the much-fabled family compound, touching the sacred chords of Kennedy memory in those with nostalgia for Bobby and Jack.

"What Kennedy excels in is raising money," wrote Michael Barone. "He is probably the biggest single draw at fundraisers

around the country . . . the draw, of course, is that he is a Kennedy."
"Around the country, he is treated like royalty," said Dreyfus, who
quotes a Democrat saying, "They want to touch a Kennedy. It's like
seeing a work of art." In Congress itself, he seemed less of an art-
work, given to overheated attacks on the opposing party and
repeated iterations of the family names.

Joe II was less blatant, but he continued to suffer from chronic
emotional turbulence. "He couldn't get along with his colleagues,
and had an uncontrollable temper . . . got upset over seemingly
minor matters . . . exploded like a tornado out of a summer sky."
Some colleagues were irritated to the point where they got up and
left when he began speaking, but his staff indulged him, for the
sake of his name and the golden future he was assumed to
have: they "not only excused Joe, but considered suffering his out-
bursts a small price to pay." In the end, he would pay, but only
much later, and under conditions no one could begin to foresee.

Among those conscripted for backup in Patrick's first race was
his cousin John Kennedy Jr., although, as observers noted, he
seemed half-hearted and had to be pressed into doing his job. Later,
he sought out the assemblyman Patrick had challenged, telling him,
"I don't like being here. I don't think it's fair for me to be here. . . .
The only reason I'm here is for my cousin. But I don't believe in it."
From details such as these, it soon becomes evident that this most
courted grandson of Joseph P. Kennedy spent his short life trying
to fend off the sort of career and condition his young cousin Patrick
embraced. Stunningly handsome, appallingly rich, heir to his
mother's glamour as well as to the mystique of the father he could
not remember, he seemed terribly wary of being tempted by more
fame than he had already, of being in some way made use of by
others or of being steamrollered by the ambitions of others into
something he might not himself want. John's cousins, especially the

senators' children, had been brought up around Washington in largely political households, but when he was three his mother had withdrawn him from Washington and from the Kennedy ambience, away from the pressures of public ambition and the increasing disarray of the Kennedy's personal lives.

"One of the most important decisions Jackie made in her life was to get the children . . . away from the Kennedys," said her friend Peter Duchin. "One summer, Jackie sent John on a diving expedition to Micronesia. . . . She said to me, "Do you think that's far enough away?" Pursued all his life by political suitors, he learned early on to intrigue and evade them, making crowds swoon at the 1988 Democratic convention and then slipping back into his more private pursuits. He dealt with the pressure, and the exposure, by eluding them gracefully, wary of being entrapped.

"He was always thinking, how do I define myself as a person and not just as a Kennedy?" said his friend John Barlow Martin. "He had a strong sense of Irish loyalty, but he felt he was different, and he was." He did not rule out politics, but he did not rule it in, either, deferring it to an indefinite future, whose conditions were never stated exactly and before which presumably other things would be done. He defined himself as having a curious, as opposed to a partisan, nature, which led him into working one summer for the conservative William Bradford Reynolds, to find out what the other side thought. "I have a slightly contrarian impulse I can't seem to shake," he said once. "It's always sort of fun to try and play with blocks and see what you can come up with that's a little bit different."

What he came up with in the long run was *George*, a magazine that tried to give the star treatment to politics but was interesting to many largely for what it said about John.

As the *National Post* would write when John died, "*George* ... did give Mr. Kennedy a role in which he could be a Kennedy without being too much of a Kennedy, a role on the sidelines of politics in which he could yet wield the family sword. And it gave him a precariously balanced perch between the lifelong quest for a measure of privacy and the public life." Carefully maintained as nonpartisan, the magazine was an ingenious way to both be in politics and yet stay above it, a place in which he could weigh and explore the risks and rewards of a life spent in public before deciding to do it himself. As an editor, he assigned himself a monthly interview with some famous figure, in which he grilled them about the pressures and perks of their lives. "Again and again he asked his subjects about the costs of public life," said one of his editors. "What sacrifices . . . were required of those who ran for office? He posed his queries in myriad ways, but in truth there was only one question. . . . Here was the great drama of John's life, played out in plain sight."

"In many ways, *George* was most interesting as a reflection of the career pressures and conflicts that buffeted its editor," wrote Hendrik Hertzberg in the *New Yorker*, suggesting that the magazine had "rechannelled those conflicts" while not quite resolving them. For the staff, it became a psychoanalytical exercise, in which John tried to work out his future while his associates indulged their own curiosity. "If *George* provided a template in which John could hash out his identity conflicts, it also became a forum in which my colleagues and I debated everything we wanted to know about John, but were afraid to ask," said Richard Blow, an associate. "Conspiracy theories, sex in politics, assassinations . . . we redirected the questions we could not ask John into [article] ideas." The magazine became a road map into his preoccupations as he tried to work out his feelings in regard to a father who was at once an object of gossip as a philanderer of epic proportions and a worshipped slain leader who was now a Lost Prince. Sometimes he seemed to be tweaking his father, as when, on the birthday of President Clinton, he put on the cover an actress dressed to resemble Marilyn Monroe, the reigning sex queen of the Camelot era, who had made an iconic performance at President Kennedy's birthday fund-raiser in a skin-tight nude-colored dress. He also ran a long article by the mother of the man who had shot Yitzhak Rabin, the Israeli prime minister, in an act that resembled his own father's murder. But nothing raised quite so much stir as the editor's letter that he ran in his July 1997 issue, in which he chided Bobby's sons, Joe II and Michael, for problems in their publicized personal lives.

For the Kennedys, the year had begun on an upswing, with Joe about to make his big move in the run for the statehouse, a move expected since he had first run for office and one in the planning for years. Then in March his first wife published a book, in which she detailed his attempts to force her to let him have an annulment and called him a bully and a hypocrite. "By the end of our marriage I had simply become afraid of him," she would write. It was the same problem with temper he had battled for years, but for the first time in his life a price was exacted: assailed in the press as aggressive and arrogant, he had started to slip in the polls. But this was innocence itself compared to the scandal that broke out in April concerning his brother—his campaign manager, the father of two, and widely seen himself as a potential congressional candidate—and an affair with an underage girl.

Five years younger than Joe, the fourth in the line of the RFK brothers, Michael was once seen as the best and most balanced—quicker than Joe, more stable than Bobby, the one who had seemingly sustained the least visible damage from their father's traumatic and terrible death. But under the surface, something was cracking, and as he passed thirty, the cracks seemed to spread. The first sign was his behavior at Citizens Energy, the company Joe passed on to him when he went to Congress. Joe had paid himself a modest salary, but Michael had changed that, turning the largely charitable concern into a cash cow for himself and his partners, paying himself salaries as high as $600,000 yearly while Joe, on a small trust fund and a congressman's salary, lived in a small apartment on Capitol Hill. His greed was soon matched by other excesses, some seen before in lesser degree in previous family members; some new, and his own.

"Michael had not one addiction, but three: alcohol, sex, and danger," wrote Lawrence Leamer. "He treated his addictions as interchangeable, drinking until he was high, getting it on with a new sexual partner, taking extraordinary chances on the ski slopes, in his car, or out in a boat. Each addiction gave him a great rush, followed by a crashing letdown that he got out of by heading into one of his addictions again, as often as not using his Kennedy name to indulge himself. . . . He wanted others to sense what he was doing, and either to applaud or tolerate whatever conduct he felt like exposing them to."

He began to womanize in the style of his grandfather and of his uncle, the president, and then he went beyond them: After going through many of the friends of his wife, he seduced the daughter of friends who looked after his children, beginning the affair when the girl was fourteen. This was bad enough, but he made no attempt to conceal it, and as time went on, he became more and more brazen. "In full view of the family, [he] took the girl on three summer rafting trips," write Collier and Horowitz. "There was heavy drinking and naked partying. . . . Michael rigged up a tent as a sauna, generating an intoxicating steam by dashing vodka on to the hot rocks." By the fall of 1996, rumors were flying, and Michael's brothers had tried to confront him, to no effect whatsoever. In November, the story came close to breaking out when the girl's mother climbed out in her nightgown to the roof of her town house, threatened to jump, and had to be rescued by firefighters. And in April 1997, the *Boston Globe* broke the story that a Kennedy nephew had had a long-standing affair with a schoolgirl who had worked in his household and might even stand trial for rape.

The immediate victim of Michael was Joe, who as a candidate could not hide, like his brother, but was raw meat for a ravenous press. May 29 was John Kennedy's birthday, the date of the presentation ceremony for the Profile in Courage Award, established by the family to honor his memory (and be a showcase for oncoming talent), which always before drew a large showing of family members. This time it was different: John Jr. was present but not Joe and Michael, "Michael because he was being investigated for statutory rape by the district attorney's office, and Joe because he didn't want to be asked about Michael, about his first wife, or anything else." Relentlessly battered, Joe left the race in August, unable to change the subject from his brother's behavior, which was now the subject of media frenzies. Michael escaped prosecution and trial when the girl refused to press charges, but he had been found guilty in the eyes of the public, which, adding his conduct to a bill that included Chappaquiddick, the William Kennedy Smith rape extravaganza and trial, the numerous drug busts, and the conviction of his cousin, Michael Skakel (son of one of Ethel Kennedy's brothers), for the 1975 murder of a Connecticut neighbor, began to see this next tier of the Kennedy family in a new and unflattering light.

At the state convention in June, Joe apologized to the public, the girl, and the family. Michael, however, made no apologies, and he continued to act as if none were required, carrying on with a manic exuberance. He went square dancing at a family barbecue. He went on a bike trip in Ecuador. He went with his family for New Year's to Aspen, where they indulged in the perilous sport of touch football, this time played on skis. There, on the last day of the year, with park police trying to usher them back to the chalet, he reached for a pass and slid into a tree, dying at once of massive head injuries. A wake at Hyannis tried to cast him as yet the next in a long line of Kennedys who died tragically young, but this time no one outside of the family was buying the story, and the heroic themes seemed increasingly ludicrous. This was also the last straw for Joe, who, devastated by the events of the year, announced two months later that he was leaving the family business, the first Kennedy ever to bow out of politics. Pushed into it in the first place by his famous father and uncle, pushed out of it by a brother who had become infamous, he would not be the last.

At Michael's wake, John appeared ill at ease and defensive, still under suspicion from some of the mourners for breaching the code of family closeness with the piece he had run in July. But Joe's retreat had opened a space in the family sweepstakes that John now appeared about to consider because his problems with *George* had increased. Poised uncertainly between glitter and substance, the magazine had a foot in both worlds but a foothold in neither, and, after the initial burst of excitement, circulation and revenue had begun to decline. The year 1998 would be key to his publishing fortunes: John had always believed in the fusion of gossip and power—in power explained by the personal story—but when the perfect example appeared on his doorstep, Bill Clinton's affair with the star-struck young intern and the impeachment that flowed from his lie in a lawsuit, he would find himself tangled in family history, conflicted and stricken and mute.

To address the questions of Clinton's excesses—and the misdeeds of some of the people pursuing him whose own skeletons would soon tumble noisily out of their closets—he would have to confront not only the crimes of his cousins and the scandals and public affairs of his uncle, but the central mystery of his father's life that still puzzles biographers: the seemingly inexplicable incongruity between his stoic, serious, sometimes heroic persona and his unbridled and sybarititic side. In this mystery, a whole line of inquiries seemed to present themselves for public discussion: What was the line between public and private morality? Was there a connection? Could a failure in one sphere damn one completely? His father, and others, had been both faithless husbands and inspirational leaders. Were there different ways one could be a good man?

In private, John seemed to ponder these questions, but in the end, they would prove too demanding: John ran two tough issues and then backed away from the story, thereafter treating only obliquely a drama that for the rest of the year would mesmerize the general public and all other arms of the press. "John was on the cusp of success with *George*," writes Lawrence Leamer. "There was a natural connection between Clinton's sex scandal and his father's career. . . . He could have written an essay that was equally about Clinton and his father. He could have picked up the phone and gotten to some of the major players. . . . He could probably have reached Monica Lewinsky, who had wanted to intern for *George*. . . . He could have pushed *George* into the fray." But John stepped away and doomed the magazine to irrelevance and himself to an uncertain future. For if *George* failed, had he?

Early in 1999, as an impeached Clinton was acquitted by the Senate in a party-line vote, *George* was facing a hazardous future, and John, the crown prince of the Kennedy family, was facing the fact he might fail. Despite his brave front, he had always been self-conscious in regard to his father, who in his day had been something of a problem child, but who by John's age—thirty-eight—had long since found himself. By that age, his father had been a war hero, written a book, and served three years in the Senate and six in the House, become a serious and increasingly listened-to voice on international policy, and was already thinking of running for president.

John, in contrast, had failed the bar exam twice, had had a short, undistinguished career in the office of the attorney general, and had run a magazine about to go under that had failed to win public respect. Rumors were rampant that he was like a dumb blonde—stunning, but lacking in substance and intellect—and the tabloid headline "The Hunk Flunks" had hurt. "When John failed [the bar] the second time, it seemed to precipitate a crisis of sorts regarding his father," wrote his friend Robert Littell, who had known him since college, adding that after a slighting remark from a colleague comparing his accomplishments to those of his father, he drove alone one weekend to a remote upstate cabin, where he listened to self-help tapes and drank. "He did get a therapist not long after," Littell related. "He found it a great help, allowing him to articulate the enormous complexities of his life without sounding ungrateful or weak." The imminent extinction of *George* now revived all these feelings. "How's it gonna look if we fail?" he asked friends. As Blow writes, "He believed that his future was inextricably linked with *George.* If the magazine proved to be a long-term success, John could move on to the next phase . . . with a win under his belt. If *George* went bust, he would be an unemployed former editor . . . that would be more than a perception problem. It might make John himself wonder if he really was capable of greater things." "John was obsessed with the magazine, not only with what he might do to it, but what he had done wrong," writes Leamer. "If *George* fails, am I a failure?" he asked.

As his parent company announced its intention to stop funding the project, John took off on a frenetic round of meetings with other possible backers, often flying to them in his Piper Cub plane. He found few solid prospects but did not stop trying, and soon he looked exhausted and strained. "John took the blow hard," Littell tells us, after one possible backer had passed on the project. "He'd gained weight, he looked tired, his hair was noticeably grayer. . . . He was becoming resigned to the fact that it [*George*] would close." There were rumors his marriage was also in trouble. "He told a friend who was doing particularly well that their lives were going in different directions, and then changed the subject," as Leamer says. Friends would claim later he was making plans then to go into politics—he had discussed a Senate run with one party chairman—but he was at the same time starting to think of new business ventures, including an Internet version of *George*. He was preoccupied, stressed, tired (and recovering from an ankle injury) when he took off in his plane with his wife and her sister two hours late into a hazy twilight on the warm night of July 18, 1999. They never arrived. Five days later, after a well-publicized search, his plane was found in the waters just off Martha's Vineyard, with the passengers strapped in their seats.

In the days just before and after the plane was discovered, the press was filled with pictures of the three-year-old boy saluting his father, making it clear that whatever John Kennedy Jr. had done, planned, or wanted, he was seen most of all as the son of his father, one more in the long line of Kennedy offspring who had managed to die much too young. But others remembered a man who had been good, if not great or remarkable, and one with a large gift for friendship. "Very fair, very witty, and very loyal," a friend and coworker told Christopher Hitchens. "He was a good man, quite simply . . . given the context in which he lived, a really extremely good man." "He did not so much draw on the Kennedy legend as add to it," said Tony Blankley, who had written a magazine column for him. "Oh God, how he sparkled. He was both luminous and warm." His end, and the pressures he had been under increasingly as he had begun to slowly edge up on his forties, seemed to pose the question of whether a normal life would ever be enough or be possible for the son and namesake of a dynastic and idolized president. But if his accomplishments were in the range of the normal as compared to those of his father and uncle, for him, being normal was surely an accomplishment, and if he had not become president or a great politician, neither had he been a public embarrassment, and no one had ever accused him of rape.

He was mourned especially in contrast to some of his cousins, who continued to make the wrong sort of headlines when they made them at all. This was especially true in relation to Patrick, whose election to Congress had not brought the peace that he craved. In November 1999, he confessed to the *New York Times* that he was under a psychiatrist's care for chronic depression and taking numerous drugs to control it. Whatever he took, it did not seem all that helpful: in March 2000, he was caught on videotape shoving a guard at an airport, who sued him the next year for assault. Meanwhile, he piled up a series of colorful nautical mishaps for doing what was called "rock star damage" to a series of boats. In the space of a year, three rented pleasure boats became tangled in nets, had their engines ruined, or were abandoned off Martha's Vineyard, and the Coast Guard was once summoned to rescue a girlfriend he had abandoned after a noisy and clamorous fight.

As a result, he faced what had once seemed unthinkable—a serious challenge in the 2002 midterms—as his poll ratings fell twenty points. He was not the only one of his family's connections to face trouble in the 2002 cycle: in New York, Andrew Cuomo, married to an RFK daughter and hoping to avenge his father's 1994 loss to George Pataki, shot himself in the foot with a feral attack on the governor, and then he ran a campaign so abysmal that it had to be ended by Bill and Hillary Clinton before he had a chance to lose in the primary to the November loser, Carl McCall. And Max, another RFK child, announced his candidacy for Congress in Massachusetts but stumbled so badly in his very first outings that he was forced to pull out of the race.

In critical ways Max was like Patrick: a "soft kid" in a chaotic and traumatized household, who had had breathing problems from numerous ailments and who had serious problems with drugs and drinking and had struggled to fight his way free. But where Patrick grasped early on at what he saw as a lifeline, Max bounced in and out of a series of interests until suddenly at age thirty-three he honed in on a seat being vacated by the ailing Joe Moakley in the suburbs of Boston, bought a five-bedroom house in Moakley's blue-collar district, and, in the magic way possible only to sons of great families, suddenly found himself surrounded by a network of donors and the most expensive and famous consultants in the liberal universe. Overnight, he had become the front-runner. And then he opened his mouth. On May 17, he gave his first major speech to a political audience, and people expecting a new RFK got a shock to the system. Max pulled at his ear, mumbled, and erupted in giggles; at a later speech he identified Byron White, appointed in 1962 by John Kennedy, as a current member of the U.S. Supreme Court.

"Nothing in the meandering text was itself disastrous," wrote Matt Bai in a *New York Times* story. "It was the delivery—the stumbling over words, the compulsive ear-scratching, the mumbling and sudden laughter. . . . The next day's stories mauled him. . . . The Senator [Ted Kennedy] began to have his doubts." "Ted sensed a major problem," wrote Karen Tumulty, and slowly he began to pressure his nephew. In mid-June, the *Boston Herald* dug up a nineteen-year-old arrest for a fracas on the campus at Harvard, and a poll showed that Max's large lead had now vanished. Politics no longer seemed quite so exciting. Four days before he was to make his formal announcement, Max instead would bow out.

A more inexplicable fate befell Max's cousin Mark Shriver, a golden-boy son of the president's sister, the son on his father's side of a great Maryland family, an eight-year veteran of the state assembly, and, in the words of a family intimate, "the most talented political candidate I have ever seen." Running for a congressional seat in the suburbs of Washington, he had a $2.5 million bankroll, a lead of nearly thirty points over his primary opponent, and expectations that he would roll into Congress as a rising superstar, and land on a national ticket in several years. But as the campaign progressed, air seemed to seep ever so slowly out of his effort: he made no mistakes, he did not flame out, and he did not embarrass himself, but he did seem to lack some vital element, the drive and intensity that had marked Jack and Bobby, which his less glamorous primary opponent seemed to possess more than he did. In the end, he would lose by three points, the third Kennedy of five running to be wrung out in or before the primary season. And there were two more to go.

By September 2002, the only two Kennedys running were Patrick, fighting his way up from the depths of his swan dive, and Bobby's first daughter, Kathleen. As the boys fell away, she emerged as a comer, and even their opposite: clean, sweet, pious, and scandal free, called in the conservative press "a poster girl for good behavior, friendly, humble, and thoroughly decent," with a "wide-eyed desire for good government . . . that recalls a more innocent time." "She is not just a nice person," wrote another conservative. "She is perhaps the nicest person I've ever encountered in her line of work." A sweet-natured mother of four, married to a quiet and supportive superprofessor, she had not been picked out when young to be groomed by her family, scouted in her teens by political vultures, or parachuted into a safe seat by her family. Instead, she had run for Congress in a Republican district in Maryland, lost, and then paid her dues in a series of dull jobs in government until 1994, when she was picked out by Parris Glendenning to run on his ticket and became the state's lieutenant governor at forty-three.

It was a powerless post in a fairly small state, and she had lost the only race she had ever run on her own, but she was touted as a political star of the very first magnitude, a potential running mate for Al Gore in the 2000 election, and the undisputed next governor in 2002, if she was not tapped for high office first. All at once, she became "the next Kennedy," especially after the death of John Kennedy Jr. both ignited nostalgia and opened a gap. "Bobby's Girl Could Lead Al Gore to the White House" ran one of the thousands of gurgling articles. Democratic national chair Ed Rendell hoped to be chief of staff in her White House. "Maybe some day I'll be knocking on doors for her when she's running for national office," Bill Clinton opined.

As she geared up her governor's campaign for the 2002 cycle, cash flooded in at the many posh fund-raisers held in a series of family mansions: at Ted's house in Washington; at the Hyannis Port compound; at the Shrivers' estate in Maryland, where traffic backed up for five miles and five hundred people gathered on the spacious green lawn to look at celebrities and stare at the fabulous Kennedys. They were there to do more than merely support a potential state governor. As one woman said who had flown in for a fund-raiser at the home of Ted Kennedy, she had come all this way so that she could say later, "From early on, I have supported the person who will become the first woman president of the United States."

Kathleen entered the governor's race with an unheard of $6.6 million, a firm lead in the polls in a state that had not had a Republican governor in twenty-five years, and a stated belief that she was bound to be the next governor. And then things began to go wrong. "All these premature coronations have left many long-time Townsend watchers in Maryland baffled," wrote Matt Labash in a June 2002 profile. Says a reporter who's covered her for years, "There's a real disconnect between her national reputation and that in the state, where it's quite mixed." Her political record had not been remarkable, and her persona, although pleasant, was small.

"She's normal," said Clinton friend Lanny Davis. "Even in a power suit . . . she's a small, bird-like presence," said the magazine *Capitol Style*, calling her "more like an elementary school librarian" than a big-time politician or star. "Some of the big boys of Maryland politics are uneasy with Townsend's ascendancy," the *Washington Post* reported one year before the election. "These concerns have only mounted in recent months. Her skeptics point out that Townsend has never won a campaign on her own. Nor has she run a government. . . . Even Townsend's admirers fret about her tendency to misspeak or garble her message. . . . Her policy blunders have left a sour impression. . . . One Republican campaign consultant told me, 'There's a widespread perception that she's an empty dress.'"

She was inept on the stump (she once forgot at a fund-raiser to introduce guest star Bill Clinton), her main policy program was mired in scandal, and she failed at projecting an aura of competence. Her one asset seemed to be her family background, played up in ads featuring shots of her father and a televised movie based on his life. But her opponent, Bob Ehrlich, a hometown boy from a working-class suburb of Baltimore, had cleverly turned this advantage against her, contrasting her background of un-worked-for privilege against his own blue-collar roots. When Townsend threw a fund-raiser at two thousand dollars a head at her family's Hyannis Port compound, Ehrlich countered with a twenty-dollar crab roast in Arbutus, the Baltimore neighborhood where he was raised. "Obviously, some folks love the Camelot legacy," Ehrlich said to reporters. "But that world contrasts with the one we live in as night differs from day."

By the end of October, Ehrlich had pulled even, surged to a lead among independents, and even erased Townsend's huge lead in funds. "Townsend's campaign seems to be unraveling from a combination of political blunders, speech slips, and Kennedy scandal," *Insight* magazine reported. "If Townsend should lose, it will be a remarkable upset and a huge frustration for many within the Democratic Party who see 'Bobby's girl' as vice presidential material for Al Gore's 2004 campaign." By ten thirty on election night, it was clear this had happened; the verdict was pronounced by the *Washington Post* in this statement: "The votes were not tallied on election night when Gov. Parris Glendenning pronounced his lieutenant governor's bid to succeed him 'one of the worst run campaigns in the country.' . . . In the three weeks since KKT lost the governor's race, few dispute he was right."

Left standing were Ted and his younger son, Patrick, one old and neither inspiring, both mirroring the exhaustion of the family enterprise. "The Kennedys" as a concept and a viable force had died with Robert F. Kennedy, and over the next thirty-five years the image, hollowed out from within, had slowly collapsed on itself. The most dramatic and tragic of American dynasties had finally come to an end.

CHAPTER 5

Their Three Sons

When John Kennedy entered the Senate in 1953, he was joined there by two other freshman members of the upper body, Tennessee's Albert Gore and Prescott Bush of Connecticut. In time Kennedy would become friendly with his fellow Democrat and his fellow New Englander, but he would share with their children the burden of great expectations, of ambitions imposed from above. The year 1948, when Kennedy began fitfully to feel his way into the career his father had wished on him, would be critical too for the Bush and Gore families: it was the year that Prescott's son, George Herbert Walker, left New England at twenty-four to seek his fortune in Texas, taking his wife and son with him. And it was the year that Gore and his wife, Pauline, had their only son and second child, whom they would name Albert Jr. and raise to become a great man.

Gore and his wife were from Appalachia, where they had been born obscure and hungry, whereas Prescott's son George and John Kennedy were both children of New England privilege, sons of millionaires who had held high public office, Kennedy's father entertaining FDR in happier times at his rented mansion in Maryland and Bush's father golfing with Ike at Burning Tree. Both grew up cushioned by comfort and privilege. Both saw hard times for the first time at war in the navy, and each thrust himself head on into danger: Kennedy hiding his health problems (or lying about them), Bush volunteering on his eighteenth birthday, the youngest pilot to serve in the war. Later, both nearly drowned in the Pacific Ocean: Kennedy when his boat was sunk by a destroyer, Bush when his plane was shot down. Both came home with medals to public applause. Both came from large, frenetic, and ambitious families that mingled raw hunger with hunger for service; and the endless activity and rough verbal ragging were oddly similar at the Kennedy compound at Hyannis Port in Massachusetts and the Bush family compound some miles distant, up north at Walker's Point, Maine. The formative Kennedy was Jack's father, Joe Sr., who had a burning desire to show up the Yankees; the formative Gore was Albert Gore Sr., who had a burning desire to bury his roots as a country boy; and the formative Bush was George Herbert Walker (whose daughter Dorothy was married to Prescott), a fierce entrepreneur not unlike Joe Kennedy, who had a burning desire to win at all costs.

The Bushes and the Kennedys lived in a world of long summer holidays at family compounds, recurring contact with the rich and world famous, guaranteed entrée to Ivy League colleges, and scores of rich friends in many professions eager to lend their young men a hand. Albert Gore, in contrast, was born on a farm in the Tennessee hollows, not far from a village named Difficult. George Bush and

John Kennedy got up early at times to sail or play golf with their families. Gore got up early, at four in the morning, to help with the chores on the farm. George H. W. Bush and John Kennedy went to Yale and to Harvard, and paying the bills there was never a problem. Gore took seven years to go through a small country college, driving trucks and waiting tables to pay his tuition, and it was three more years before he could afford to go to law school in Nashville, driving the 100-mile round trip from Carthage three times a week. Bush and Kennedy married debutantes from social register families (although both would turn out to be very strong women); Gore married Pauline LaFon, whom he met when she was waiting tables to pay her way through law school at the hotel where he stopped for coffee before driving home. She too came from a struggling family, and her upbringing—she had cared for her siblings, including one blind sister—had been even more straitened than his.

When Prescott Bush, George Bush, and John Kennedy had made it to Congress, it was no more than what was expected of bright boys from good families whose doting parents had given them every conceivable chance. But when Gore made it to Congress (in 1938, and to the upper house fourteen years later), it was an incredible triumph of grit over circumstance; of ambition and striving and will. As a result he determined to dress, talk, and act like the people who really belonged there, like the Bushes and the Kennedys, or like Cordell Hull, his role model, an FDR cabinet member and another Tennessee farm boy made good. "Hull's public manner was invariably formal and correct, as if to insist that he never be taken for a hillbilly," writes David Maraniss. "Gore consciously modeled himself on Hull, adopting the same formal manner for the same reason, but then slightly exaggerating it . . . speaking in full sentences full of Latin-sounding words." For the same reasons, he would raise his children as if they had come from a long line of establishment figures, used over time to wield power. They would have every incentive, every credential, every chance possible. If he had come so far from such low beginnings, how far could a son of his—given all that he now had been able to give him—possibly be able to go?

"If I have a boy baby, I don't want the news buried inside the paper," Congressman Gore told the editors of the Nashville *Tennessean* before the birth of his second child, and the paper obliged with the following headline: "Well, Mr. Gore, Here HE is." It was an announcement fit for a prince—or a possible president—second only to the declaration made by Honey Fitz over thirty years earlier, and exactly as serious: with the single exception of Joe Kennedy Jr., no American child would be aimed at the White House with such intense precision as was the younger Al Gore. As he grew, young Al was immersed in the culture of politics, exposed to the leaders he was expected to emulate, dandled on the knees of John Kennedy and of Richard M. Nixon, meeting the greats at family parties, listening in on a 1962 phone call to his father as President Kennedy cursed out U.S. Steel. The expectations were open and obvious. "There may be another Gore on the way to the political pinnacle," ran a story in the Knoxville *News Sentinel* when young Al was six.

He never complained. "As he marched through his cameos at dinner parties . . . he was less a kid than a miniature grown-up," writes Bill Turque, his biographer. "While his peers tested the forbearance of the adult world, Gore instinctively looked for ways to comply with its requirements. He epitomized the 'easy child,' pleasant . . . reluctant to complain." He did not complain in the winter about the exactions to perform well at the best private schools in the city, and he did not complain in the summer when they went back to Carthage, and Al, in his parents' attempt to build the character of a possible president, was set to clearing a field with an ax. "Anything his daddy told him to do, he did," said a maid who had worked for the family. "He was a child who always listened to his parents; never talked back." "He made himself the son that his parents wanted," explains Maraniss. "[He] presented himself to the world as serious and earnest, always striving to do right." At school, his classmates teased him for being too perfect and made fun of his plans to be president. His fitful attempts to do something else—a stint at divinity school, never completed; a stab at reporting on a paper run by a friend of his father's—were not taken seriously by others and possibly not by himself.

As Maraniss writes of Gore's life as a journalist, "six of his newsroom friends . . . spent one night drafting a plan for Gore to be president, replete with timetables of when he had to run for the House and the Senate. They had him in the Oval Office in 2008." As it was, he ran for his father's old seat in the House in 1976, when he was twenty-eight; and for the Senate four years later, when he was just thirty-two. Through it all, there were some signs of stress in the picture, signs that politics and Al Gore the younger were not the fit they appeared. Classmates and teachers sometimes thought he was playing a role. He was bright enough, but his intellect appeared geared to abstractions and science, fields that seldom attract politicians. Making his first speech, he had thrown up beforehand. Unlike his father, he did not crave mass approval, and he did not love the sound of his voice. In the Senate, he had made few friends and passed little or no legislation, preferring hearings in which he showcased his knowledge of technical matters in exotic fields.

Nonetheless, he had gone far and seemed primed to go further. Looking in fact rather like Superman (or instead, rather like Clark Kent without glasses), with a lovely blond wife and a picture-book family, he seemed the very model of the upright young leader in training: central casting for the sort of person who ought to grow up to be president. "Are you too good to be true?" TV host John McLaughlin asked him in a 1986 interview. "You've got the magical name . . . you're intelligent, you're well informed. You've got a Vietnam war record . . . you're almost too good to be true." And so it all seemed, at least on the surface, when his father came to him at Christmas vacation and urged him to run in the upcoming cycle. The elder Gore was then pushing eighty and feared he might not live to fulfill his ambition. So did the younger, who wrote out a note in which he placed himself in a long line of lofty historical figures: "A 28 year cycle—TR 04—FDR 32—JFK 60—AG Jr 88—Great presidents . . . Harvard grads . . . prep schools . . . political families. . . . young."

Gore planned to run in the same electoral cycle as Prescott's son, George Herbert Walker, who would then be sixty-four to Gore's forty, was in his second term as Reagan's vice president, and had run for president one time before—in 1980—and lost. But whereas the Gores had moved from Tennessee to the Fairfax Hotel in Washington and there become easternized, this Bush had gone in the other direction: from Greenwich, Connecticut, to the Permian Basin, to reconstitute himself as an oil man and a westerner. The "anointed one" in the Bush-Walker clan for his generation, he was a golden boy and an overachiever, a star athlete and a Phi Beta Kappa, a war hero at twenty, a father at twenty-two, and a millionaire by age forty, having made his fortune in the oil business in Texas, and being ready, as his father bowed out of the Senate, to launch his own public career. He would be pressured by his father's success as he would lose in two tries for the Senate (1964 and 1970), but he did manage to serve two terms in the House between them, a foot in the door that would prove most effective as a springboard to further success.

It was a big career, and an impressive one, and his achievements in turn would pressure his two older children, Jeb and George W., who from an early age had viewed their father as perfect and felt compelled to repeat his accomplishments. It was Jeb, the second son, an academic star like his father, who would copy him by marrying young, leaving home early, and seeking his fortune in another state (Florida), where he would go into business (banking and real estate) and work his way up through the state party, with an eye always on running for office. But most of the pressure would fall on "Little George," the firstborn and namesake, who was the natural focus for the expectations on both sides of his family that was already some layers deep. He had been happy enough as a schoolboy in Midland, but at fifteen he was packed off to Andover, his father's old prep school, and there he had his first taste of what it meant to follow a man who was still looked at and recalled as a war hero, a role model, and one of the best athletes and scholars the school had ever had. George W. tried to achieve, but he always fell short of his father's accomplishments: he did not fail, but he did not excel either, and in his family, this meant the same thing. He went to Yale because his father had gone there, and the same thing happened: his father had been a star athlete and a Phi Beta Kappa; he, George W., was a cheerleader and an average student, hardly a failure, but a failure compared to his father (and brother), who had set the bar very high.

As John Kennedy had done at Choate when confronted by an ideal older brother, Bush began to concoct a rebel persona and for much the same reason: to depreciate the standards he wasn't sure he could meet. When he left Yale, he appeared at a loss, intimidated by his father's example and unsure how to match it. "George W. would spend those five years after Yale drifting," Paul and Rochelle Schweitzer write in their family study. "He held three different jobs, and had many girlfriends. . . . He had seven apartments in three different states." One thing he did do was enlist in the Texas Air National Guard, largely because his father had also flown fighters. But where his father had flown overseas in a great war and come home a hero, he would stay stateside in a war that was both small and ugly, and the plane he trained on was phased out. The one thing he did do that his father did not was go to business school at Harvard, where he distinguished himself by wearing cowboy boots and an old leather jacket and by chewing tobacco, which he spat into cans. But when he returned, he went into the oil business in Midland, exactly as his father had done almost thirty years earlier, although the conditions had utterly changed. His father had gotten in at the start of the oil boom in the Permian Basin when the field was opening up and it was possible to make fortunes. Thirty years later, the big strikes had been made; the market itself was in a depression, and the business in some ways was not really suited to the skills George W. would show later on. Still, he would stay in it through ten years of frustration, as he tried to break even, and failed.

Why he did this would seem to defy explanation, except for this comment an aunt would make later: "He was battling in a way between imitating his father and going in a different direction. I think he almost felt disloyal if he went on a different path from his dad." He had begun drinking at Yale, and he drank more and more as the frustrations mounted and he stood in one place, or even stepped backward, as his father was moving ahead. George H. W. lost a race for the Senate in 1970 but had moved on through ever-widening circles of power, from chairman of the Republican National Committee to ambassador to the United Nations, to ambassador to China, to director of the CIA. He would lose again in 1980 when he ran for president, but Ronald Reagan would pick him to be his vice president, the perfect spot from which to launch another campaign. When John Kennedy began his career, his brother Joe Jr. was dead, and his father had failed as a diplomat and retired from politics. With Little George, his father's career was still building and would continue to do so until he won the presidency at sixty-four in 1988, when "Little George" had already turned forty-two. He would remain "Little George" as long as his father kept rising, which he did long after some men had entered retirement. "Everywhere he went, his father was there," said his cousin, John Ellis. "He was really high up there on a pedestal. . . . Every year the pedestal seemed to get bigger and bigger. . . . As a young man, how do you compete with that?"

A related problem was his brother, who at age eight had announced he planned to be president and was working steadily toward his goal. A Phi Beta Kappa, just like his father, he breezed through college in two and a half years, married a Mexican girl he had met in the Peace Corps, headed to Florida, and was well on his way to his first million dollars. "When they were young, Jeb was somebody for George to torture," said the boys' cousin. "Then he grew up to be 6'4" and that got complicated. . . . Now all of a sudden his brother . . . is married, has kids, is making a good living . . . and George was floundering around."

John Kennedy had been pressured by a seemingly faultless brother two years his senior who was his parents' favorite; but in Bush's case the perfect brother was eight years his junior, and he was positioned between him and a young father just twenty-two years his senior, whose career was still on the rise. As time passed and Bush moved up into his thirties, the pressures became more intense. He dreamed of a big strike he christened "the Liberator" that would free him from financial and family strains. "In his quest for the Liberator, W. tried everything," write the Schweitzers. "He tried to convince the owners of the famous Waggoner Ranch . . . to let him drill on their property. . . . He tried joint ventures with other oil companies. . . . He even ventured overseas. . . . The underlying problem was . . . the tumultuous oil market. Even when he was able to find oil, prices were so low it often didn't pay to bring it up."

Nothing worked. As he reached forty, his life was a "study in failure," of hopes disappointed and expectations unmet. "[He] was named for a father who excelled in everything," David Frum would write later. "He tried everything his father had tried—and succeeded at almost nothing. . . . [He] scraped through Andover and Yale . . . never made a varsity team, earned no distinction in the Air National Guard, and was defeated in a run for Congress. . . . He lost millions in the oil business, and had to be rescued by his father's friends in 1983. It was after that last humiliation that he began drinking hard." A low of some sort was reached in a Dallas restaurant when he insulted and almost assaulted reporter Al Hunt who was there with his family, cursing him out in front of his children. "The incident was the latest in what had been a long chain, and the family was growing weary of it," write the Schweitzers. "He was becoming an embarrassment. And the family let him know that things needed to change." "There's a famous story about him being introduced to Queen Elizabeth . . . and joking, 'I'm the black sheep of the family,'" David Frum would write later. "People who make jokes like that are not always joking." "George is the family clown," his brother Marvin would tell an associate. In 2000, Jeb's son George P. would tell a reporter, "If you came up to any close member of my family six years ago, and said my uncle wanted to be president, they'd probably laugh in your face."

One candidate at whom no one was laughing was Albert Gore Jr., ready at thirty-nine to make his first run for president, and, in the opinion of many, not acting too soon. "Gore Senior began 'putting the bite on him,' as one family friend put it, during the Christmas break in 1986," as David Maraniss informs us. "Father and son went down to the basement. . . . 'Son,'" said the father, "'I want to see you elected president before I die.'" "Daddy wants me to do this, really wants me to run," Gore said to his friends. A group of rich backers agreed that he looked like a president. "I had a feeling the first time I got to know him that he was presidential material," said one moneyman, stunned by his looks, voice, and carriage. "I . . . thought he was a shining star." The rationale was that he was an expert on defense and on arms control, a new face, and a southern moderate in a party dominated largely by liberals, who by then had managed to lose four of the last five presidential elections. But it was the first time that he faced an audience outside of his home state as anything more than the son of his father, and troubles began to arise.

To start, he could not assemble a team of people who were loyal to him and worked well together but instead amassed layers of high-priced consultants, who gave him conflicting advice. Perhaps as a result of this, he did not stay with a message but moved erratically from foreign policy to environmentalism and then to populism, depending on his audience and on the day's polls. He lied, clumsily, in making his switch from being a moderate state candidate to being a national one who had to appeal to the base of his party denying he had once been pro-life (and had supported a bill declaring the fetus a person) and had backed tobacco and guns. In his first strongly contested election, he unveiled a penchant for overkill, breaking what some thought were the rules of civility in his frequent and heavy attacks. These did not endear him to some of his fellow Democrats (including Dick Gephardt, who would one day become the House minority leader), and who, when Gore needed him twelve years later during the Florida recount, would be less than impassioned in his support.

All these things would hurt Gore (and reemerge twelve years later), but they were not quite as damaging as a fourth major failing: he tended to inflate his curriculum vitae, claiming credit for the achievements of others or experiences he never had. Usually, these were not lies as much as exaggerations, but they were enough to have his staff send an anguished memo after he had been caught and corrected several times by the press on his claims to have been a home builder, a farmer, a pioneer in moving several issues in Congress, and a combat veteran in Vietnam.

"Your major pitfall is exaggeration," the memo said. "There was, in these cases as in others, a factual basis to every claim Gore made, but none of it really rose to the level of what he was claiming. He had a financial connection to a home-building enterprise, but he was not a home builder. He owned farmland, but he was not a farmer. . . . In Congress, he had publicized the issue of hazardous waste in a series of hearings, but it was his colleague . . . James Florio . . . who actually authored the Superfund legislation." He had indeed been a Vietnam War veteran, but he had created the impression he had been a combat soldier on a long term of duty, though in reality he had served seven months as an army journalist. He had also enhanced his record as an investigative reporter, claiming, falsely, that he "got a bunch of people indicted and sent to jail." The odd thing was that Gore's record itself was extremely impressive and he had a well-earned reputation for hard work and diligence, but he seemed under such pressure to live up to expectations and billing that nothing could seem good enough.

The constant need to boost himself was so strong and so ingrained that he told Richard Ben Cramer, then writing his book

What It Takes, an account of the men who in 1988 tried to be president, that he decided to run for the office only because "thousands of people" had written him letters, begging him to come save the country. As Cramer told Maraniss, that was when he decided to leave Gore out of the story. "It wasn't the fact that he wasn't telling me the truth, it was the pallid bankruptcy of the lies, all in the service of a picture of himself that wasn't even interesting. That was the kiss of death for me." For all of these reasons, his campaign failed to resonate, and on Super Tuesday—the southern state primaries apparently made for his purpose—he fell well short of his first expectations, coming in behind two other candidates. His staff wanted him to leave gracefully but failed to contend with the candidate's father, who refused to let him bow out. "Arlie! Arlie! Do you realize that boy is going to be president?" he cried to an aide as his son was losing. Against the advice of the staff, he pushed his son into Illinois, where he won 5 percent of the vote (and lost $250,000); and New York, where he embarrassed himself, spent a million dollars, and came in a poor third. Days later, close to his fortieth birthday, he bowed out of the race. "I was doing great until I turned forty" was the way he put it, and he would call the experience "horrible." One aide had a different take on the matter, wondering, as so many would later, "how you can take a guy with so much potential, and see his campaign get blown to smithereens."

The 1988 campaign would shake Gore up greatly, as the first sharp check in his march to the White House, and the first sign he had that he might not in fact make it, or that getting there might take more than he thought. One year later, he would be shaken still more: on April 3, 1989, Gore's six-year-old son was struck by a car outside Memorial Stadium in Baltimore, and, as his father watched in stark horror, hurled twenty feet in the air. It would take the boy more than a year to recover; and this near-death experience, following so soon on his first public failure, set off a crisis for Gore in which he would question, for the first time in public, what he was doing, where he was going, and what he wanted to do with his life. Central to this was a critical disconnect between who he was and the job he was doing, an arranged marriage that had never quite fit. There was an overlap at times, as when his Senate duties led him into technical pursuits and he could lose himself in the study of toxic waste or arms control issues, but more often there was a growing chasm that could be bridged only with a strenuous effort that most of his colleagues did not need to make. He was happy alone, not in crowds or when dealing with people. And, although he had a wide range of interests about a large number of subjects, they were often concerned with things outside of the purviews of politics, such as inanimate objects or abstract ideas.

In the 1980s, he had made himself into an expert on nuclear weapons and thrived on a series of rigorous seminars, winning high praise from the experts who taught him. James Woolsey recalled he had never before had such an informed discussion with a member of Congress: "[Gore] was one of the few in the House to have read the literature, and learned the theory. This is a guy who rolls up his sleeves and masters the technical details like nobody else." (Lamar Alexander had a different take on the subject: "He knows more things in detail than it is necessary for a decision-maker to know.") But if he was bursting with facts and technological data, he was oddly lacking in the political sense that translated facts into action or, in his case, into law. Stories would grow of his curious gaucheries. At a fund-raiser in the campaign of 2000, he left without thanking the host, pausing only to ask how to get to the bathroom. Late in 2003, he endorsed Howard Dean without first telling Joe Lieberman, his 2000 running mate who also was running for president, enraging many ex-aides. He was also a stranger to bargaining. "Clinton was constantly luring the Republicans with hints of a possible compromise, while Gore held an unyielding position from which he hectored his opponents about the waywardness of their reasoning," wrote David Maraniss. "His oldest friends often lament in private that he seems not to want to listen to them if he knows they are going to disagree."

"Al Gore is at home with ideas but deeply wary of people," said Bill Turque, his biographer. "He was at once competent and self-confident about anything that he could translate into what he considered a question of fact, yet often insecure and riddled with self-doubt when it came to perceptions and emotions and aspects of life that could not be established with mathematical certainty," said Maraniss. "[He] could deliver an hour-long extemporaneous lecture on global warming, and yet need index cards as a crutch when saying a simple thank you and good-bye." In the 2000 election, John Harris would write, "Perhaps never in modern times has a candidate for president been so conversant in the realms of science, technology, communications and international economics . . . but rarely has a candidate labored so doggedly with such uneven results to find the right voice."

The right voice would remain elusive, whether in personal bargaining, speech making, or debate. "He doesn't often 'inhabit the role,'" Nicholas Lehmann would write in a sympathetic profile in the *New Yorker*. "He lacks any middle range. He'll be speaking animatedly, and then . . . abruptly shut down and become lifeless. . . . When Gore has to come down to the ground level of daily politics, he over calculates, or he too obviously ingratiates, or he brutally attacks." Later on, it would become axiomatic among people who knew Gore or even observed him that Gore was very bright in a number of ways not useful in politics—a smart person caught up in the wrong line of work. "Politics was a terrible career choice for him," a former aide told the *New Yorker*. "He should have been a college professor or a scientist or an engineer. He would have been happier." Nobody doubted this, including Bill Clinton, who noted that "but for his father, he would have been a professor, or something more solitary" while wondering aloud how Gore could have gotten so far in politics, when he liked and understood it so little. Eventually, such questions would also strike Gore.

"The most turbulent part of Gore's midlife reassessment took place privately," as Turque tells us. "For the first time the 'real little politician' of the Fairfax began to examine the emotional costs of meeting the grand expectations set by his parents. . . . What began as a spring and summer of discontent grew into a broader midlife examination . . . a serious reassessment of what it was he really wanted to accomplish as a politician and a man." He talked to Lance Laurence, a Knoxville psychologist, who gave him books about children and parents that he read, internalized, and quoted to others as being especially relevant. One was Allen Wheelis's *How People Change*, whose story of a son being forced to clear fields with a razor paralleled some of Gore's chores on the farm. But he seemed most impressed by *The Drama of the Gifted Child*, Alice Miller's account of children whose personalities had been distorted by parents who demanded they bend to their will. "Accommodation to parental needs often . . . leads to the 'as if' personality," Miller wrote. "This person develops in such a way that he reveals only what is expected of him. . . . He cannot develop and differentiate his true self because he is unable to live it." The same themes are put forth in *Earth in the Balance*, the book that Gore wrote in this period, which is about the environment but also is filled with metaphors of dictatorial fathers, of psychological wounds whose pain lasts a lifetime, of "artificial patterns" into which children are forced by their parents, of the harsh effects of patriarchal oppression, and of mysterious power-ful forces, against which it is futile to fight. He complained about being forced into patterns of life against his real inclination. "Children in dysfunctional families . . . often construct a false self," he wrote, in a rehash of Miller, "controlling his inner experience—smothering spontaneity, masking emotion, diverting creativity into robotic routine." ("Robotic routine" was a frequent descrip-tion of his public performance, of which he could not have been unaware.) He ended with pledges to change and to become more "authentic." But of course, he did not.

For a moment, Gore appeared poised on the edge of rebellion, then teetered, and pulled himself back. He would not—or could not—do anything radical. He had been proclaimed at his birth as an oncoming president, touted at age six as a political comer, teased by his schoolmates for his plans to be president. A wall of one room in the Gore home in Carthage was left bare for the many pictures of the Gore administration (planned to begin in 2001). He had been told he was on the "agenda of history," that he could lead and should lead, that the presidency was something he owed to his parents and he was owed by the country, and the main ques-tion that concerned his ascension to power was much less an "if" than a "when." He was young, he had his seat in the Senate, his future still seemed filled with promise. In the end, the one result of his brief insurrection was that it would from now on force him to work even harder: having admitted if only obliquely that he did not like politics, he had to win to justify the sacrifice he had made. ("I'm not like George Bush," he would say during the 2000 elec-tion, "If he loses, life goes on. I'll do anything to win.") And so he would. From the mid-1990s on, when he began his next run for the White House, comments would focus on how hard he found it and how hard he still worked.

"He wants very badly to be president," Bill Turque would say in 2000. "He's a career politician who doesn't enjoy politics. . . . Politics for him has always been sort of a chore." "He works like a dog—but it's excruciating," a Clinton aide told Joe Klein, then of the *New Yorker*. "When I watch what he does, it's heroic. . . . Gore is the most introverted person I've ever seen in public life." "He'll work on weaknesses and work on them, until he gets past them," an aide, Carter Eskew, would tell the reporter. "It's like one of those white basketball players who may not have the natural ability, but he has a lot of desire. He'll keep practicing the game until he's good enough to play." But there would always be limits to what will could do. "It can be agonizing to watch Al Gore jump through the hoops of a profession he might not be suited for, in pursuit of an ambition that was chosen for him," as Klein would continue. "It may be significant that not one of the several dozen Gore friends and staffers I spoke with thought that the Vice President would have chosen to be a politician if his father hadn't been one, and hadn't so ardently wished for his son to be president. And neither did Gore."

It was around age forty that Gore, whose life to that point was a string of successes, had his first setback, poised for a time on the brink of a life change, and then slowly pulled himself up. At about the same age, George W. Bush, whose life until then was a series of failures, touched what for him was a personal nadir and started to pull himself back. The first in a series of steps that would finally rescue him took place in 1985 at Walker's Point, where the unhappy thirty-nine-year-old son of the vice president had a chance talk with Billy Graham, the evangelist who was a longtime companion to presidents and also a family friend. This led in turn to still more conversation, and soon the hard-drinking, directionless family problem was reading the

Bible, attending study groups, and going to church. What he found in these activities were the traditional things that have drawn people to faith since time immemorial, but also something unique to his personal crises: the antidote to the dynastic dynamic and its ongoing pressures and claims. Faith, as Graham explained it, posed a new set of standards; if the dynastic creed claimed ambition was everything, faith said there was something above and beyond it. If the dynastic creed measured a life by public accomplishment, faith said there were other ways of proving one's value. If the dynastic creed said he had disappointed his earthly father and mother, faith maintained that there was a still greater father in heaven, in whose eyes he had worth. Bush was not the first dynastic son to slip into a trap where despair fed on failure, but he was the first to be able to pull himself out of one, and in his revival, this insight was key. In 2002, Bush would tell a group of clergymen visiting him in the Oval Office that his faith was the reason he was then in the White House and not in a bar in west Texas. In his book *The Right Man*, David Frum cannily picks out Bush's favorite Psalm from the Bible of holding the key to his final salvation: "Cast me not off, forsake me not, O God of my salvation! For my father and my mother have forsaken me, but the Lord will take me up."

This was the first in a set of developments that would lead the eldest Bush child out of the wilderness and into his own promised land. It was his faith that gave him the strength to stop drinking (which he did on July 6, 1986, his fortieth birthday), and this in turn determined that he would be sober and focused when his father approached with his big opportunity: the chance to work with him on his presidential campaign. This gave him the chance to move out of the oil patch (importantly, with his father's permission and blessing) and into a field where his footing was surer and his father required his help. The elder George Bush was a transitional figure, awkwardly poised between Walker's Point and west Texas, between his westernized sons, who had warmed to the cowboy in Reagan, and his father, the personification of the establishment banker, who used to go golfing with Ike. He understood the world scene more than he did his own party, now well along in its transition from East and Midwest to the Sunbelt, from old to new money, and from the established big-unit corporate forces to the bottom-up entrepreneur. George H. W. Bush, an Episcopalian and a transplanted Yankee, had no idea how to deal with or appeal to this party. George W., brought up in Midland, a Methodist who had worn boots and chewed tobacco at Harvard, could, and he did. He fit in at once with the new wave of consultants who understood this dynamic, reassured Reaganauts who were cool toward his father, and stroked the evangelicals, to whom he appealed with his personal saga and who were becoming a critical part of the base. "For the birth of the politician, you have to look at 1988," *Time* magazine would write later. "He discovered things about his father and himself and the oily workings of national politics that cleared the way for all that would come after. . . . He got to perform the ultimate act of synthesis—take his father's weaknesses . . . and apply his own instincts to solve the problem. . . . He wasn't being asked to compete with his father, he was compensating for him," working with him, if not quite as an equal, at least as another adult. He emerged a changed man who had found his vocation and resolved his conundrum regarding his father. For the first time in their lives, he had found something they both did that he could do better: this was the "Liberator" that he had been seeking, and the impact would alter his life. It would take a while for his family members to fully absorb what had happened, but the professionals he worked with had come to be fully aware of his talents.

By the time he left Washington, they were starting to think he could one day run for office. And by then, so was he.

Jeb in Florida had been biding his time, following his father's path much as his brother had done, but with more success at it and in a new place. He had left home, married young, made money, and now, nearing forty, just like his father, was planning to make his first run. He had a fortune of nearly two million dollars, a long history of working his way up through Florida's nascent Republican Party, and a handsome clutch of Hispanic-WASP children, including his oldest son, George Prescott or "P" (known to hopeful pros as the "Republican JFK Jr."), recognized as the "anointed one" in the next generation, its rising political star. Jeb had vowed not to run while his father was president, but his father's defeat in 1992 by Bill Clinton would open the door to his own aspirations, and in February 1993, barely a month after his father left office, he announced he was running for governor. Everyone expected this and expected him to win handily.

What no one expected was that later that year George W., who had spent the past five years with the Texas Rangers, building his bankroll and his name recognition, would announce that he too was running for governor, in his home state of Texas, and against Ann Richards, the immensely popular incumbent governor who as Texas state treasurer had famously insulted his father at the Democrats' national convention in 1988. Jeb, who had moved five hundred miles away in his desire to steer clear of domestic entanglements, felt that his race had been stepped on and reduced to the level of family drama. The others, who thought George was in over his head and would surely be beaten, were quietly horrified. They were not quite aware of how much he was changing, how he was addicted now not to drink but to discipline; that he exercised now as if doing penance and had made an obsession out of punctuality, as if aware he had wasted much too much time.

At the time, no one, not even his mother, believed that George Bush could beat Richards, a national celebrity who raised vast sums of money from out-of-state liberals, frequently moved with an entourage of film stars and rock stars, and was famed for her white hair and her razor-tongued put-downs, such as her dismissal of George Bush's father, "Poor George. He can't help it. He was born with a silver foot in his mouth." Faced with "Poor George's" son, Richards treated the race as an insult, appalled at being asked to contest this political neophyte. Persistently angry and a little too shrill, she railed at the man she considered a child of privilege and a wastrel and hothead, whom she tried to goad into making a scene. Her problem was that the man she described bore no relation at all to the one voters saw out campaigning, a composed, sober figure clad trimly in dress suits, who was calm and soft-spoken as he intoned his prescriptions for what had emerged as his four major issues, revolving around welfare, criminal justice, and court and education reform. Relentlessly civil, he refused to rise to her baiting. She called him "Shrub"; he called her "Governor Richards." She called him "Junior"; he called her "Governor Richards." She called him a jerk; he said he found her "interesting" as a psychological study. To her relentless assaults on him and his family, he made no responses at all.

As the only parents in American history to have two sons running at one time for governor (much less the first former First Couple to do so), George H. W. and Barbara Bush sat down on election night in their home in Houston to watch election returns. What they saw would astonish them: Jeb was losing (by four points) to Lawton Chiles in Florida, the victim of a last-minute phone blitz about Social Security, while George was beating Ann Richards in Texas by a seven-point, or 335,504-vote, margin, the largest spread in two decades. "Can you believe this?" a shocked Barbara Bush would say later. Her husband was so stunned that when he called George to congratulate him on his victory, he could talk about nothing but Jeb and his problems. "Almost the entire conversation had apparently been about Jeb's loss," said the Schweitzers, who quoted George as saying plaintively, "Why don't you feel good about me?" No one could quite believe that the erstwhile recurrent family problem had come in eight years from abject disgrace to his place as current political head of the family, its crown prince and new hope.

On January 21, 1995, the first son and onetime black sheep of the family became the only Bush then holding office as he was sworn in as governor wearing cufflinks worn by his grandfather when he served in the Senate and by his father as president. He was succeeding them as the third in their line to hold high public office; perhaps more important, he was succeeding Sam Houston, the state's first governor, who had pulled himself out of alcoholic despair to become the father of Texas and in whose life Bush found parallels. (As governor, Bush would hang in his office in Austin a monstrous portrait of Houston dressed up as the emperor Marius. "He must have been in a drunken stupor to have done this," Bush explained.) *The Raven*, Marquis James's biography of this first Texas governor, had become, next to the Bible, Bush's favorite book. "His first thought, his constant thought, was to atone for the period of his delinquency," James wrote of his hero. "He would do something grand."

CHAPTER 6

Bush versus Gore
versus Bush

Al Gore was at the Capitol with his fellow senators on January 20, 1989, as George H. W. Bush was sworn in as the forty-first president while Jeb and George W., several yards distant, looked on from the family seats. Four years later, Bush and Gore would be back as Gore himself was sworn in as vice president, his golden boy image repaired and embellished, and the Bushes prepared to go home. Coming off his loss, Gore had worked harder than ever on his liabilities, hiring a speech coach and even a choreographer to help him get over his stiffness in public. But in 1992, his stiffness was exactly what Bill Clinton wanted, adding depth and stability to the Arkansas charmer, who was facile and nimble but seemed to some people too glib. As it was, the choice of the wonkish and somber forty-four-year-old from Tennessee to run with the wonkish and raffish forty-six-year-old from neighboring Arkansas appeared nothing short of inspired, a double infusion of youth and vitality, running against an administration that was trying for its fourth term in power and that now appeared tired and stale.

It was the exception that was proving the rule of one of the prime maxims of politics: the ticket might not have been "balanced," but it was surely enhanced. "Those of us who thought the choice of Gore would be a good one had no idea how soon it would turn out to be . . . magical," trilled Hendrik Hertzberg in the *New Yorker*. "The ticket seemed to be vastly greater than the sum of its parts."

Bill Turque was less lyrical but no less impressed. "If there was a pivotal moment in the 1992 campaign, it may have been the scene on the verandah at the governor's mansion . . . as the two men and their young families came out, the image resonated with an energy that even Gore's boosters couldn't have predicted. Just like that, it seemed a generational page had been turned." It was not merely Gore's assets that buoyed Clinton—the foreign policy background, the military background, the placid personal life— but his liabilities as well. Gore's formality and rigidity added reassuring "increments of maturity" to his sometimes too bad-boyish boss. The convention was a celebration of youth and vitality, as was the bus tour that followed, as the strapping young candidates made their way through the heartland with their bouncy blond wives. Never before had a presidential campaign looked so much like a double date from an old 1950s movie: every time they plunged into the crowds, the four of them looked still more young and more vibrant, and President Bush, old enough to be father to all of them, looked even more tired and worn. Originally, the Gores were supposed to have spent only a few days on the bus tour, but when the tour was successful, Gore dug in his heels. This set up the template for the eight years to follow: Gore saw the campaign— in fact, Clinton's entire eight years in office—as mainly the setup to his own term in power and insisted he be treated and seen as a peer. His friends had the feeling that the studious veep was a more worthy man than the man at the head of the ticket. Gore may have felt the same.

Gore spent most of his two terms in office in a state of anxiety, carefully nursing his prospects and dignity, having struck an agreement in writing with the new president that gave him unprecedented powers and influence. "Gore came into the White House determined to hold the Clinton staff to every part of the bargain," wrote Marjorie Williams, "an inviolable weekly lunch alone with the president, a staff presence in all important West Wing meetings, and a say in all major appointments." Gore aides studied Clinton's schedule intently, so that the vice president could be at any important meeting. "He had people there all day long telling him what was going on," says a former Clinton staffer. . . . "Gore would cancel meetings of his own in order to shadow the president . . . even if it meant sprinting down the hall to make it to a meeting he had heard about at the last minute."

Sometimes this was carried to an extreme some would find curious, as when Gore demanded a four o'clock lunch in Nashville as the president was about to embark on a tiring overseas mission. "Gore insisted on it, despite the fact that Air Force One was standing by to take the president to visit U.S. troops in Bosnia," Williams writes. "Aides eyed their watches incredulously as Gore marched through his agenda, not at all daunted by the knowledge that Clinton faced a nine-hour flight into a tense situation." "He wouldn't let Clinton skip one of those lunches if the f——ing missiles were coming in from Russia," said one former aide. Gore had a scare in the 1994 midterm elections, when it looked for a time as if he might face a future as the former second in command to a failed one-term president, but Clinton adroitly regained his (and

Gore's) footing and won a second term for what was then a slightly more weary golden-boy ticket. But the last race for Bill Clinton, a master campaigner, was the start of the race of his life for his anxious vice president, who this time would run all alone.

Gore began his 2000 race before the last one had ended, trying to use his last term to burnish his standing, but, once out of the orbit of Clinton's protection, few things appeared to go well. In his speech in August 1996 to his party's convention, he tried for rapport with a detailed account of his sister's death from lung cancer and his vow at her deathbed to fight Big Tobacco, forgetting that for years after her death he had fought for subsidies for that industry and four years later had given an impassioned speech to tobacco growers in which he had bragged of planting and reaping the plants with his hands. In March 1997, he was fingered for his role in a political fund-raising scandal, having made dunning phone calls from the vice president's office. His response was to stage an impromptu press conference in which he swore he had done nothing wrong and would never repeat it. Gore repaired seven times to what would survive as a great comic mantra: "My legal counsel advises me . . . there is no controlling legal authority that says that any of these activities . . . violated any law."

With these stumbles under his belt, he was wholly unable to navigate the rapids of the Lewinsky scandal when his president and senior partner was caught out in an affair with an intern only slightly older than his (and Gore's) daughters and in a lie under oath to a legal panel investigating a previous claim of harassment. Gore's first response was hysterical loyalty. "He is the president of the country! He is my friend!" Gore screamed to an audience in his first appearance with the president after the scandal went public, causing even Clinton himself to stare at him quizzically. In December, after Clinton had been impeached by a Republican

Congress, Gore joined a gaggle of Democrats on the lawn of the White House in a show of defiance, calling Clinton one of the greatest of presidents. All this was remembered about six months later when Gore made his formal announcement of candidacy, declaring three separate times in televised interviews that he found Clinton's behavior "wholly inexcusable." Many people began to wonder where all of this outrage had been six months earlier, and which of these two Gores was real.

In no time at all, his campaign turned into a replay, on steroids, of his failed previous venture, as all his old problems resurfaced in force. He hired layer on layer of expensive consultants who fought with one another, often in public. He continued to exaggerate (some called it lying), and in his debates with Bill Bradley, his single opponent, he showed his old unappealing ferocity. He moved back and forth between issues and viewpoints, running alternatively as a populist and as the heir to Bill Clinton's more centrist agenda. He had successive makeovers in substance and style, in which his clothes, message, and general appearance would change overnight without warning. He took strange advice from still stranger people: a furor arose when it leaked out that he had paid fifteen thousand dollars a month to a friend of his daughter's who dressed him in earth tones for a soothing appearance, and he traced his low poll ratings to his image as a "beta male."

Around this time, Democrats began to realize that they were stuck with an oddity, a man who had risen effortlessly by winning eight big elections but who was nonetheless a bad politician, who could win as his father's son or as Bill Clinton's running mate, but who on his own had serious problems in addressing the public, framing his issues, and trying to run a campaign. Without Clinton to play off, his magic had vanished. And it was now much too late to go back.

. . .

Stunned by his loss, Jeb Bush had regrouped and won four years later, only to find the goal of his lifetime stepped on by his brother's career. He had been elected by six points in Florida, a promising start for a new politician. But in Texas, his brother had won in a landslide, a stunning twenty-seven-point sweep that demolished his rivals and gained votes hugely in each demographic, even those that usually had gone to the Democrats. There was no doubt now as to who was the star of the family: after forty-plus years of frustration and failure, George W. Bush had found something he could do very well. To anxious Republicans, eager to break a two-term losing streak for the White House, the appealing young governor appeared as a godsend, someone whose profile—a governor from a southwestern state with interesting ideas about education— appeared, well, Clintonesque. It was always uncertain how much Bush longed to be president, but he always had wanted to emulate his father, and when the chance came to follow him into the White House only eight years after he left it, he could not pass it up. "When the decision [to run] was finally made, the pressures and expectations he had felt for much of his life seemed to evaporate," said the Schweitzers. "It wasn't an elaborate plan to exact revenge for his father," said his biographer. "It certainly wasn't to satisfy an obsessive yearning. . . . People who had been watching Bush through the prism of the family dynasty said that in the end he had to become president in order to finally achieve some peace." The "obsessive yearning," it seemed, was to follow his father, and the office itself appeared less important. "What makes him tick?" A friend of both men would remark to the *New York Times* in 2000. "It's Daddy. . . . Daddy is the motivation. . . . Daddy allows him to do things and achieve ambitions he would not do on his own."

Bush was a golden boy in his home state and a standout among the Republican governors, but when he emerged as a national figure, a different take on his prospects began to reveal itself. He had spent only five years in office, with no experience in foreign affairs and a record of failure in his life before politics. He was not articulate and had a mild form of dyslexia that made him sometimes misuse words, confuse words, or assign to some words rather more syllables than they were commonly thought to possess. People got used to seeing him stop, search for a word, and then come up with the wrong one or at least one that seemed engagingly different: inventive new words such as *strategery* and *misunderstimate* slipped into the lexicon via his tongue. This, added to a fairly poor memory, led him to sometimes do poorly in interviews and fed the suspicion that he was in over his head. His Texas style did not endear him to the urbanites who made up the media, and stories began to assert that the "wrong" Bush was running for president.

"There is an odd thing about watching the brothers together," wrote Marjorie Williams. "The man on the left (George W.) with his bunched, ruddy face, is the habitual C- student, who barks out his bullets of verbiage with a striking vehemence. . . . You can't help noticing that the man on the right (Jeb)—smarter, deeper, and in many ways more admirable—was supposed to be his generation's shining star." Stories such as these led Jeb to pull in his horns even further, compromising his attempts to win his state for his brother, a task made more difficult early in August when Gore named Joe Lieberman as his running mate, which would ensure a heavier-than-usual turnout of Democrats in the southernmost part of the state.

For Jeb, it was a conundrum with no way out whatsoever: when he campaigned, the press said that he outshone his brother;

when he did not, the press said that he was jealous; and all the time the press harped on how unjust it all was that his klutz of a brother had gotten to run in his place. "Had he not lost the first time, Jeb Bush might well be the presidential hopeful," the *New York Times* wrote in July 2000. "Instead, if his brother is elected, Mr. Bush will find himself precluded from fulfilling any aspirations for the White House for four, or perhaps even eight, years." Confessing that he had become in fact almost a recluse, Jeb complained bitterly about being used to tear down his brother—and being used with his brother to tear down their father, often described as a poor politician—but he seemed unable to affect or alter the process. He had planned his career around that of his father and had run only once his father left office, a situation not exactly novel in politics. But he never had planned to deal with a brother, and so took his place in a trio of dynasts, caught up in their—and their own parents'—dreams.

Gore and Bush had entered the contest matched eerily evenly, in many ways opposites, in some ways alike. Both had been born at the edge of the baby boom to political families and were raised in competing loci of influence, with ties to both eastern establishment centers of power (New England and Washington) and to the more rural Southwest. Both went to the best schools (Andover and St. Albans, and then Yale and Harvard, respectively), where they failed to distinguish themselves academically. Both were unusual in their rebellious age cohort for the way they revered and respected their fathers and families. While in college, both avoided involvement in politics and were largely bystanders to the cultural wars of the era. Both were ambivalent about Vietnam and managed to serve while minimizing their exposure to danger: Gore serving in Vietnam for seven months as an army journalist, Bush flying fighter planes stateside in the Texas Air National Guard. Both had fathers who lost Senate races in the 1970 cycle, breaking the hearts of all of their children. And both had the experience of being drawn because of their fathers into pursuits they would find uncongenial: Bush following his father into the oil fields, where he would be unsuccessful; Gore being forced by his into electoral politics, where he would at first seem to flourish but at higher levels would founder and fail.

In some ways alike, they were still very different, and these characteristics would come more and more to the fore. Gore was the model son, polite to a fault; Bush had gone out of his way to make trouble. Gore seemed a small adult as a child; Bush seemed a boy almost into his forties. Gore came from two poor hardscrabble families yet acted like someone whose ancestors for generations back had all gone to Harvard; Bush came from generations of bankers and statesmen yet acted like the public school boy from Midland, Texas, he at one time had been. Gore had been a rising star early, in the Senate at age thirty-four and a candidate for president a mere five years later, two years younger than Bush would be when he merely helped run a campaign for his father. But it was in this campaign—at thirty-nine, and then forty—that Gore had his first taste of failure; as Bush, at the same age of forty, began to turn his life up and around. In 2000, Gore had been in public service for twenty-four years and was deeply immersed in the arcana of government, whereas Bush had one of the shallowest backgrounds of any man ever running for president and was wholly ungrounded in foreign affairs. Gore had never run anything (and worked poorly with others in the House and the Senate), whereas Bush had emerged as an outstanding and creative governor and had run two impressive campaigns. Bush had political skills but little experience and, in some fields, little knowledge.

Nobody doubted the depth of Gore's knowledge, but his political skills appeared thin. If Bush's past disturbed some, so did Gore's present, as his political blunders became more and more obvious. Pundits joked that together the two might add up to one wonderful president, but this did not appear attainable, and the voters seemed torn, moving back and forth between the two candidates, who seemed unable to hold or maintain an advantage. And as the polls swung back and forth between the two dynasts, it began to occur to a number of people that the best of both worlds might be Jeb.

Jeb in some ways seemed the Al Gore of his family, the good seed who bloomed young and who never caused problems, who had all of the virtues of both of the dynasts and added a few of his own. A Catholic convert, married to a Mexican woman, with three handsome Hispanic-WASP children, he had access to the two biggest swing blocs in the country, with no prior record of failure and no embarrassing things in his past. Like Gore, he was steeped in the details of policy; like his brother, he had an eye for the overall picture, and he was more articulate than both men combined. With Jeb, there would have been no jokes about verbal entanglements, no stories of drinking or rumors of drug use, no incidents such as the radio interview in late 1999, when Bush failed to name four foreign leaders (whose names, two years later, would have rolled off his tongue). With Jeb, above all, there would have been no such embarrassments as the drunk driving arrest from his brother's blue period (his period of angst in the mid-1970s), which surfaced in the last week before the election, just in time, in the views of his handlers, to cost him a state, a "clean win" in the election, and his tenuous lead in the polls.

But if Jeb had avoided the many slips made by his brother, he would also have skirted those made by Al Gore. With Jeb, there would have been none of the exaggerations that had been a problem for Gore since the 1988 venture, which he had been warned of repeatedly and seemed unable to stop: the claims that his mother-in-law paid more than his dog for the same kind of medicine, that schools were criminally overcrowded in Jeb Bush's Florida, that he had played a critical role in disaster relief. "I don't know, I'm not a psychiatrist," one Democrat snapped when asked about this habit. "Biographers have posited an enduring desire to please a father whose expectations were seemingly endless," the *Washington Post* would add in October. "Whatever the explanation, years of warnings have not cured Gore." Nor had the warnings done much to curtail his aggression. In the first debate, Gore rolled his eyes, sighed, and snorted while Bush made his arguments, appalling the audience. Ripped by the press (and battered by polls), Gore was so subdued in the second debate as to be almost invisible, but in the third, the aggression resurfaced. As Bush was speaking, Gore left his place, walked over, and loomed up behind him, arms dangling awkwardly. Bush looked up, nodded, and then went on speaking. The audience laughed. Two and a half weeks later the campaign was over, Bush ending a fourteen-year search for redemption, and Gore, in a state of exhaustion (and Jeb Bush's Florida), ending a quest that had consumed his whole life.

George and Jeb Bush and their families were at dinner at an Austin restaurant shortly before seven o'clock central time on Election Day when they heard a television set that was on in the dining room call the state of Florida, and thus the endgame, for Gore. Jeb Bush had not only lost his state for his brother, but with his state his brother had lost the election, because with the pending loss of the other swing states of Pennsylvania and Michigan, Bush was facing a deficit he could not make up. And almost as bad as the news was the timing: 7:50 on the East Coast was 6:50 in the central time zone, 5:50 in the mountain time area, and 4:50 on the West Coast, prime voting time in all of these venues, when office workers, released from their jobs, would stop on their way home to vote. Within minutes of the networks' call for Gore of Florida, Bush aides in Austin had begun to receive phone calls from their captains in California and elsewhere that volunteers were getting up from their phone banks and voters were walking away from the polls.

"We were worried about the West, absolutely," one Bush aide would say later. "For two weeks, voters across the country had been told that whoever wins Florida wins it. . . . And when you called Florida for Gore, that was it—you could feel the air go out of our headquarters . . . you could feel it go out of Republican voters in California and New Mexico, and places like that." Worse still, Florida was a state with two time zones, and the polls were still open in the Panhandle, a prime Republican area. Worse than that, for nearly an hour the networks had been saying repeatedly that all the polls in Florida were closed. The Panhandle was the one part of Florida that would lag behind the rest of the state in the percentage of those voting, and officials reported an unforeseen falloff in the last hour.

Bush would lose the popular vote by 537,000, less than half of 1 percent of the one hundred million votes cast in the country. He would lose states in the West and the Midwest by minuscule margins. Three states would be too close to call days after the election was formally over. He would lose New Mexico by 344 votes. In the weeks to come, as they fought over handfuls of votes in South Florida, Republicans' stomachs would twist into knots as they thought of the phone calls not made in the West, the people they thought had gone home without voting, the strangely empty polling places in the Panhandle in the last hour of the voting day.

Democrats too had their teeth-gnashing trials. An election official in Florida's Palm Beach County (a Democrat), concerned for
the eyesight of elderly voters, had designed a ballot, the "butterfly,"
that spread ten candidates' names over two facing pages, with
punch holes by the names of the candidates down one central
spine. The problem was that about 4 percent of the voters would
confuse the hole for Al Gore with the one just above it—for
Reform Party candidate Patrick Buchanan—and punch the hole
for the wrong person or, in their confusion, punch both. The result
was that nineteen thousand punch cards in Palm Beach County
would register overvotes, or double-punched ballots, three times
the rate of the usual number, and the vote for Buchanan, an ultra-
conservative, would balloon to 3,400 in a district populated almost
exclusively by elderly liberal Jews. For the next six weeks, when the
difference between the two candidates would be measured in
spoonfuls, the thought of the twenty-thousand-plus votes they had
lost to ballot confusion would drive Gore and the Democrats mad.
The result was to shave thousands of votes from both candidates'
totals and to send each side into the melee that followed with
nerves frayed already, a very strong sense of frustration and grievance, and a belief that in a just world it would have won an unquestioned victory. And then things would get even worse.

Shortly after nine o'clock in the East, after a series of furious
phone calls from Bush and his people, the four major networks
got their first indication that the Florida call had been wrong. Exit
polls had overestimated Gore's totals, and as the real votes poured
in, his lead shrank. By ten, two hours after the first call, the networks pulled Florida back. With that, what had looked like a
rout turned into a squeaker as Bush began picking off states in the
core of the country that had seldom before gone for Republicans,
such as West Virginia, Bill Clinton's Arkansas, and even Al Gore's

Tennessee. At eleven, the polls closed in the West, but this made things no clearer, with a great many states still locked in squeakers, and the popular vote and the electoral tallies in seeming dead heats. Pundits began discussing a tie, then discussing how either side could win without Florida. By one in the morning, it was clear that no one could win without Florida. By two, it looked as if Bush had a thirty-thousand-vote lead and could not be overtaken. At 2:18 A.M., the networks began calling Florida, and thus the election, for Bush.

About three-thirty, Gore was about to step on stage in Nashville to concede the election when he was pulled back by hysterical aides. While he was in his car, Bush's lead had been melting: an hour later, he would lead with a little more than a thousand votes out of six million, a margin of two-hundredths of 1 percent. Asked to choose between the two heirs, the voters chose neither: it was, by any description, a tie. It was not only a tie but a tie all the way down through the system: it was a tie in the Senate, a near tie in the House, and so close in the states that three were too close to call days after the election was over, and thirteen were won by less than 4 percent. It was so close that minute swings in a number of states would have altered the outcome or brought about ties of a different description.

"A swing of just 269 votes from Bush to Gore in Florida would have given Al Gore the presidency," write Andrew E. Busch and James W. Ceaser in *The Perfect Tie*, an account of the 2000 election, adding that even if Gore had won Florida, "modest swings from Gore to Bush to 183 votes in New Mexico, 2,854 votes in Wisconsin, and 2,072 votes in Iowa would have resulted in an electoral vote tie, while those same changes in Wisconsin, Iowa, and Oregon would have given the presidency back to Bush." In Florida and New Hampshire, the vote total racked up by Green

Party candidate Ralph Nader was many times Bush's margin of victory, for a total of twenty-nine electoral votes, which would have made Gore the president. But there were four states won by Gore, for a total of thirty electoral votes, where his margin of victory was less than the vote for Bush and far-right-wing candidate Patrick Buchanan combined. Given the justified claims of both sides that they may have lost thousands of votes because of strokes of bad luck not of their making, it is possible to posit a tie of a new configuration, in which Gore narrowly wins Florida while Bush ties the popular vote or narrowly wins it and picks up some states in the West.

As it was, the tie was a stunning development, "a long shot wrapped in a longer shot," wrote David von Drehle in *Deadlock*. "The virtual tie in Florida was a once-in-every-few centuries proposition, and so was a presidential election that hinged on a single deadlocked state." For weeks, months, and years after, the principals would torture themselves wondering what might have occurred if they or fate had handled things differently, but by the dawn's early light, George W. Bush was clinging to the thousand-plus votes that would allow him to follow his father, Al Gore was stopped three electoral and one thousand–odd Florida votes from his and his family's lifelong obsession, and it was all coming down to the state run by the second Bush brother, the one everyone thought would someday be president, and the one who, had he been running, might have won it all going away.

Early in the morning of November 8, a plane filled with recount experts from Nashville touched down at the airport near Florida's state capital, next to a small plane on its way in from Austin, bearing Jeb Bush and his son. The next day, Gore's campaign manager arrived in the state to declare that Gore "should be awarded a victory" and maintain that "with so much at stake, steps should be taken to make sure that the people's choice becomes our president. . . . We will be working with voters from Florida in support of legal action to demand some redress." At least since 1984, when a bloody six-month battle had been waged over a seat in the House from Indiana's 8th district, the politics of recount procedures had become almost a science, and the Gore people had on hand two of the three people who had literally written the book. The book in this case was *The Recount Primer*, and it laid out in prescient detail exactly the routes to be followed by the differing camps. "If a candidate is behind," it instructed, "the scope of the recount should be as broad as possible, and the rules should be different from those used on Election Night. . . . If a candidate is ahead, the scope of the recount should be as narrow as possible, and its rules and procedures . . . should duplicate the procedures of Election Night."

Thus, as *Deadlock* explained it, "Gore would gamble, Bush would stall. Gore would preach a doctrine of uncounted ballots, Bush would extol the dependability of machines. Gore needed more: more counting, more examination, more weighing and pondering of more ballots. Bush needed it over while he was still ahead." In the 1984 recount, Democrats had begun with a slight lead and clung to it. "They fought to keep the scope narrow and pushed the case into a friendly federal jurisdiction: Congress, then controlled by the Democrats." Now the roles were reversed, and so were the strategies. Gore could only gain by change, so he would go to court repeatedly to push for more changes: more recounts, more extensions for recounts, more loosening in the standards by which votes were measured. Bush had everything to lose by change, so he would sue to restrict it, to keep to the laws established before the election, and to keep the standards for reading a ballot close to those used by machines.

Gore's first move was to ask for hand recounts in four heavily Democratic South Florida counties, hoping that with ballots read by sympathetic local officials, they could "recover" a sufficient number of votes in the process to make up for the ones they had lost. His people began in a state of euphoria, drawing on precedents from previous contests to issue predictions precinct by precinct of the votes that they planned to pick up. But the projected "yield rates" had been too optimistic—a local race in an obscure county was very different from a presidential contest under contention and fierce public scrutiny—and they had been forced soon after to scale their hopes down. Under pressure, officials in Broward County changed their standards in midvote and gave Gore a windfall, but Palm Beach stubbornly clung to its own stricter standard, while Miami-Dade County, reluctant to start in the first place, stopped counting completely on November 22, citing time pressures and the noisy objections of the press and Republicans when told they would not be allowed in to watch.

Democrats became "delirious with impatience" as the canvassing boards stalled, bargained, and finally churned out Gore votes at a much slower rate than they ever thought possible. Gore sued the canvassing board of Miami-Dade County to force it to resume counting. He sued the canvassing board of Palm Beach County to make it accept his "dimpled chad" standard. By this time, both sides had flooded the state with literally hundreds of observers, activists, and the de facto equivalent of two major law firms, featuring some of the most high-priced and well-known legal names in the nation, fighting in all some sixty-plus lawsuits in varied state, local, and federal courts.

The problem for all—and especially Gore, who was on the side that was looking for more and more remedies—was that this was both a case without precedent and one in which precedents failed to apply. "Mr. Daley," one of Gore's experts told his campaign manager at the start of the process, "the recount procedures in Florida are designed to resolve contests in sheriff races and county commissioner races. They never contemplated something the size of this." Most recounts took place within one district or county—would public opinion, or the higher courts, permit a presidential election to be resolved on a recount in only four of a state's sixty-seven counties and ones that had been handpicked by one party? What about standards for judging the ballots? Standards now varied from county to county; they even varied within counties and sometimes from table to table in one canvassing office because each party's observers, hanging literally over the counters, fought back and forth for each vote. And what about time? Florida's elastic election law posited an endless amount of time in which to decipher the "will of the voter" through repeated perusals of ballots. But with the presidency this would hardly be possible, because the law had established a series of deadlines by which time the race had to end. Seven days after the election, the vote of the state had to be formally certified. "Safe harbor" occurred on December 12, the last date on which a state's electoral vote was guarded from challenge. On December 18, the vote of each state had to be read out in its capital. On January 6, the vote of each state was read out in Congress, and on January 20, the president was sworn in in Washington, a date that no court seemed likely to change.

"There were plenty of state cases where officials had been removed months after taking office," Jeff Greenfield wrote later. "How . . . would this work in the case of a presidential election? Would a clerk from the Florida circuit court show up at the Inaugural platform, armed with a subpoena? Would a team of Florida state troopers storm the northwest gate of the White House sometime in mid-March?" Unless something could be made to change quickly, Gore's demands for change and more recounts would run head-on into the stone wall of deadlines and produce a collision that would be up to the courts to decide.

In Washington, Gore had entrenched himself in the vice president's mansion, where he ran the campaign as a war. "He truly believes he had at least a 10,000 to 20,000 vote lead in Florida among the people who intended to vote for him, but were somehow thwarted," the *New York Times* reported. "With each passing day, Gore has grown more adamant in the view that he is trying to 'vindicate the truth.'" From command central at his dining room table, Gore ran through his days, calling supporters, conferring with lawyers, scanning the news to see how his efforts were playing, raising money to finance his fight to survive.

"His behavior during the astonishing post-election struggle found him mostly playing to type," wrote David Maraniss, "dogged in the pursuit of the 25 electoral votes that would make him president, insatiable in his hunger for the latest news from Florida, realistic about the power play at the core of the struggle, absorbed by the smallest legal or political detail, and alternatively preternaturally calm or uncomfortably frenetic. . . . He surfed the channels and pored over the newspapers, keeping tabs of who was saying what about him. . . . In the face of unpromising prospects, he could impress his staff as seeming 'unmovable.' . . . But then he might disappear into a back room and start dialing a round of desperation calls to opinion-makers, pleading every nuance of his case." He spent one day berating the mayor of Miami-Dade County, who he thought had betrayed him, and another urging a network anchor to put an exposé of what he called rigged voting machines on the air.

Behind all of this was a growing frustration on two different issues: his inability to put a convincing face on a visible enemy or to find a remedy to address his real wrong. "If an election is stolen, then someone has to be stealing it," write Busch and Ceaser. "Yet this was just the problem that Gore and the Democrats faced. . . . Who had disenfranchised the citizens of Palm Beach County? Not the Republicans, but a Democratic election official trying to do her best to help those she harmed. Who had decided not to count the ballots in some of the counties? Not a plot of Republican officials, but Democrats or neutral civil servants. Who had installed the sub-par voting equipment? Mostly Democrats in Democratic counties. And so it went. . . . Every time they looked for a 'thief,' it turned out to be a Democrat, or an impersonal force." And if Democrats complained they were injured by fate, Republicans too had complaints of this nature: they firmly believed that their loss of the popular vote (and perhaps a few western states) was the likely result of the first call of Florida and that the claims of the networks that all the polls in Florida had closed at what was only six o'clock central time had kept some of their voters away from the polls.

A more serious problem was the fact that what Gore designed as his remedy—counting the undervotes—did not apply to the genuine grievance at hand. His real complaint was that some of the ballots had confused some of his voters into voting twice, or for the wrong candidate, neither of which were errors a recount could rectify. Voting twice was likely to result in two clean distinct punches, from which no honest observer could discern a clear preference, and a vote for the "wrong" person was simply . . . a vote. As the recounts stalled, or were stopped, or kept coming up empty, Gore became more and more desperate, to a degree that even his rivals could now see was tragic in nature. "One by one, the last doors are slamming shut on Al Gore's lifelong ambition," Marjorie Williams wrote in early December. "If Gore is finally forced to concede defeat, it will be the hardest of all the spectacles we have witnessed in this month-long electoral endgame, the one most like driving by a wreck on the highway and recognizing in a burst suitcase or scattered toy the sudden ruin of a life." Whatever he thought in his heart, no canvasser on the face of the planet was going to look at a clean punch for Buchanan and assign it to Gore.

The other life strongly assumed to be ruined was that of Jeb Bush. On all sides, it was widely agreed that no matter what became of Gore or his brother, the second Bush son had a great future behind him, guilty of being in the wrong state at the wrong moment, with, of course, the wrong name. If Jeb had been annoyed when his brother decided to run for the first time in the same year he did, unsettled when he was elected in the same year his brother emerged as a national figure, and unnerved when his state emerged as a key one in the 2000 election when the tie of all times dropped down in his bailiwick, his very worst dream had come true. "If George Bush wins the presidency in a race that comes down so clearly to the arcana of Florida politics, Jeb will be accused until the end of time by a sizeable number of people of being a dynastic hack who stole the election," wrote Williams, who was speaking for many. "And if Al Gore somehow manages to emerge the winner, then Jeb Bush is the sorry bastard who failed to deliver his own state." If Jeb failed decisively to come to the aid of his brother and party, he would be forever damned by his brother and family; if he did, he would draw down on himself the full wrath of the Democrats, who, when he faced reelection in the 2002 cycle, would vent all of their rage on him. At any rate, his career was widely assumed to be over. Fate could play no stranger trick on the reluctant dynast who had tried all his life to flee family drama and now was caught up in its midst.

Jeb's hope had been to try to fly quietly under the radar, coordinating his efforts with his brother's in Austin while keeping himself as much as possible out of the sight and the mind of the public. This came to an end on December 8, when in a 4–3 decision, the supreme court of Florida, which had previously smiled on Gore's pleas for recounts, overrode a slew of lower court decisions and ordered a statewide recount of undervotes, awarded Gore almost four hundred votes from prior and incomplete recounts, and erased and extended some prior state deadlines into an indeterminate and unstated future—December 12, or perhaps 18. This thunderbolt revived the Gore campaign, which had been quietly dying; stunned the Bush camp, which appealed to the U.S. Supreme Court for redress; and drew an anguished dissent from the state court's chief justice, who this time agreed with the U.S. Supreme Court and the Bushes that Gore, with the backing of the supreme court of Florida, had been extralegally rewriting state law.

"My succinct conclusion is that the majority's decision . . . has no foundation in the law of Florida as it existed on November 7, 2000, or at any time until the issuance of this opinion," the chief justice thundered. "The court's action 'propels this country and this state into an unprecedented and unnecessary constitutional crisis.' . . . That would do 'substantial damage to our country, our state, and to this Court.'" It also aroused and drew in the Florida legislature, which believed that its power to make election law for the state, granted by Article II of the U.S. Constitution, had been attacked and usurped by the court. It had been preparing for some weeks for just such an outcome, and now announced that if Gore took a lead under what it saw as an illegal recount, it would send its own slate of electors—for George W. Bush—to Washington and to the state capitol and let it be settled by law.

What the law could come up with in these conditions threatened to stagger the mind. "With this decision," Greenfield wrote later, "all of the wilder fantasies of we Constitutional Catastrophists appeared to be just around the bend. Two slates of electors? If the hand recount produced enough Gore votes to give him the lead, that scenario was a near certainty. A presidency hanging in the balance until Congress convened?" Several scripts appeared to present themselves, each more bizarre than the next. If the two slates of electors were tied up in lawsuits, surely a possibility under these circumstances, then Florida's votes would go missing, and no candidate would have the needed majority. If nobody had a majority, then the House would choose the president and the Senate the vice president, thus electing George W. Bush and Joe Lieberman, the first time the executive branch would be split between parties since Thomas Jefferson served under John Adams two hundred years earlier.

If two slates at once arrived before Congress, the two houses together would select the president, the House voting for Bush on a party-line ballot, the Senate tying, with Joe Lieberman voting for himself and his running mate, and Al Gore, as vice president, breaking the tie, and selecting himself. In case of a split between House and Senate, the election would go to the slate signed by the governor of the state in contention: in this case, Jeb Bush. Gore would then have voted to make himself president while Jeb Bush would have installed his own brother, a turn of events never foreseen by James Madison. Gore, of course, would have nothing to lose, but Jeb, in indicating that he would in fact sign such a document, had in effect put his neck on the block for his brother and put an end to his own aspirations. No matter what happened, he would be the prime target for Democrats in the 2002 midterms, damned if he didn't, or did.

At nine in the morning on Saturday, December 9, 2000, recounts began in canvassing rooms in all Florida counties. Five and a half hours later, at two-thirty in the afternoon, the Supreme

Court of the United States, which a week before had slapped down the Florida court for overreaching, halted the recount pending a hearing on the appeal brought by the Bush side, to take place on Monday, two days away. At ten thirty on the night of Tuesday, December 12, Gore was in the vice president's mansion writing an op-ed piece asking the public for patience when the Supreme Court reached its decision. The recount was compromised by the lack of a standard, and the process had run out of time. There were bitter dissents by four of the justices, and Gore partisans assailed the five who concurred in the 5–4 opinion as corrupt, biased, unhinged, and treasonous—precisely the same terms that Bush's friends had used days earlier to describe Florida's court.

Some claimed that the Court would pay in lost honor, but much of the country seemed relieved and exhausted, much as if the Court had seized the wheel of a runaway vehicle and steered it to a bumpy landing in the side of a haystack, minutes before it would have plunged over a cliff. One reason was that the race was so close that most people realized that any outcome was bound to have been inconclusive; another was that that almost six weeks of recounts and wrangling had produced no real change in the outcome; and a third was that the damage suffered by institutions and people was judged to have been quite enough. Most races have only one loser at a time per position, but this one appeared to have three: it was the consensus at the time of the political classes that Al Gore had suffered the most painful loss in all of American history, that Jeb Bush had martyred himself for the sake of his brother (who many people implied was not worth it), and that the presidential life of George W. Bush, the nominal winner, would be nasty and brutish and short.

Through the course of the recount, predictions had flown that the election's ultimate winner would be the real loser, that he would reap the whirlwind in terms of rage from the opposite party, that he would lose between twenty and forty seats in the midterm elections and be ousted himself two years later. Like John Quincy Adams, the only other president's son to have reached the same office, Bush would arrive in a weakened position, having lost the popular vote by a small margin, having won the electoral vote by the smallest of margins, and having been helped at the end by a Supreme Court decision, something his rivals would see as a deal. As Democrats were fond then of saying, the second Adams's term was not productive, and he lost four years later to his earlier rival, a Democrat from—where else?—Tennessee. Making things worse for Bush was the fact that he was on the short end of a larger left-wing–right-wing schism: put together, the combined vote of Gore and Ralph Nader outpolled him by three million votes. This, it was thought, would tie his hands more than they were tied already, and his reign would be brief and lacking in consequence. The one bright spot was that times appeared calm, and no crises seemed imminent. Or so people thought.

CHAPTER 7

2001

On January 6, 2001, in one of the worst days of his life, Albert Gore Jr., in his role as vice president, presided over the formal reading of the electoral vote in the House chamber, standing there as die-hard Democrats tried to enter a protest. Worst of all, he had to listen stoically as the crucial twenty-five votes from the state of Florida were formally given to George W. Bush. Then, on January 21, again in his role as outgoing vice president, he stood on the dais on the west side of the Capitol as Bush was sworn in as president, in close company with the other two men he blamed for his problems, Bill Clinton, the outgoing president who had given the new President Bush an issue to run on, and the new president's younger brother, Jeb. After that, he went to the Democrats' send-off for the ex-president and the new Senator Hillary Clinton, where his name barely appeared in the filmed retrospective. After that, he seemed to disappear. With his wife, he went on vacation to Europe, returning bearded and thirty pounds heavier, looking nothing whatever like the trim, forceful figure who impressed people in the mid-1980s with his serious grasp of affairs.

"He went completely inside," Donna Brazile, one of his handlers, told Liza Mundy of the *Washington Post.* "He completely cut off people as if we had a disease." "He was saddened, and he was reeling a little bit," said an associate. "He was adjusting to a whole new set of assumptions: how he thought about himself, what he could rightly assume about the structure of day to day life." A lifetime of disciplines had been suddenly ruptured: for the first time in eight years, he was not in the White House; for the first time in twenty-four years, he was not in office, running for office, or planning a run for an office that was higher still. The wall in his parents' house set aside for his final accomplishment was blank and might stay so forever. The obligation that had been laid on him at birth—to one day be president—had been suddenly lifted, leaving him unencumbered, but ungrounded and lacking in context. Without it, he seemed to have no frame of reference; worse, he had not only lost, he believed that he had won and been cheated, that he had been deprived by a combination of sinister forces of something he won and deserved. The effort to cope with this while pretending that nothing was wrong appeared to exhaust him. "He really looked like walking death," said a friend who came on him unannounced at a party. "You saw the look on his face when he thought he was alone. . . . You could see the effort it took him to look like he was alive."

Stoic in public, Gore feigned composure, much like the boy he had been as a child, who had pleased his parents by never complaining or making "an unhappy sound." In private, however, he and his aides vented loudly, blaming the Supreme Court, Bill Clinton, and the Bushes, but apparently never themselves. No retrospectives were held to discuss the campaign or its management; there were no suggestions that he might ever have made a mistake. But what he did not do for himself, others did for him. Democrats were enraged that he had managed to tie an election they believed he was set up to win. "Even as the recount battle was playing itself out . . . Democratic leaders were reaching an informal but pervasive consensus . . . that Al Gore had no political future," wrote Jack Germond in the *Los Angeles Times*. "The anger at Gore's failures is intense enough that expressions of commiseration . . . should be taken with a grain of salt." As one leading Democrat told columnist Robert Novak, "This is the worst presidential campaign that I have seen in my lifetime. . . . It's the candidate. He's horrible. How could he lose Tennessee?"

In the fall, when Gore began his tentative movement back into political circles, he was met with skepticism in even the most friendly of papers. "It is one thing for Mr. Gore to be disliked among the Washington elite, although that must be a bitter enough pill for someone who spent so much of his life inside the Beltway," wrote the liberal *New York Observer*. "What's more remarkable is the level of animosity among politicos in a place like New York, where Mr. Gore defeated Mr. Bush in 2000 by almost a 2–1 margin." The *New York Times* wrote of the "deep reservoirs of anger and resentment about the way Mr. Gore conducted his campaign. In interviews conducted with more than two dozen contributors and strategists, most said they believed Mr. Gore was robbed of Florida . . . but that his own missteps made the race much closer than it should have been."

Gore did not answer these charges or even acknowledge them. In time, he took the traditional highly lucrative and not very tiring jobs on the boards of large corporations that are par for the course for retired or defeated political figures, signed on to teach a few college courses, and planned to write a book along with his wife, all steps commensurate with an eventual return to politics, although not necessarily indicative of it. It was in these teaching jobs that one caught a glimpse of the person whom Mundy would call "OtherGore"—as opposed to "PoliticalGore"—the Gore who was easy, relaxed, and wholly at home in scholarly settings, free to write, think, and ruminate with congenial peers. In a better world, perhaps, OtherGore might have taken him over, but not after a race so protracted and grueling and an end so traumatic and close.

"Who in the world is guaranteed to have choked on his corn-flakes at the sight of President Boy George gallivanting into Buckingham Palace and then on to the G8 summit in Genoa?" asked the *New Statesman*. "Who has put on more than two stone in the past six months? . . . Poor Gore remains in self-imposed exile at his home across the river from DC in Arlington, . . . fuming over the unfairness of a system that gave him half a million more votes than Dubya . . . yet consigned him to teach in New York and Kentucky [*sic*], and write another boring book with his wife." Soon after this, he would move back to Tennessee, where he too would live in a white house with pillars, comforted perhaps by the historical footnote that the last time a former president's son had won the presidency without the popular vote after a contested election, the loser, Andrew Jackson, had come back four years later to become a two-term and significant president. Jackson too was a Tennessee Democrat. No president before who lost the popular vote had been reelected. If Jackson came back, so might he.

As of the spring, Democrats looked to a recount of all the votes cast in Florida undertaken by a consortium of newspaper publishers that they clearly expected to prove beyond doubt that Gore had won the state by at least a ten-thousand-vote margin. But the results when they appeared were just as inconclusive and close as the original tallies and just as subject to change based on varying standards. And by the time they were published, the country's attention had shifted, and few people would notice or care.

On September 11, 2001, Al Gore was in a hotel in Vienna waiting to give an address about the Internet when a bulletin came over a television set in the room that a plane had flown into the top floors of the North Tower of the World Trade Center in New York City. In the next few hours, he would watch with the rest of the world as a second plane minutes later hit the South Tower, as another plane hit the Pentagon in suburban Virginia, as the towers collapsed, leaving a great steaming crater in lower Manhattan, and as reports came of a fourth plane, forced down by passengers in a field outside Pittsburgh, that had seemed headed for either the White House or the Capitol. After that, it would take days before he could get on a flight into Canada, where Mounties took him across the closed border and into New York State. There, he was able to connect with Bill Clinton (flown home days before from Australia on a government transport), and the two went down on a government aircraft to Washington for a memorial service for the three thousand casualties, held in the National Cathedral on the morning of September 14. There they sat in a packed house of past and present political leaders as President Bush, in the first of a series of ringing pronouncements, rallied the country to a new and fierce fight. Then Gore went home while Bush got on a plane to Manhattan, where he got his first look at the wreckage of ground zero and reached the iconic moment of his presidency when he climbed on a pile of rubble and, his arm around a fatigued firefighter, vowed that American vengeance would reach round the world.

For the next weeks, months, and years, Gore, who had been brought up to think he was destined to lead in great crises (and who in college had once played the part of John Kennedy in a reenactment of the 1962 missile crisis with Cuba), had to stand by as a man he looked down on proceeded in the course of a year to (1) clear the terrorists out of their fief in Afghanistan; (2) extend the meaning of the new war on terror to include states suspected of backing or arming the terrorists; (3) assert a preemption doctrine that assumed the right to act to forestall an attack, should one be suspected; and (4) last, but not least, launch an attempt to rip up the dark roots of terror by introducing the elements of democratic institutions into the despotic and impacted Middle East. Expansive and bold (not to say rash and breathtaking), this was the last thing people expected from Bush, who before this had shown little interest in foreign relations and had come into office pledging a restrained foreign presence.

Only the first of these four was predictable, and the last three provoked wide debate. When critics claimed it was rash to have linked Iraq, Iran, and Syria in an "axis of evil" when none had a clear tie to 9/11, Bush claimed that they were part of a pattern of terror that included Iran's year-long seizure in 1979 of the American embassy and Iraq's attack on Kuwait, that they possessed or were pursuing nuclear and chemical weapons, and that they had long records of bankrolling terrorist acts. When critics claimed that preemption was the road to unprovoked, lawless, and endless aggression, Bush replied that attacks had come without reason or warning from an undeterrable enemy; that with box cutters and jet fuel the terrorists had killed thousands and cost billions of dollars; that with chemical or nuclear weapons the terrorists could have killed millions, wiped out whole cities, and dealt a blow to the country it could not survive. When critics claimed that trying to bring democracy to the Middle East was a futile and perilous exercise, Bush replied that the Middle East, the main remaining source of terror and violence, was the one place on earth without working democracies and that this was not a coincidence; that Spain, Latin America, and much of eastern Europe had not been democracies before the past several decades, and that Japan and Germany had been expansionist and tyrannical before being defeated in 1945.

"It is presumptuous and insulting to suggest that a whole region of the world—or the one-fifth of humanity that is Muslim—is somehow untouched by the most basic aspirations of human life," Bush would say later. "The world has a clear interest in the spread of democratic values, because stable and free nations do not breed the ideologies of murder. They encourage the peaceful purpose of a better life." "The difference between retaliating against al-Qaeda and declaring war on terror is the difference between a response and a doctrine," said Nicholas Lemann, lifting Bush to the level of James Monroe and Harry S. Truman, at least when it came to audacity. "He sees this as the nation's moment of destiny. . . . Bush is going to use September 11 as the occasion to launch a new, aggressive American foreign policy that would represent a broad change."

To rub it in all the more, *The Economist* ran a feature positing an alternative universe, in which Al Gore had very narrowly won in the Florida recount, the inexperienced, unimaginative, and unprepared Bush had thankfully gone back to Texas, and the superbly credentialed former vice president rose to the challenge he had been born and raised for, and became a great leader at last.

In February 2002, the actual Gore, minus the beard, but still thick in the middle, went back to the scene of the crime (or, at least, the confusion) to denounce the current Republican government and urge Florida Democrats to channel their rage at the 2000 recount into a drive to oust Governor Bush. A defeat for Jeb, he insisted, would be just the beginning, the run-up to the great act of ultimate vengeance, which would be the defeat of the president. "At that point," he had said to his audience, "there will be one down and one to go." The tone for the year had been set early in 2001 when Clinton friend Terry McAuliffe, the newly elected head of the Democratic National Committee, told a wildly cheering crowd of Washington Democrats that he would make Jeb's defeat the number-one goal of his party.

"We will transform the anger about Florida into energy about politics," he had told them. "We will prove there is victory after denial, democracy after Florida . . . and justice after the United States Supreme Court." Barely a week after Gore had conceded, the teachers' union of Florida had mortgaged its headquarters, freeing up $1.5 million that it would earmark to be used for ads to bring down the president's brother, and an added $15 million would be raised out of state. "There won't be anything as devastating to President Bush as his brother's losing in Florida," McAuliffe said, quite correctly. "Jeb is gone!" he would cry periodically, envisioning what would be for Bush the ultimate nightmare, not only losing a state that he would need for the 2004 showdown, but having to realize that, having first stepped on his brother's larger ambitions, he had now cost that brother his job.

Brotherly love seldom beat stronger than in Florida 2002. "No federal grant, no business loan, no tinkering with federal policy that might give Jeb a political leg up is too small to merit White House attention," wrote Ryan Lizza, adding that every week brought a new example of policy altered on Jeb's behalf. Bush banned oil drilling off the coastline of Florida, poured money into projects to rescue the Everglades, loosened travel restrictions that hurt Florida's tourism industry, kept the Pentagon's Special Command stationed in Tampa, and moved a major space shuttle program to Florida from California, along with its hundreds of well-paying jobs. Cabinet members flew in and out of the state regularly, as did the president. At his urging, Texas Republicans took a sudden interest in Florida politics and flooded the state with their money. Five million dollars, to match the cash flowing in to the Democrats, was raised out of state. Gore had to beat Jeb to gain vindication. Bush had to save Jeb to gain authenticity, maintain job security, and avoid a family problem of a sort never before faced by a president. Jeb, who had moved to Florida to escape family shadows and stayed miles away to avoid complications, found himself once again at the core of a multifaceted drama, in which public and personal themes intertwined.

If Florida was a state to Jeb Bush (and a state of indebtedness to his brother the president), to Al Gore it was a state of mind that he could not get out of and talked about wherever he went. "If anybody ever tells you that one vote doesn't make a difference, ask them to come talk to me," he roared to voters in Florida. In the Midwest, he "urged Democrats to keep the anger from the 2000 presidential race in mind" during voting and whipped crowds into frenzies with his attacks on the U.S. Supreme Court. "Are you completely over that?" he cried, referring to the controversial decision. "No!" the crowds shouted. "God, no!" Adam Nagourney of the *New York Times* reported one such appearance before college students in Iowa. "'Do you remember where you were when they stopped counting the vote in 2000; do you remember how you felt?' he asked. 'Cheated!' a few of the undergraduates roared back. . . . His decision to invoke the issue explicitly suggested that after a long silence by many Democrats, Mr. Gore, at least, continued to look on the disputed vote in Florida as a source of continuing anger. . . . 'You were robbed!' one man shouted out when Mr. Gore raised [the issue.] . . . Mr. Gore beamed as he stoked up his crowd." Gore did rouse his base, but not all of the voters were angry, and the candidates, not to mention their issues, were obscured by him and his rage.

Days before the election, Kathleen Kennedy Townsend was up a few points over her opponent, Bob Ehrlich, in a close race for Maryland's governor. "Then Al hit the road with her," wrote the *American Spectator*'s "Washington Prowler" the day before the election. "His campaign speeches focused almost exclusively on his loss in 2000, with barely a mention of Townsend. Gore's speech received major play across the state. And a day later, Democratic tracking polls showed Townsend had lost three points in the polls and trailed Erhlich going into today." On November 5, Townsend would lose in a staggering upset, part of a historic performance by Bush's Republicans that had seen the president' s party gain seats in both the House and the Senate in his first midterm election for the first time in decades. Jeb Bush won Florida by a thirteen-point margin, in spite (or because) of the Gore exhortations. "You can pretty much correlate the Democrats' worst results on Tuesday with Al's travel schedule," wrote Mark Steyn in Canada's *National Post*. "Everywhere he went, [he] had a consistent message: 'This election isn't about the war or the economy, it's about me.'" A staffer at the Democratic National Committee told Americanprowler.org, "He was just a disaster. . . . All he talked about was himself. No upbeat message, no rallying cry for the candidates. Just him."

Three days after the election, Gore was interviewed by *Time*'s Karen Tumulty, who was surprised at his stridency. Bush's policies, he told her, were "'catastrophic,' 'horrible,' even 'immoral,'" and were "taking the country to a very bad place." By this time, Gore was absorbing bad news from two other quarters: two speeches he gave on Iraq had gone over badly, and the book he had counted on to fuel his reemergence was not selling well. "Mr. Gore has now made two speeches attacking Mr. Bush, and both featured more attitude than substance," said the *Washington Post*, which had endorsed Gore in 2000. "Bitterness is not a policy position," wrote the *New Republic*, his career-long supporter, which had been as bitter as he at the 2000 outcome, adding that his speech "sounded like a political broadside against a president who Gore no doubt feels occupies a post he himself deserves."

On top of his grievance, Gore had misread the new mood of the public: in a wartime world, his stories of psychic stress failed to resonate, and his book—a treatise on families—seemed to speak to a more carefree age. "Since the September 11 terrorist attacks, Americans seem less interested in a president who will understand their ordinary stresses than one who will protect them against extraordinary dangers," wrote Ronald Brownstein in the *Los Angeles Times*, correctly. "His focus here seems to embody a moment that has already passed." This was the wholesale rejection he had not seen in 2000, and the impact was crushing. "The Gores are taking news of their tanking books as if this were Florida all over again," wrote the "Washington Prowler." "'They are marshaling the troops, getting all their old friends to speak up and spin for them,' says a former Gore staffer. 'They're even looking into bulk purchases . . . that could be donated to libraries . . . anything to boost sales.'" In the face of this, fund-raising dried up, and old associates failed to support him. "Democrats knifed him," wrote Andrew Sullivan in the *New Republic*. "For a month of campaigning and touring, it was as if Gore kept pulling every lever for political lift-off, while staying firmly fixed on the ground." On December 15, two years and three days after the Supreme Court decision, Gore gave up the struggle, citing as a cause the curious reason that a repeat performance would focus too much on past happenings. There would be no rematch and no vindication. His main chance had come and was gone.

. . .

Florida was not the only place where George W. Bush found himself enmeshed in domestic relations; the Middle East too was a family affair. For the elder George Bush, the pride and the peak of his long life in politics had been the Persian Gulf War, when in the third year of his presidency he had conjured up, led, and directed a broad coalition of twenty-six nations that expelled Saddam Hussein from Kuwait after his August invasion, successfully ending the first post–cold war crisis and (temporarily) checking Iraq's ambition to extend its influence over the Persian Gulf region and gain control of its oil flow to the West. He was proud of this and proud too of his decision to leave Saddam in power, claiming that a change would unsettle the region and involve his own country in extended and unending war. For a time, Saddam seemed contained, boxed in by overflights, weapons inspections, and American troops stationed nearby in Saudi Arabia. But as time went on, and he went on making trouble, it began to seem like a lost opportunity, especially in 1998 when he forced UN inspectors out of the country, who were unable to say with any authority where Saddam's stores of material for the making of nuclear, biological, and chemical weapons had gone. It was after this that the Senate passed and Clinton signed the Iraq Liberation Act, earmarking $79 million to aid insurgents inside that country and making Saddam's removal a fixed goal of American policy.

This was the policy Bush had inherited, and for his first nine months he did little to press it. But with 9/11, things changed. "All [Saddam's] terrible features became much more threatening," Bush said to Bob Woodward, citing Saddam's ambitions, his invasions of neighbors, the atomic reactor he had built (and Israel had leveled), the poison gas he had used on his Kurdish insurgents, and his increased hostility toward the American nation upon his defeat in Kuwait. A small coterie in the administration had always considered Saddam's eviction of the arms inspectors sufficient cause for a movement against him, and an attack on Iraq concurrent with that on the Taliban had been considered the first weekend after 9/11 and dismissed at the moment. But after Afghanistan, Bush looked once again at Iraq and its possible dangers and decided the time had arrived to finish the process and end what his father had begun.

The problem was that in the view of his father, the process was fine as it was. Father and son saw the world differently, a fact obscured in the immediate aftermath of the attack but increasingly obvious as time passed and the emerging Bush Doctrine—clearly applied to only one family member—evolved. "There is an alternative Bush I view of the world that is now engaged in a death struggle with Bush II," said Jeffrey Bell in the *Weekly Standard.* "It has a micro, not a macro, interpretation of what happened on 9/11. It sees Osama and Islamism as limited and aberrational. It mildly supported the invasion of Afghanistan, but would favor no other significant military actions, backing mainly police actions geared toward catching Osama. . . . In the Islamic world, Bush I favors economic development through trade and internal, top-down reforms. While it does not oppose attempts to achieve democratic reforms in Islamic countries, it has little hope that this will be much of a factor in the immediate decades ahead." Bush I was a professional diplomat, steeped in tradition and protocol; Bush II was not. "Bush the father was steeped in arms control, détente, international organizations, and balance of power," wrote Nicholas Lemann in the *New Yorker.* "Bush the son . . . has gravitated consistently toward moralism, grand ambition, and a broad, simple way of seeing the world, . . . stressing intuition over intellect, right and wrong over strategic considerations, and simplicity over detail."

Bush I was unnerved by regime change and preemption, and he cherished stability, restraint, tradition, and the preservation of the existing order. Bush II thought the existing order was part of the problem. "Who truly believes, after the attacks of September 11 . . . that the status quo in the Middle East was stable, beneficial, and worth defending?" his second secretary of state, Condoleezza Rice, would query rhetorically. "How could it have been prudent to preserve the state of affairs in a region that was incubating and exporting terrorism, where the proliferation of deadly weapons was getting worse?" She was responding to Brent Scowcroft, her mentor, who had been national security adviser in the Bush I administration and was still Bush I's best friend. For their part, Scowcroft and Bush I had put forth their own views in a memoir of their own term in office. "While we hoped that a popular revolt or coup would topple Saddam, neither the United States nor the countries of the region wished to see the breakup of the Iraqi state," they wrote in a book published in 1994, before the younger Bush had won office. "We were concerned about the long-term balance of power. . . . Breaking up the Iraqi state would pose its own destabilizing problems. . . . It would have been a dramatically different—and perhaps barren—outcome. . . . We would have been forced to occupy Baghdad, and in effect rule Iraq."

In August 2002, as Bush was making his case to the world and the nation, Scowcroft and two other Bush I officials—Lawrence Eagleburger and James Baker (who had been Bush II's main strategist during the Florida recount)—burst into print to urge caution, presumably with the consent of the president's father or at least without his stated objection. Publicly silent, the ex-president fretted in private as his son plunged into the uncharted seas he had pulled back from confronting. "Family members could see the former president's anguish," the Schweitzers inform us. "But do they have an exit strategy?" he asked.

Also involved was a legacy battle, in which just one of the two could prevail. If Iraq fell apart or if war swept the region, the decision of Bush I to stay out would be borne out as prudent, and he would be hailed as a model of mature, reasoned judgment. If, however, Iraq were to stabilize (and become, like Afghanistan, an American ally), it would be seen instead as a mistake and a lost opportunity, a chance to have cut off Saddam with less blood and less money, a hand-off to the future of an intractable problem and a needless sacrifice of the Kurds and the Shia, who rose up against Saddam when he was retreating to Baghdad and whom Bush I had refused to aid. There was also Osama bin Laden, who gave as an ostensible cause for the 9/11 attacks his resentment at the stationing of American troops on the sacred soil of Saudi Arabia. Why had Bush I sent American troops to Saudi Arabia? To guard against Saddam Hussein, who was still then in power, kept there by Bush. "If the Bush II view of the world is vindicated," Jeffrey Bell would continue, "Bush I will no longer be the administration remembered primarily for decisively winning the Persian Gulf War. It will be remembered as the administration that left Saddam Hussein in power, inadvertently leading to a chain of events culminating in 9/11 and a far-flung world war."

This was somewhat unfair, because the Persian Gulf War was a solid achievement, but it did cast doubt on an accomplishment its authors wished to be seen as an unblemished triumph, and with this it was not too surprising that some of those supporting the Bush I decisions would now try to downplay those of his son. CIA spy spouse Joseph C. Wilson, who announced his ambition to be "the Bush I administration political employee who did the most damage to the Bush II administration," spoke warmly of his admiration for the first Bush president, who in turn had once described Wilson as a "truly inspiring and courageous diplomat" for his role in evacuating American citizens from Iraq before the war in 1991. It quickly became a matter of course for critics of the current President Bush to heap praise on his father for foresight and prudence, finding in the older man a long string of virtues that had somehow eluded them while he had been president.

Among them, of course, was John Kerry, who in the presidential debates of 2004 tried to turn Bush's father against him, saying, "You know, the president's father did not go into Iraq . . . and the reason he didn't is—he wrote in his book—because there was no exit strategy. And he said our troops would be occupiers in a 'bitterly hostile land.'" And Brent Scowcroft continued to hammer him, once with a long interview in the *New Yorker* in October 2005, an especially difficult time for both the war and the president, in which he repeated all the old arguments, and, in view of the prevailing problems, seemed to be rubbing them in. Writer Jeffrey Goldberg also described the strains this had caused in the Bush family, where the ex-president tried to mediate unsuccessfully between his old friend and his son. According to friends of the elder Bush, the estrangement between his son and his best friend has been an abiding source of unhappiness, Goldberg wrote, adding that the unknown factor remained the extent to which Scowcroft expressed what ex-President Bush had been thinking. That, said Goldberg, only Scowcroft and Bush himself knew.

Among those who supported the Persian Gulf War but opposed the Iraqi invasion was Gore. In August 2003, he had approached Moveon.org, a liberal group that opposed the war on the Taliban (and had rallied for Gore in the Florida recount) and began to make speeches under its auspices. In December, he endorsed Howard Dean, the most outspoken and angry of the Democrats' candidates, a move widely seen as ensuring Dean's nomination and marking Gore's return as a figure of influence. But Dean soon imploded, taking Gore's future with him, and Gore returned to the hustings, now once again his own man. Between February 2004 and the November election, Gore would give a series of speeches that built on his themes of the 2002 midterms and took them to stunning new heights. In these, he compared Bush to Richard M. Nixon (forced in 1974 to resign to forestall certain impeachment), who to the Democrats was the symbol of ultimate evil and who to Gore himself was the author of family trauma, as Nixon, president in the age when the South turned Republican, had helped end his father's career. Sweating and shouting, "sounding like the second coming of Huey Long," the onetime reserved and robotic vice president accused his ex-rival of a train of abuses, among them robbing the poor, raping the planet, and starting a war for political purposes.

"He betrayed this country!" Gore roared to his audience. "He played on our fears!" In subsequent months, in speeches and interviews, he would describe Bush as a coward, a bully, a liar, a tyrant, the "worst single president in American history," a religious fanatic supported by bigots and "digital brownshirts" leading a party of "vengeance [and] brimstone" that was less like a party than a cult. A crescendo of sorts was reached on May 24 when he traced abuses by a small group of prison guards to the "moral cesspool" that lay at the dark heart of power, or, more precisely, the dark heart of Bush. "What happened at the prison, it is now clear, was not the result of random acts by a few 'bad apples,'" he shouted at his audience. "It came from twisted values and atrocious policies at the highest levels of our government. . . . These horrors are the predictable consequences of policy choices that flowed directly from this administration's contempt for the rule of law." The "twisted values," it seemed, flowed from the "twisted" result of the 2000 election, the one that had stymied his parents' ambitions, the one that had twisted his life.

In July, Gore took time out from a campaign stop in Florida to inject himself into that state's senate primary, taking revenge on Alex Penelas, the Miami mayor he thought had betrayed him, firing off furious e-mails to a series of papers that described Penelas as "the single most dishonest and treacherous person" he had met in the course of the Florida recount and the entire campaign. "Gore has gone on quite a bender during this election cycle," wrote a conservative Web site, citing the endorsement of Dean, the speeches, and then the Penelas explosion. "Gore has turned the sliver-close vote [in 2000] . . . into a world-class conspiracy of destruction aimed at him personally. For four years, he dragged the Democrats into his psychosis. Now, he's accusing the Democrats of being in on the plot." In a long and carefully worded news story on the eve of John Kerry's convention, *USA Today* wrote of Gore's "unorthodox, surprising, and sometimes even bewildering approach" to his postrecount role as his party's titular leader, including a "stark departure from his button-down image" that stupefied even his friends. "Strategists in both parties privately acknowledge confusion about Gore's actions since the 2000 election," the story continued, "and remain uncertain of whether the 'new' Gore . . . represents the true colors of a politician who has moved from hawk to dove and populist to deficit buster over a nearly 30-year political career."

"Since losing," wrote James Taranto on opinionjournal.com, "Gore has undergone a metamorphosis. Once a moderate DLC type . . . Gore has become a full-fledged member of the angry Left. It's hard to avoid the conclusion that Gore's rage springs less from ideology or even partisanship than from personal bitterness over losing. . . . This is a man filled with fury and indignation over the world's injustice . . . the injustice that was done to him."

"The angry white male is back. Do the Democrats really want him?" asked Chris Suellentrop of *Slate*, a left-leaning weblog, after watching the former vice president emote in full throttle. "Gore is still popular with the Democratic base, but . . . the question for the party's nominee has to be, do you want this man to speak at the convention in Boston?" he asked. The answer was no, at least not in prime time, and at least not in front of a sizable audience. In the event, he was carefully watched by the Democrats, who gave him instructions to tone down his performance and slipped him into an afternoon slot on the convention's first day, surrounded by other ex and failed candidates, where he got little media coverage. Democrats "seemed intent on hiding him," David Remnick wrote in a *New Yorker* profile. It was all a very long way from 2000, when Gore had thrilled a huge crowd with a prime-time oration, taken his lap in the victory circle, and then come roaring out of Los Angeles, with what appeared as a large and unbeatable lead.

On October 18, 2004, once again unconstrained by authority, Gore delivered a speech about Bush that was yet another cascade of indictments, ending this time in the recourse to Florida, the source of original sin. "The widespread efforts by Bush's political allies to suppress voting had reached epidemic proportions," Gore said, without citing examples. "Some of the scandals of Florida four years ago are being repeated in broad daylight even as we meet today."

Throughout the year, he had often returned to two prior elections that had been critical points in the life of his family, comparing his father's loss in 1970 to his own loss in 2000, and 2004 as the possible corollary to 1976, when his father's loss was avenged indirectly. Another Democrat retook his father's seat in the Senate, and he himself won his father's old seat in the House. In Gore family lore, Albert Gore Sr. was a "pure" politician, destroyed by an attack machine crafted by Nixon to which the younger Gore claimed to see present-day similarities. "They tried to make out like my dad was an atheist because he didn't want a constitutional amendment putting the government in charge of telling children how they ought to worship God in the public schools," Gore had said earlier. "They came out with accusations that he was unpatriotic because he was opposed to the Vietnam War." If Gore saw himself in the place of his father, and John Kerry as himself and James Sasser (the Democrat who first won the Gore seat in the Senate), then George W. Bush was Richard M. Nixon, a corrupt and unprincipled national leader who destroyed people who were better than he was and held power by illicit means. If Kerry won, Gore implied, it would be more than a win for the Democrats: it would be an act of revenge on behalf of himself and his family, one that would inflict the punishment on Bush that had been inflicted on Nixon when he was forced to leave office and would restore the moral order Gore thought had been ruptured when Bush, instead of himself, became president.

"Al Gore will not bleed for public consumption," wrote David Remnick, referring to Gore's refusal in interviews to address directly the events of 2000. But each time Gore spoke in the 2004 cycle, he stood up in public and opened a vein. "The truth shall rise again!" Gore would shout at the end of his speeches, repeating the vow that his father had sworn upon losing. The torch of grievance had passed to the new generation. But the truth never rose quite in time for his father, who would die embittered almost thirty years later, having never held office again.

Gore by this time bore no resemblance to the man who campaigned in 2000, nor to the prim and substantive vice president, nor to the sober young man who had impressed so many with his serious grasp of events. Gone was the defense hawk, gone the politician who had been the restrained, sober moderate; gone the model son, the model vice president; gone the man once described as the superego to the unbuttoned id of Bill Clinton; gone the model young rising political figure, described as "too good to be true."

Gone too was the old—or the young—Bush who had once run against him, changed now almost beyond recognition, his hair gray, his face deeply furrowed, his mouth often pinched and turned down. The erstwhile prankster was frequently grim, tense, and testy. The "irresponsible" man who seemed a boy in his forties had willingly piled the weight of the world on his shoulders. The insular governor, who had seldom traveled abroad and in 1999 could not name many world leaders, was now wholly immersed in west Asian politics. The frat boy, who had been mocked for his presumed lack of care for ideas, much less for big ones, had come up with one of the biggest ideas of the century and was wholly consumed with his effort to turn it into reality. If the rap against Bush in 2000 was that he was immature, inexperienced, provincial, and lacking in gravitas, the rap four years later was that his thoughts were much too big altogether and that he was trying to impose on the world a grandiose and improbable blueprint. If the word for him in 2000 was "affable," in 2004 the word was "relentless," regarding the tenacity with which he clung to his objective and the ferocity with which he tried to make it prevail.

Gore, who had first won respect as a hawk and a centrist, who was one of ten Senate Democrats to back the Gulf War of Bush senior, had now moved to the very far left of his party, joined at the hip to a fringe organization that once had protested the war in Afghanistan and backed protests against the World Bank. Ted Kennedy, whose brother Jack always ran to the right of his rivals, had also migrated leftward, circling back to the isolationist views of their father, while the franchise to his brother's "Ask Not" agenda had been taken over by Bush. Bush, in turn, had jumped over his pragmatist father to go back to Presidents Reagan and Kennedy, the most crusading of all cold war executives, who also believed in the power of freedom and saw clashes of powers as great moral fights. As they all headed into the 2004 showdown, Bush would be speaking the language of Reagan and Kennedy, while his main opposition would come from Al Gore, a onetime defense hawk, who had once stood with his father; from the one living brother of President Kennedy; and from his father's best friend.

Three dynasties had huge stakes in the 2004 outcome, a pivotal year for them all. If Gore sought revenge for himself and his father, Ted Kennedy was seeking rebirth for his family's interests, at a new low since the 2002 midterms, which had destroyed the second wave of the third generation and left the family without visible heirs. Ted Kennedy had now buried three nephews and had seen other nephews and nieces lose, bow out, or be forced out of politics, and he realized that if a return were to happen it would come through somebody not in the family, one of the numerous army of Democrats who had tried for the past forty years (as had he) to rebottle John Kennedy's magic. John Forbes Kerry was literally a new JFK; he was a senator from Massachusetts, he had been photographed as a young man with the late president, and he had served in the navy in the southern Pacific, where he had run a small boat. Flattery had no form more sincere than this, and the baby of the Kennedy family, then seventy-two, became the "big brother" of the candidate, then sixty, in what shaped up as perhaps the Kennedys' last White House run. At stake for him was new life for the Kennedy dynasty: a Kerry White House would seed its departments and agencies with Kennedy heirs who had failed to win or to seek office, giving the stalled members of the third generation a chance to jump-start, or restart, careers.

But at issue also was something less tangible: a chance to rekindle a Camelot redux, to end his career, as he began it, in the small select number of White House insiders, at the uppermost branch of the tree. "It's the view from the back of the White House . . . that sticks in Ted Kennedy's mind," wrote the late David Nyhan, a Boston reporter. "He's lived 43 years, more than half his life, since first kicking back there in a rocker with Jack." "You'd have the dinner prepared for just the two of us," Kennedy remembers. "You'd go out on the Truman porch, and you'd eat looking out at the monument and the sweep of the lawn." Since then, the president's brother had been back many times, but most often downstairs and always on business, with presidents often of the opposite party, to whom he had never been close. Declaring the election the most critical one of his lifetime—"more important . . . than 1960, more important than 1968, more important than 1980," the year he himself had run for the office—he plunged into the fray with a zeal that stunned even the candidate, picking him up when he foundered in Iowa, lending him his longtime speechwriter and strategist, sending him his chief of staff during a shakeup to run his campaign. "Kerry is Teddy's ticket back to Harry Truman's balcony, and to the same kind of congressional clout you can have with a relative in the Oval Office," Nyhan added. "More than anything else, this explains why Kennedy has embraced Kerry's cause as his own."

George W. Bush had been on the balcony too, as a son and a resident, and the lease that he wished to extend was his own. His brief was as deep and emotive as Teddy's but far more complex in its nature: he had to avenge, and then better, his father, erase the question mark left from the Florida recount, erase the asterisk left from the loss of the popular vote in 2000, and validate his first election by winning the second, without which it would be seen for all time as an accident. The stars, and the precedents, all seemed against him: the one other Bush to be president—his father—had lost when he ran for a second term. The one other president's son to be president—John Quincy Adams—had lost when he ran for a second term; and his father too was a single-term president. "Like father, like son, one term, and you're done," John Kerry had taunted him, and it seemed all too prescient. No president who lost the popular vote had been elected again.

And if Bush lost after the 2000 outcome, he would be less than the others, as his first election would be then judged in retrospect as a fluke and an error, a mistake that the country had hastened to rectify. This was, of course, what Gore longed to see happen, even if he could not benefit. As for Kennedy, for whom little had gone right since June 1968 (or since July, a year later), it too would be an indirect vindication, as Nyhan explained. "If Kerry beats George W. Bush—whose family dynasty has now surpassed Kennedy's—Kennedy will have the last laugh in a presidential process that has dominated his life for half a century." A proxy for Gore, an unlikely "stepson" for Kennedy, who could find no true heir among his vast numbers of children and nephews, Kerry found himself the stand-in for two fading dynasties, against one that could still hope to rise.

In 2000, Bush had expected to win, and he had a nasty surprise around noon on November 5 that stretched out to an ugly five weeks. In 2004, he feared he might lose, and for most of the day his opponents were jubilant. It was not until late in the night that he and the country would know he had won, that he won this time without reservations and with an incontestable edge in the popular vote. The truth did not rise for Al Gore, who for the second time in a row failed to find vindication. The sun did not rise for the Kennedy family, which still remained heirless and marginal. The son who was rising was Bush. He was the first Bush president to have won reelection, the first president's son to have won reelection, and the first president to have come back to win reelection after first losing the popular vote. He had avenged and surpassed his own father, having first dispatched his father's tormentors and enemies: Ann Richards in Texas; Al Gore, who attacked him as Clinton's vice president; and Saddam Hussein, the Iraqi dictator, who was now in prison and whose two sons and heirs Bush had killed. Bush had won a total of sixty-two million votes, more than anyone else in American history, added more than ten million new votes to his 2000 total, increased his percentage in forty-eight states, and become the first president in sixteen years (since his own father) to win more than 50 percent of the vote.

In 2002, he had made history by winning congressional seats in his first midterm elections; he now added new seats in both houses. In 2000, the combined vote for Gore and Ralph Nader added up to a three-point deficit that was not in his favor. Four years later, he turned it around. "Whether you are a Democrat, a Republican, or an independent, it is hard not to look at President Bush's re-election last week and not conclude that he is probably one of the three or four most talented politicians of the last half of a century," a posting on CNN.com would say six days later. "In 10 short years, George Walker Bush has won not just one but three high profile races that most able politicians would have lost. In 1994, with no real political experience, he beat a popular incumbent governor in the nation's second most populous state. Six years later, he beat a sitting vice president during a time of peace and prosperity. And last week, with a mediocre economy, an unpopular war, and a well-funded and unified opposition, he not only won his race but also helped increase Republican majorities in the House and the Senate. . . . If you are a serious observer of politics, it is worth your time recognizing a rare political talent when it is in your midst."

Twenty years earlier an alcoholic and a failure, the unlikely visionary of the Bush family would have a new chance to enact his ideas, to test his Middle East vision against that of his father, and to determine if the legacy he passed on to his brother and nephew would be one worth having. In 1952, Al Gore was four years old, George W. Bush was six, and his father, George, was twenty-eight when Prescott Bush, then fifty-seven, went into the Senate with Albert Gore Sr., who was then twelve years younger, and with John F. Kennedy, twenty-two years his junior. What would become of them and their children, nobody then could have dreamed.

Epilogue

From 1775, when the Adamses began raising their sons to be president, to 2006, in the second term of the second Bush president, this country has been through 230 years of dynastic ambition, with fairly uneven results. Taken together, four families have given us five presidents, three vice presidents, five senators, four governors, four ambassadors to major foreign powers, and four members, including one past and one future president, of the House of Representatives. This sounds impressive, and is, until the downside is counted: one certain and one probable suicide, multiple deaths in what can be called young adulthood, numerous lives either warped or distorted, and more alcoholics and drug users than one can easily count. Well-meaning dynasts have pushed sons to accomplish large goals that they might not have dreamed of achieving, but they have also pushed sons till they broke, pushed them into the wrong line of work, where they were embarrassed, or set them adrift at levels of fame and temptation that exceeded their power to cope.

Dynastic sons have been president during the two scariest moments of the current half century: on September 11, 2001, when Islamist terrorists struck New York and Washington, and in October 1962, when atomic missiles capable of striking New York and Washington were discovered in Cuba. Dynastic sons—no fewer than three of them—helped steer the country to the edge of a constitutional breakdown after the 2000 election was tied. Dynastic dynamics had combined with partisan interests to create a near shipwreck. Would it have been fought with such murderous passion if the three men concerned in it did not have so much to prove to their kin?

Dynasties start with an impulse to power that transcends the life of one man. In the case of the Adamses, the Gores, and the Kennedys, they began with the will of one founding father, who pointed his children at one place—the presidency—and began rigorous training in childhood. The Roosevelt drama began in reverse—a son-driven dynasty—with the wish of two "sons," Franklin and Ted Jr., to seize and latch on to the mantle of Theodore, the hero and "father" to both. Between these two poles, we encounter the Bushes: a dynasty , not quite so dynastic, a low-key dynasty, an "accidental dynasty," a reluctant dynasty, a dynasty that denies that it is one. Most dynasties are top-down, and begin with a bang: the decision of a Gore or a Kennedy male to create a succession. The Bushes are bottom-up, and built up by increments: Prescott Bush was a New Englander and a gentleman banker who dabbled in politics as almost an afterthought; George H. W. Bush was a transitional figure who moved from New England to Texas and seemed more of a diplomat even while president; Jeb and George W. are pure politicians, and products of the south and the west.

Beginning as lower-middle-class or outsiders, the Adamses, the Gores, and the Kennedys tended to become or to mimic aristocrats, with the later Adamses becoming snooty and uppity Brahmins, Al Gore being known as "Prince Al" of the Fairfax Hotel, and Jack Kennedy's sister marrying the Marquis of Harting-ton (which would have made her a duchess, had he lived). The Bushes, on the other hand, have become more middle-class over time, while becoming more powerful. George H. W. Bush married a debutante from Greenwich, Connecticut, in a society wedding; George W. married a Midland librarian. George H. W. Bush summers in Maine, where he likes to go sailing; George W. sum-mers in Crawford, where he likes to clear brush. The Adamses and the Kennedys have been chained to the Northeast and mainly New England; the Bushes have been migrants and entrepreneurs, mov-ing the franchise into different markets as new openings seem to arise. "George Herbert Walker Bush alighted in Texas and began sensing that there was a true political opportunity here for the fam-ily," says Bill Minutaglio, his son's biographer. "This is a very for-ward-thinking clan." Thus, as the focus of economic growth, population, and political power began to move to the South from the North and the Rust Belt, the Bushes moved with it. "The Bushes are political migrants," Mitchell Moss of New York University told the *Washington Post.* "The Bush family understands the political geography of the nation. They maintained their polit-ical hegemony by moving west."

They have also avoided a different nature of pitfall by not forc-ing a calling on unwilling heirs. They have been more flexible in this regard than the Kennedys, who, with their rigid hierarchical structure, focused attention (and pressure) on the oldest male living. With the Bushes, a younger son would often jump over a first-born. George H. W. Bush was the second son in his generation, and in the next Jeb was for a long time considered the star of the family. "It was Joe Kennedy who called the shots in his clan, determining for as long as he was alive which son would run for which office," the Schweitzers inform us. "The Bushes operate more like a high-tech start up. . . . Instead of a line of dynastic succession, they follow a process of natural political selection. The young charges are never told or pushed to run." The elder Bush sons plotted their political moves without the instruction of family members, and George W. made his first big run, in the 1994 race for governor, against the wishes of both of his parents, who firmly believed he would lose to Ann Richards. But in spite of this lack of direct interference, the implied pressures were strong enough to imprint the two older Bush sons in childhood with the obligation to follow the path of their father, and for much of his life drove the elder, George W., down the path to destruction that once claimed no fewer than four Adams sons.

In its prime, a dynasty may have a great name, and it may also have money, but the prime asset it has to bestow on its children may be the help of its friends. By the time a George H. W. Bush or a Joseph P. Kennedy has built his career—making millions in business, befriending a president, heading a number of government agencies, or holding down the embassy to a great foreign power—he has also accumulated a web to acquaintances of the most powerful people in several countries, ready and willing to repay his favors, find jobs for his children in fields of their interest, invest in their businesses, and help fund and man their campaigns. Serving as parties inside the parties they nest in, invaluable founts of connections and money, networks like these were key in the breakouts of John Kennedy in 1960 and of George W. Bush forty years later, allowing them to compete on equal terms with more experienced rivals who had institutional backing inside their own parties or from one or more strong interest groups. It is not fair to say that their families made them contenders for president, as they were talented enough to emerge sooner or later, but their families helped to make sure it was sooner. The families didn't make them president necessarily, just president in 1960 and then in 2000, while under different conditions they might have had to wait for more seasoning. By that time, circumstances might have been different. And each one's chance might have come, and gone.

That said, one must say also that this does not happen too often, and there are limits to what dynasts can do. Theodore Roosevelt had four sons, at least one of whom, it was assumed, would one day hold high public office. It didn't happen; nor did it happen with Franklin and Eleanor, whose children were laughingstocks. For the twelve years after the assassination of Robert F. Kennedy, it was assumed that Ted Kennedy could have the White House whenever he wanted. In 1980, he ran against a stunningly weak Democratic opponent and lost. George W. Bush lost in his first run for office. His brother Jeb lost in his first run for office. Their father lost often: he lost races for the Senate in 1964 and 1970 and the Republican nomination to Reagan before becoming vice president. George Bush the younger was selected to run for president by his party less as the son of his father than as a break with tradition, a "new kind of Republican," and he patterned his campaign on Clinton's campaign against Bush senior, a young southern governor who took on a creature of Washington. (It was Al Gore who was often compared to George Bush the elder, as a two-term vice president with impressive credentials, but lacking political skills.) In 2000 (with Gore) and then two years later,

Democrats were burned badly by children of major political talents who got their first jobs on the strength of the names of their families, rose by being picked as running mates by different executives, and proved unequal to tough races in more exposed venues, where family feeling carried less weight. State Democrats are doubtless still ruing the day they forced Baltimore mayor Martin O'Malley out of the 2002 gubernatorial primary to make room for an "unbeatable" Kennedy daughter, who managed to lose, even in Maryland, where Democrats held a huge lead.

Ironically, while his family name can help launch a candidate, he must transcend it or change it in order to rise. Theodore Roosevelt got his start as the son of his father but rose on the strength of his own personality. Franklin Roosevelt in turn spun off from his cousin but quickly established his singular presence. The three Kennedy brothers who had major careers were markedly different, not just from their father, but from one another, with exceedingly different styles and backers and policies. George H. W. Bush was not like Prescott Bush, and Jeb and George W. are not like their father, with George W., much like John Kennedy, defining himself in opposition to most of his father's ideas. Theodore Roosevelt Jr. was widely mocked as a candidate for seeming to do nothing beyond trying to mimic his father, and the younger Kennedys who were flushed out of politics also failed to emerge as distinct personalities. Despite a massive investment of money and effort over the past quarter century, the Kennedys have in the third generation exactly one minor member of Congress, who does not seem likely to rise very far.

If dynasties start when someone decides that the whole must be more than the sum of the parts that it comprises, they start to decline when the process reverses: when the family unit becomes too large and unwieldy, when the family spines become rotten with privilege; when the parts begin to assert their importance over the claims of the whole. In each family story (except, so far, that of the Bushes), it is possible to point to the juncture at which what began as a joyous adventure becomes an obligation that has to be shouldered, and then is a burden, or a curse. To John Quincy Adams, it was both a burden and a pleasure (or he would not have gone back into politics after losing the White House); to Charles Francis Adams, it was a burden alone. It was a burden and a puzzle to Ted Roosevelt Jr. Bobby Kennedy ran for president as if he were bearing the cross on a terrible pilgrimage. To his brother Teddy, it was a fate to be feared and evaded.

Dynasties move through three major stages of increasing privilege and often declining effect. The founders (John Adams, Joe Kennedy) rise by sheer force as they blast their way out of semiobscurity and are followed in turn by the privileged strivers (John F. and Robert F. Kennedy, George W. and Jeb Bush), who are given a hand up but are not handed anything, and who, after a big boost at the start of their efforts, have to go out and win on their own. After these two classes come the inheritors, who coast along in the wake of the strivers' efforts, and it is here that the rot—and the problems—set in. Elected in effect on reflected achievement (as someone's son, brother, nephew, or cousin), they are swept into safe seats in safe states or districts, in coronations that mask any absence of talent and in which character flaws are indulged. Mistakenly classed with his brothers the strivers, Ted Kennedy belongs to the inheritor class, along with his sons and nephews, and has seen his stature diminish in office. For the young Kennedys, now closing in on their fifties, public life has been largely a snare and an illusion, luring them in at too early an age or lifting them up beyond their capacities, where their shortfalls in skill become clear.

As they decay, dynasties tend to alter their nature, ending up, in the course of extinction, far from the heights they once held. The Adamses—who began with John, blunt, fierce, ambitious, and bursting with energy—went out with a whimper three generations and many drunks later with Brooks and Henry, who gave the words "effete snob" new weight and new meaning, feared the democracy John helped establish, and became obsessed with their own enervation and decadence. The public-spirited and productive Franklin and Eleanor Roosevelt produced Jimmy, Elliott, and FDR Jr., who in their turn produced mainly embarrassments. As a state of mind, Camelot began in August 1943, with Jack's swim into Blackett Strait to try to get help for his wounded compatriots, and ended in August 1969, with Ted's swim from Chappaquiddick to Edgartown, leaving his brother's assistant to die in his car.

Ted Kennedy has now racked up a stellar career in the Senate, serving for a longer time than his brother Bobby lived, and has projected the political life of his family into the twenty-first century. He has also damaged the brand name of that family, drained it of all of its moral authority, and reverted in tone to the bombastic and heavily partisan manner against which his brother Jack had rebelled so effectively. "I just do not believe the clichés a politician must utter," Jack had said when beginning his career. "A speech where you ascribe only the good to yourself and only the bad to your opponent has a synthetic quality. . . . Those guys who can make the rafters ring with hokum . . . I guess that's okay." But in modern politics, it wasn't okay, and for this cause among others Ted failed to emerge as a national figure. As a result, he has narrowed his sphere of influence to the Senate itself and the shrinking liberal base of his party. The family itself is back to where it began with Honey Fitz at the start of an earlier century, a local brand that sells well in its restricted home market, but that beyond it has little or no market share.

Dynastic sons all grow up in reaction to pressure, and they react in some typical ways. There are the weak boys gone bad, who give up at the start and are seen later in drunk tanks or drug busts. There are the bad boys gone good, George W. Bush and John Kennedy, the only two recent dynastic sons to be president both paradoxically brought up in the orbit of dynastic ambition but never considered the heir. Both for a while were underachievers who made up with huge growth spurts in their thirties or forties. Both were compared to Prince Hal and King Henry. Both burst upon the political world with upset victories over popular incumbents who had seemed unbeatable (Henry Cabot Lodge and Ann Richards), and both won the presidency with well-run campaigns against more experienced two-term vice presidents and with controversial razor-thin margins that gave rise to charges of electoral larceny. "GWB and JFK were both elected on narrow margins," writes *Weekly Standard* contributor David Gelernter. "Neither was a born politician; neither was an ideologue; both grew up wealthy in decidedly over-achieving families, got Ivy League educations and (when all is said and done) wound up president because of their fathers. As young men, neither seemed remotely cut out for the job. Both came out of nowhere to bear down on American politics like a speck in the rear-view mirror that suddenly turns out to be a 40-ton tractor trailer right on top of you with the driver cheerfully leaning on his horn." Both as president defined themselves in opposition to the foreign policy views of their fathers, and both took breathtaking risks in the interests of long-term stability, being ready to wage or threaten preemptive war to forestall a possible nuclear strike at their country.

Faced with perfection in the form of his brother, Kennedy at Choate became a cutup and a rebel, mocking the things that his brother excelled at. Faced with perfection in the form of his father,

Bush did the same thing at Yale. Kennedy told the psychiatrist called in to examine him that his brother's example made it harder for him to do anything. "Jack is apparently avoiding comparison and withdraws from the race, so to speak, in order to convince himself that he is not trying," the doctor concluded. So did George W. Bush. Each had to wait for his model to die or to lose before he could fully achieve his potential, suggesting that their models' successes had to some extent suppressed or weighed down on their characters. Kennedy blossomed only after his brother moved out of the picture. And it was only after his father had lost to Bill Clinton that Bush could begin his ascent.

The opposite number to the bad boy gone good is the good son who loses, who shoulders the family burden in childhood, gives it his all, and then fails. These unhappy souls include Ted Roosevelt Jr.; Al Gore, who won the popular vote in 2000 but still lost the White House; and John Quincy Adams, who won the White House in 1824 under the old rules, when the State Department or a major embassy was the high road to power, and lost it four years later when the rules were changed on him and it became a post needing political skill. All took it badly. Adams blamed Andrew Jackson for being a demagogue; Ted Roosevelt blamed Teapot Dome and cousin Eleanor; and Gore blamed the Supreme Court and a cast of thousands, including, above all, Jeb Bush. But in the end, all lost because they were poor, or even non, politicians, who failed to connect with the general public and made more than their share of mistakes. None wanted to be politicians, and each wanted to be something different: Ted Roosevelt wanted to be a great soldier, an ambition he later realized. "Literature, the arts and science were what genuinely interested him," Andrew Jackson biographer Robert V. Remini wrote of John Quincy Adams. "He really yearned for the life of the mind." So did Al Gore, who was as at home and as happy in an academic environment as he was awkward and stilted in public affairs.

Having been told all their lives that the White House was their birthright and destiny, these good sons were all but destroyed when they lost. According to Brooks Adams, his grandfather's loss "injected into his mind the first doubts as to whether there were a God, and whether this life had a purpose." Judging by the way that they later reacted, similar thoughts seem to have occurred to Gore and Ted Roosevelt. All spoke of those who defeated them with an excessive bitterness. As Richard Brookhiser tells us, "When Harvard announced that it would award President Jackson with an honorary degree, Adams announced that he would skip the ceremony: 'As an affectionate child of our Alma Mater,' he could not 'witness her disgrace in conferring her highest literary honors on a barbarian who could . . . hardly spell his own name.'" For years, Ted Roosevelt's comments on Alfred E. Smith would scald the ears of his listeners, and he nurtured a smoldering long-term resentment of Franklin and Eleanor. In this context, and against these examples, Gore's tirades against George W. Bush do not seem exceptional and are not unexpected at all.

Comparisons of the good sons who failed with the bad boys gone good leads to the question of why, under parental direction and prodding, the bookish and introverted John Kennedy was turned in time into a great politician, while the bookish and introverted Al Gore was not. Part of the answer lies in the things they were bookish about. From childhood on, JFK was a history buff and a news junkie, wholly absorbed in the subject matter of politics. At Choate, while neglecting his studies, he absorbed volumes of newsprint, which he faithfully analyzed, winning all quizzes on current events. "World affairs were very important to him," recalled a girlfriend at Stanford. "He listened to every radio news broadcast. I think he was thinking of politics all along." In the war zone in the Pacific, he would take shipmates aside and grill them about political events in their home states and districts. "We'd sit in a corner, and I'd recall all the political problems of New Jersey and Long Island," recalled one such companion. "He did that with everybody—discussed politics." At Harvard, his first scholastic breakthrough came when he was assigned a paper on the career of an obscure Republican congressman from New York State. "His final report was a masterpiece," said his professor. "He got so interested that he went down to Washington, met some of his father's friends, and got a further line on his congressman. . . . Jack was interested in it, did a superb job." Even before the death of his brother, it was always assumed that politics of some variety would be his life's work. His parents thought he might work in an embassy. When he talked of spending his life writing or teaching, it was always assumed that current affairs or history would be what he would be teaching or writing about.

When his brother died, the big change in his life was not to a different milieu, but to a different place in it. It was the salesman aspect alone that caused him uneasiness: "Jack . . . hated . . . the handshaking, the back slapping, the phony smile, the small talk," wrote Ralph Martin. "For all these reasons, [his cousin] did not consider him prime political material, as young Joe had been." Part of his problem would be solved by television, an intimate medium that would serve as an empowerment measure for intro-verts. The rest he would continue to hate but would come to accept as the price of admission. Soon, he would find that politics "fit the Greek definition of happiness. A full use of your powers, along lines of excellence in a life affording scope."

"Fascination began to grip me," Kennedy said of politics in 1959, when he was already running for president. Fascination of this variety never seemed to grip Gore. Kennedy's interests were people and power; Gore's were technology, theory, and natural science. Kennedy read history and biographies of powerful leaders; Gore read psychological and sociological tomes of limited popular interest, of the sort that would have bored Kennedy, and most politicians, to tears. Now and then, politics would allow Gore to indulge his real interests, as when he made his name in the 1980s as an arms control expert, but he showed little interest in working with people and had little feel for the matrix of power relationships that make up the political enterprise. Kennedy improved dramatically with every campaign that he ran in, and by 1958 he had thoroughly mastered the process of politics. Gore's first national run, in 1988, was an utter catastrophe, and when he began to run again ten years later he repeated every early mistake he had made.

Gore would later blame Clinton for having lost the 2000 race for him with his dalliance and the scandal that followed, but Clinton had also left him a roaring economy, and a world that people thought was at peace. It was not Clinton who urged Gore to make a speech about how his sister's death from lung cancer in 1984 had made him a staunch foe of smoking, when he knew tape existed of a speech he made praising tobacco a full four years later. It was not Clinton who told him to pay fifteen thousand dollars a month to a friend of his daughter's to dress him in earth tones, and it was not Clinton who told him to roll his eyes and sigh loudly in the first debate, or to stalk Bush and then hover above him. It was not Clinton who told Gore to change messages, change advisers, or commit any one of the many large and small errors made between July 1996 and November 2000 that worked to undo his campaign.

"The only way to make sense of Al Gore," wrote *Washington Post* columnist Marjorie Williams, "is to see him as a man for whom politics is an ill-fitting trade, adopted under the duress of family legacy. . . . Politics has always had, for Gore, the quality of a second language, learned by the class grind not naturally gifted in this area, mastered by rote and sheer force of will." Politics was a first language for Kennedy, who had to be coaxed into speaking in public but understood from the beginning its texture and syntax. Gore never did. It would have been better for him if he had lost at the outset and then gone to work at a college or a think tank, but his curse was that he always looked so good on paper, and when carried by others—as his father's son and as Bill Clinton's vice president—had always seemed to do well. But it was his bad luck, which for a time seemed his good luck, that he was born to two well-placed and fiercely ambitious political players, who thought that by sheer force of will they could bring up a president. Instead, they damaged their son and their party, because it turned out they were wrong.

Pressures bear down on dynastic children from different quarters and in different ways. There is the pressure that tends to come down from a parent—an elder Al Gore or a Joe Kennedy—who wants to fulfill a private ambition, and there is the pressure that tends to push up from the crowd. It was not pressure from family (by that time, almost no one was left to exert it), but from his party and agonized fans of his brothers that drove Ted Kennedy into the near-breakdown that produced Chappaquiddick; pressure from fans of TR who decided Ted Jr. was his second coming (until they decided he wasn't, and dropped him); and groupies longing for a rebirth of Camelot who set up a clamor that "Bobby's Girl" (Kathleen Kennedy Townsend) would make a wonderful president, until she inconveniently lost her own state.

There is the pressure that comes from too good an example, that makes even a quiet success seem like failure and sets the bar of achievement too high. "The issue of work . . . was complicated for John," wrote Robert Littell, a close friend of John Kennedy Jr. "On the one hand, he had as many advantages in the form of connections and opportunities as anyone on earth. On the other hand, there were very few things he could do that would ever be enough. He couldn't just go and be a good lawyer or work at an investment bank or even run a philanthropy. . . . His father's unique contribution and sacrifice meant that John had to do something both genuinely valuable and truly big to consider himself as anything more than a failure." When John died, he had not yet discovered that "something," and the pressure was starting to mount. At that, he was better off than his cousin, Christopher Lawford, who battled major drug problems. "In my case, it was not that anyone in my life forced me to do anything, it was that the circumstances I was born into were so extraordinary that it was impossible not to be imprisoned by them. . . . It really wreaks havoc on your inner self when you realize that you have been born into a life so compelling and attractive that finding your own path and your own self feels like losing," he said.

Some people do come to terms with their fabulous forebears, but this often needs passage of time. "There is this legacy to live up to," said a great-granddaughter of Franklin and Eleanor Roosevelt, "but I'm never going to win a world war." One of the many advantages Franklin had in his epic fight with Ted Jr. was that he was not Theodore's son but his cousin, that his father was a country squire of no special distinction, and that if he had turned out to be just like his father no one would have thought it embarrassing, no one would have thought him a failure, and no one would have said a cross word. Perhaps the most desperate acts of rebellion were undertaken by one son apiece of John Quincy Adams and Robert F. Kennedy, compulsive achievers who let no moment pass unimproved in their quest for perfection. Overwhelmed by this spate of relentless activity, the sons opted out of the terrible contest, drank or doped themselves into a stupor, and then not so quietly died.

"What can a man do when he is absolutely beaten over the head with ancestry?" asked the second John Quincy Adams, introduced to a crowd as "the descendant of three men who had either been president or ought to have been, and as a prospective president himself." His father, Charles Francis (the man who ought to have been president), wrote as a young man, "Crushed by the weight of two generations of distinction . . . my life must be by decree of providence a verdict of failure against myself." "Crushed," "weight," and "failure" are the operative words. Charles was not a failure and later was able to say so: "The ambition I had to make myself a position worthy of my name and race has been satisfied," he said later. Yet even here there was a caveat. He had not excelled, just met expectations. He was a man who broke even, not quite a success. At that he was happier than his son, the second John Quincy, whose name far outran his potential, and who knew it. "I am nobody, and I know it in my heart, and I am sure to be found out," he complained. "I'm like a BB rattling around in a boxcar," said a young Joe Kennedy, Bobby's son, trying to place himself inside the family legend. "They're for him," Bobby had said, referring to John Kennedy, when he gave a speech at which people had cheered.

"When I am president, I'll make you Secretary of State," George Washington Adams told a friend at age six. "How will you handle this when you are president, Joe?" Harold Laski asked Joe Kennedy Jr. Al Gore was "Prince Albert" at St. Albans, where his parents had sent him to learn how to lead. George Washington

Adams died young as a possible suicide; Joe Kennedy Jr. died young in a suicide mission, and the saddest of all has been Gore. From the moment the recount was started in Florida, it was crystal clear that the loser would go to his grave convinced that he had won and had been cheated, and that the one man in all of American history least able to bear it was Gore. "We raised him for it," Gore's mother said of the White House, and no man had ever worked for it harder or longer or disliked it all more. Gore was the man born and bred to be president, sent to plow fields because it built character, told he was on the agenda of history, that his election was never an "if," but a "when." He was also the man for whom politics was and has remained a grind and a struggle, a grim, joyless puzzle he never decoded, the man for whom the act of campaigning was, in a dark simile, like "crawling over broken glass." "There is something about Al Gore's progress through life . . . that suggests an entire existence bent on a wheel of duty," wrote Marjorie Williams. "Born under another star, Gore would probably have pursued one of the trades for which the contours of his mind more naturally equip him: science, or teaching, or the law."

The first time—1988—Gore crawled over glass and came out of it empty, his feelings seeping out indirectly in the course of his incomplete midlife correction and the books that he read, quoted, and passed on to his friends. These books, Joe Klein noted, had one common focus: "the repressed anger of children toward their parents—especially children who devoted their lives to achieving goals set by others" and had their own goals shoved aside. This anger, expressed, suppressed, or distorted, cuts a deep swath through political families. Public life as an option, to be picked up at will or discarded, is one thing, and not always a bad one. But great expectations, pushed too hard with too little regard for individual difference, have given us desperate men.

Selected Sources

Books

Adams, Henry. *The Education of Henry Adams*. New York: Penguin Classics, 1995.

Alsop, Joseph, with Adam Platt. *I've Seen the Best of It*. New York: Norton, 1992.

Anderson, Christopher. *The Day John Died*. New York: William Morrow, 2000.

Barone, Michael. The *Almanac of American Politics*. Washington, DC: National Journal, 1994–2006.

———. *Our Country*. New York: The Free Press, 1990.

Bechloss, Michael R. *Kennedy and Roosevelt*. New York: Norton, 1980.

Blair, Clay Jr., and Joan Blair. *The Search for JFK*. New York: Berkeley Books, 1976.

Blow, Richard. *America's Son: A Portrait* of *John F. Kennedy Jr*. New York: Henry Holt, 2002.

Boorstein, Daniel. *Hidden History*. New York: Harper & Row, 1987.

Bush, George H. W., and Brent Scowcroft. *A World Transformed*. New York: Knopf, 1998.

Ceaser, James W. and Andrew C. Busch. *The Perfect Tie*. Washington, DC: Rowan & Littlefield, 2001.

Collier, Peter, and David Horowitz. *The Kennedys: An American Drama*. New York: Summit Books, 1984.

Collier, Peter, with David Horowitz. *The Roosevelts: An American Saga*. New York: Simon & Shuster, 1984.

Dallek, Robert. *An Unfinished Life: John F. Kennedy, 1917–1963*. Boston: Little, Brown, 2001.

Dionne. E. J., and William Kristol, ed. *Bush v. Gore: The Court Cases and the Commentary*. Washington, DC: Brookings Institution Press, 2001.

Donn, Linda. *The Roosevelt Cousins*. New York: Knopf, 2001.

Ferrell, Robert H. *The Dying President*. Columbia, MO: University of Missouri Press, 1998.

Friedrich, Otto. *Clover*. New York: Simon & Schuster, 1979.

Frum, David. *The Right Man: The Surprise Presidency of George W. Bush*. New York: Random House, 2003.

Goodwin, Doris Kearns. *The Fitzgeralds and the Kennedys*. New York: Simon & Shuster, 1987.

Gore, Al. *Earth in the Balance*. New York: Penguin Books, 1992.

Greenfield, Jeff. *Oh, Waiter! One Order of Crow!* New York: Putnam, 2001.

Hersh, Burton. *The Shadow President: Edward M. Kennedy in Opposition*. South Royalton, VT: Steerforth, 1997.

Jeffers, H. Paul. *In the Rough Rider's Shadow*. New York: Ballantine Books, 2002.

Jenkins, Roy. *Franklin Delano Roosevelt*. New York: Penguin Press, 2004.

Kennedy, John F. *Prelude to Leadership: The European Diary of John F. Kennedy, Summer, 1945*. Washington DC: Regnery, 1995.

Kennedy, Sheila Rauch. *Shattered Faith*. New York: Henry Holt & Co., 1998.

Lawford, Christopher. *Symptoms of Withdrawal*. New York: William Morrow, 1995.

Leamer, Lawrence. *The Kennedy Men*. New York: William Morrow, 2001.

———. *Sons of Camelot*. New York: William Morrow, 2004.

Littell, Robert T. *The Men We Became: My Friendship with John F. Kennedy Jr.* New York: St. Martin's Press, 2004.

Mahoney, Richard D. *Sons and Brothers: The Days of Jack and Bobby Kennedy*. New York: Arcade, 1995.

Maraniss, David, with Ellen Nakashima. *The Prince of Tennessee: The Rise of Al Gore*. New York: Simon & Schuster, 2000.

Martin, Ralph G. *Front Runner, Dark Horse*. New York: Doubleday, 1960.

———. *Seeds of Destruction: Joe Kennedy and His Sons*. New York: Putnam, 1995.

Minutaglio, Bill. *First Son: George W. Bush and the Bush Family Dynasty*. New York: Three Rivers Press: New York, 2001.

Morris, Edmund G. *The Rise of Theodore Roosevelt*. New York: Coward, McCann & Geoghegan, 1980.

Morris, Sylvia Jukes. *Edith Kermit Roosevelt: Portrait of a First Lady*. New York: Coward McCann & Geoghegan, 1980.

Nagel, Paul C. *The Adams Women*. New York: Oxford University Press, 1987.

———. *Descent from Glory*. New York: Oxford University Press, 1983.

———. *John Quincy Adams*. New York: Knopf, 1997.

O'Toole, Patricia. *The Five of Hearts*. New York: Ballantine Books, 1990.

Podhoretz, John. *Bush Country*. New York: St Martin's Press, 2004.

Remini, Robert V. *John Quincy Adams*. New York: Times Books, 2002.

Renahan, Edward J. Jr. *The Kennedys at War*. New York: Doubleday, 2002.

———. *The Lion's Pride*. New York: Oxford University Press, 1998.

Roosevelt, Eleanor Butler. *The Day Before Yesterday*. Garden City, NY: Doubleday, 1959.

Roosevelt, Nicholas. *A Front Row Seat*. Oklahoma City, OK: Oklahoma University Press, 1953.

Russell, Francis. *Adams: An American Dynasty.* New York: American Heritage, 1976.

Schweitzer, Peter, and Rochelle Schweitzer. *The Bushes: Portrait of a Dynasty.* Garden City, NY: Doubleday, 2004.

Searls, Hank. *The Lost Prince: Young Joe, the Forgotten Kennedy.* New York: World, 1969.

Shepherd, Jack. *Cannibals of the Heart.* New York: McGraw-Hill, 1980.

Shesol, Jeff. *Mutual Contempt.* New York: Norton, 1997.

Sifry, Michael L., and Cerf, Christoher, ed. *The Iraq War Reader.* New York: Touchstone Books, 2003.

Teague, Michael T. *Mrs. L: Conversations with Alice Roosevelt Longworth.* New York: Doubleday, 1981.

Thomas, Evan. *Robert Kennedy: His Life.* New York: Simon & Schuster, 2002.

Turque, Bill. *Inventing Al Gore.* Boston: Houghton Mifflin, 2000.

Von Drehle, David and the political staff of the *Washington Post. Deadlock: The Inside Story of America's Closest Election.* New York: Public Affairs, 2001.

Ward, Geoffrey. *A First-Class Temperament: The Emergence of Franklin Roosevelt.* New York: Harper & Row, 1989.

Wead, Doug. *All the Presidents' Children.* New York: Atria Books, 2003.

West, Darrell M. *Patrick Kennedy: The Rise to Power.* Upper Saddle River, NJ: Prentice Hall, 2001.

Whelan, Richard J. *The Founding Father: The Story of Joseph P Kennedy.* New York: New American Library, 1964.

Williams, Marjorie. *The Woman at the Washington Zoo.* New York: Public Affairs, 2005.

Woodward, Bob. *Bush At War.* New York: Simon & Schuster, 2002.

———. *Plan of Attack.* New York: Simon & Schuster, 2004.

Zelnick, Bob. *Gore: A Political Life.* Washington DC: Regnery, 1999.

Magazines, Newspapers, and Web Sites

Americanprowler.com. "Losing the Popular Vote." November 27, 2002.

———. "New Negatives," November 4, 2002.

———. "Why He Quit." December 16, 2002.

Bai, Matt. "Running from Office." *New York Times,* July 5, 2001.

Bell, Jeffrey. "Bush I vs. Bush II." *Weekly Standard,* October 13, 2003.

Blankley, Tony. "A Grief Observed." *Washington Post,* July 21, 1999.

Dreyfus, Robert. "The Inheritor: Patrick Kennedy." *Nation,* September 18–25, 2000.

Gelernter, David. "GWB & JFK." *Weekly Standard,* February 3, 2003.

Goldberg, Jeffrey. "Breaking Ranks." *New Yorker,* October 31, 2005.

Harwood, John. "Jeb Bush May Pay for a George W. Win." *Wall Street Journal,* November 15, 2000.

Hertzberg, Hendrik. "George Without Tears." *New Yorker,* August 9, 1999.

Klein, Joe. "Learning to Run." *New Yorker*, December 8, 1997.

———. "Wind on Capitol Hill." *New Yorker*, October 11, 1999.

Labash, Matt. "Patrick Kennedy: The Man and the Myth." *Weekly Standard*, June 7, 1999.

———. "The Next Kennedy." *Weekly Standard*, August 5, 2002.

Lemann, Nicholas. "After Iraq." *New Yorker*, February 17, 2003.

———. "Gore Without a Script." *New Yorker*, July 31, 2000.

———. "How It Came to War." *New Yorker*, March 31, 2003.

———. "The Next World Order." *New Yorker*, April 1, 2002.

———. "The War on What?" *New Yorker*, September 16, 2002.

———. "Without a Doubt." *New Yorker*, October 14, 2002.

Lizza, Ryan. "He Ain't Heavy." *New Republic*, July 26, 2002.

Maraniss, David. "In Tough Defeat, a Life Comes Full Circle." *Washington Post*, December 17, 2000.

Montgomery, Lori. "In Md., A Cakewalk Spoiled." *Washington Post*, August 4, 2002.

———. "Taking Heat for Townsend's Loss." *Washington Post*, December 1, 2002.

Mundy, Liza. "Mr. Resident." *Washington Post*, November 17, 2002.

Nagourney, Adam. "Gore Uses Disputed Count to Encourage Iowa Turnout." *New York Times*, October 15, 2002.

Nichols, Bill. "Gore's Hard Turn to Left May Help Ticket." *USA Today*, July 26, 2004.

Nyhan, David. "Life of the Party." *Boston Magazine*, February 2000.

Remnick, David. "The Wilderness Campaign." *New Yorker*, September 13, 2004.

Roberts, Roxanne. "Like Father, Like Sons." *Washington Post*, December 16, 2000.

Suellentrop, Chris. "That '70's Campaign." *Slate*, February 9, 2004.

Szegedy-Maszak, Marianne. "All Their Mothers." *Harper's Bazaar*, September 2000.

Taranto, James. opinionjournal.com, February 10, 2004.

Tumulty, Karen. "The New Kennedys." *Time*, August 31, 2001.

Tumulty, Karen, and Tamala Edwards. "At Last, His Own Man" *Time*, December 25, 2000.

Turque, Bill. "Why Gore Fights On and On and . . ." *Newsweek*, December 11, 2000.

Watson, Carlos. "The Political Genius of George W. Bush." *CNN.com*, November 8, 2004.

Williams, Marjorie. "Death of a Dream." *Washington Post*, December 5, 2000.

———. "Family Fallout." *Washington Post*, November 10, 2000.

Index